Daddy's Little Princess

Also by Cathy Glass

Damaged
Hidden
Cut
The Saddest Girl in the World
Happy Kids
The Girl in the Mirror
I Miss Mummy
Mummy Told Me Not to Tell
My Dad's a Policeman (a Quick Reads novel)
Run, Mummy, Run
The Night the Angels Came
Happy Adults
A Baby's Cry
Happy Mealtimes for Kids
Another Forgotten Child
Please Don't Take My Baby
Will You Love Me?
About Writing and How to Publish
The Child Bride
Saving Danny
The Silent Cry
Can I Let You Go?
Nobody's Son
Cruel to be Kind
A Long Way from Home
Where Has Mummy Gone?

THE MILLION COPY BESTSELLING AUTHOR

CATHY GLASS

Daddy's Little Princess

A confused little girl.
A broken father.
A shocking discovery.

HARPER
element

Certain details in this story, including names, places and dates,
have been changed to protect the children.

HarperElement
An imprint of HarperCollins*Publishers*
1 London Bridge Street
London SE1 9GF

www.harpercollins.co.uk

First published by HarperElement 2014

17

A catalogue record of this book
is available from the British Library

ISBN 978-0-00-756937-3

Printed and bound by CPI Group (UK) Ltd, Croydon

Acknowledgements

A big thank-you to my editor Holly; my literary agent Andrew; Carole, Vicky, Laura, Hannah, Virginia and all the team at HarperCollins.

In the Beginning

To write this book – Beth's story – I need to go back in time, to when Adrian was six and Paula was just two. I had only been fostering for a few years, and back then foster carers were given little in the way of training or support, or background information on the child. They were 'thrown in at the deep end' and left to get on with it, either swimming or sinking under the strain of it all. Looking back now, I shudder to think of some of the unsafe situations my family and I were placed in, and I also wonder – with the benefit of hindsight from years of fostering and training – if I would have handled situations differently. Some, maybe, but not with Beth. I am sure I would have made the same decisions then as now, for some behaviour is never acceptable and has to be stopped to save the child.

Chapter One

Close to Tears

I was starting to think that they weren't coming after all. Beth's social worker had telephoned me during the afternoon and had said she would bring Beth to me at about 'teatime'. It was now nearly seven o'clock – well past teatime – and Adrian, Paula and myself had eaten. I'd make Beth something fresh to eat if and when she arrived. It was a cold night and little Beth would be upset enough at being parted from her father without arriving tired and hungry. I knew that plans in social care often change unavoidably at the last minute, but I thought the social worker might have telephoned to let me know what was going on. A little while later I told Paula it was time for her to go to bed. We were in the living room, at the rear of the house, snug and warm, with the curtains closed against the cold, dark night. Paula and Adrian were sitting on the floor; Paula had been building a castle out of toy bricks and Adrian was poring over a large, beautifully illustrated book on vintage cars and motorbikes he'd been given as a Christmas present three weeks previously. Toscha, our lazy, lovable cat, was curled up on her favourite chair.

'I thought that girl was coming?' Adrian said, glancing up from his book.

'So did I,' I said. 'Perhaps her father isn't as ill as they thought and she was able to stay at home. I hope so.'

Adrian, aged six, had some understanding of what fostering meant from having children stay with us previously, while Paula, aged two, wasn't really old enough to understand, although I'd tried to explain that a girl aged seven who was called Beth might be coming to stay with us for a while. All I knew of Beth, other than her age, was that she lived with her father and that he was now ill and likely to be admitted to a psychiatric hospital. That was all the social worker had told me when she'd telephoned and I'd hoped to learn more from her when she arrived with Beth.

I rose from where I'd been sitting on the sofa and went over to Paula to help her pack away the toy bricks. 'Bedtime, love,' I said again.

'I thought that girl was coming?' Paula said, repeating Adrian's comments. She was at an age where she often copied her older brother. I heard him give a little sigh.

'I don't think she will be coming now,' I said to Paula. 'It's rather late.'

But just as I began collecting together the plastic building bricks, the doorbell rang, making us all jump. Both children looked at me expectantly.

'Perhaps it is them after all,' I said. 'Stay here and I'll go and see.'

With my husband, John, working away I was cautious when I answered the door after dark. Leaving Adrian and Paula in the living room, I went down the hall and to the front door where I first peered through the security spy-hole. The porch light was on and I could make out a woman and a child. Reassured, I opened the front door.

'Sorry we're so late,' the woman immediately apologized. 'I'm Jessie, Beth's social worker. We spoke on the phone. You must be Cathy. This is Beth.'

I smiled and looked at Beth, who was standing close to her social worker. She wore a grey winter's coat buttoned up to the top. She was pale, but her cheeks were flushed and her eyes were puffy from crying. She clutched a tissue in one hand, which she pressed to her nose.

'Oh, love,' I said. 'You must be very tired and worried. Come in.'

'I want my daddy,' Beth said, her eyes filling.

'I understand,' I said, touching her arm reassuringly. Jessie eased Beth over the doorstep and then brought in a very large suitcase.

'We stopped off at Beth's house to get her clothes,' Jessie explained as I closed the front door. 'It took longer than I expected. Beth wanted to change out of her school uniform, and then we had to pack. She was worried about washing her clothes and the food in the fridge spoiling. I've told her not to worry, that you'll wash her clothes here, and the house will be fine.'

I smiled again at Beth. 'That's right. There's nothing for you to worry about. I'll look after you.' Although I wondered that a seven-year-old had thought about laundry that needed to be done or food spoiling. 'Would you like to take off your coat?' I asked her. 'And we'll hang it here on the hall stand.'

Beth began to undo her buttons and then let Jessie help her out of her coat. I hung it on the stand and Jessie did the same with hers.

'I want to be with my daddy,' Beth said again.

'It's just for a short while until Daddy is better,' Jessie reassured her.

'Come on through and meet my son and daughter, Adrian and Paula,' I said. 'They're looking forward to meeting you.'

Jessie took Beth's hand and I led the way down the hall and into the living room. My first impression of Beth was that she'd been well cared for at home and was now clearly missing her father dreadfully. Jessie, I guessed, was in her late thirties, smartly dressed in black trousers and a pale-blue jumper. She seemed stressed, probably from running late and from all the arrangements she would have had to make to bring a child into care.

'Would you like a drink?' I offered Jessie and Beth.

Beth shook her head while Jessie said: 'A coffee would be lovely, thank you. Milk and one sugar, please.'

'This is Beth and her social worker, Jessie,' I said, introducing them to Adrian and Paula. 'I'll leave you all to get to know each other while I make the coffee.' But Paula wasn't going to be left alone with strangers and she rushed over and slipped her hand into mine.

Jessie and Beth were settling on the sofa as I left the living room with Paula to make the coffee, while Adrian had put down his book and was setting aside his embarrassment to talk to Jessie and Beth. It's always difficult when a new child first arrives until everyone gets to know each other and relaxes. From the kitchen I could hear Jessie asking Adrian how old he was and what he liked to do in his spare time. As I made the coffee I explained again to Paula who Beth was.

'Beth's going to stay with us for a few sleeps while the doctors make her daddy better,' I said.

'Why?' Paula asked. 'Why' was a word Paula had recently discovered and now used quite a lot.

'Because there's no one else at home to look after her,' I said. 'And she can't stay at home by herself.'

'Why not?'

'Because she's too young,' I said. 'She's only seven.'

'I'm two,' Paula said proudly.

'Yes, that's right, and in a few months you'll be three.'

I made the coffee, arranged some biscuits on a plate and set them on a tray. Paula followed me into the living room where I placed the tray on the coffee table within reach of Jessie.

'Thanks,' she said gratefully, reaching for the mug of coffee and a couple of biscuits. 'I can't remember the last time I had something to eat or drink. Today has disappeared.'

Jessie wasn't the first social worker who'd arrived having not had time to eat or drink. 'Shall I make you something to eat?' I asked.

'No, thank you. I'll settle Beth and then I need to get home. I have two children of my own, although you wouldn't think so for the little I see of them.'

'Are you sure you don't want a drink?' I asked Beth.

She shook her head.

'A biscuit?' I asked, offering her the plate.

She shook her head again.

'She'll need something to eat before bed,' Jessie said. 'She had her school dinner but has only had a drink since then.'

'You can tell me what you'd like later,' I said to Beth with a smile.

But she pressed the tissue to her eyes and looked close to tears. I wasn't surprised. I couldn't begin to imagine how upsetting or unsettling it must be for a child to suddenly have to leave their home and all that is familiar and live with strangers.

Beth gave a sniff and then suddenly blurted: 'It's my fault my daddy's ill. It's because I forgot to give him his tablets.' A tear escaped and ran down her cheek. Adrian and Paula looked at Beth, very worried.

'No, that's not the reason,' Jessie said kindly, slipping her arm around Beth's shoulders. 'I explained to you on the way here that sometimes tablets are not enough to make a person better and they have to go into hospital. Your daddy was taking the tablets. It's not your fault, Beth.'

Jessie cuddled Beth for a few minutes while Paula and Adrian, looking very concerned, sat close to each other on the floor beside the building bricks. I threw them a reassuring smile.

'I'm wondering if we could go somewhere private to talk?' Jessie asked me when Beth had stopped crying and had dried her eyes.

'Yes, of course,' I said. 'We can go in the front room.'

'Beth, you stay here with Adrian and Paula while I talk to Cathy,' Jessie said. 'Perhaps Adrian will show you his book. It looks good to me.'

Jessie stood and Adrian took his book and went and sat in the place Jessie had vacated. Paula immediately went too, sitting on the other side of him.

'Thanks,' I said to them as we left the room.

I showed Jessie into the front room and pushed the door to so we couldn't be overheard.

'I didn't want to discuss Beth's father in front of her,' Jessie said, drawing out a chair and sitting down. I sat opposite her. 'She's finding it difficult enough already.'

I nodded.

'Beth has been brought up by her father, Derek, since she was little,' Jessie said. 'I think she was about two or three when her mother disappeared. Beth never sees her. Derek has done a good job of bringing up Beth alone, but they came to the notice of the social services a few months ago. Derek went to his doctors saying he couldn't cope and was depressed. He was prescribed medication, which seemed to work for a while, but today he reached crisis point. I don't know why. He took Beth to school and then went straight to casualty at the hospital. He told the doctors he couldn't take any more and was thinking of committing suicide.'

'Oh dear. The poor man,' I said.

'Yes. They've admitted him to the psychiatric wing of St Mary's Hospital, but I'm hoping it won't be for long. Once his condition has been stabilized he should be able to go home with medication. If he's in for longer than a week, Beth will need to visit him. They're very close.'

'Yes, of course,' I said. 'Beth's obviously going to miss him a lot. And there isn't a relative who can look after her?' Which is usually considered the next best option if a parent can't look after their child.

'Not that we're aware of,' Jessie said. 'Derek has had nothing to do with his ex-wife's family since she left four years ago. His own mother died last year and his father is old and frail and in a care home. Derek is nearly fifty. He had Beth late in life.'

'I see.'

'That's all the information I can give you really,' Jessie said, winding up. 'You have my contact details, so telephone if there is a problem. Now, I need to get going. I'll say goodbye to Beth and leave you to it. I'm sure Beth will feel a bit brighter in the morning after a good night's sleep.'

Jessie hadn't given me much background information, but I assumed I had what I needed to look after Beth and that the rest was confidential.

We returned to the living room where the children were sitting in a row on the sofa looking at the pictures in Adrian's book as he turned the pages.

'I'm going now,' Jessie said to Beth. 'If you need anything, ask Cathy. As soon as I have news about your daddy I'll phone. But try not to worry. The doctors are looking after him and I'm sure he'll be better soon.'

'When can I see my daddy?' Beth asked anxiously.

'As soon as he's a little better,' Jessie said. 'I'll be in contact with the hospital tomorrow and I'll telephone Cathy.'

I could see from Beth's face that this hadn't reassured her. Indeed, she looked close to tears again.

'Goodbye,' Jessie said. 'Try not to worry.'

'I'll see Jessie out and then I'll get you something to eat.' I smiled at Beth.

Beth looked back, lost and afraid.

I went with Jessie down the hall and it was only as she began putting on her coat that I realized I didn't know which school Beth went to.

'Beth's school?' I asked. 'I assume she's still going to school while her father is in hospital?'

'Yes, sorry, I should have said. It's Orchard Primary School, about a five-minute drive away.'

'Oh,' I said, surprised. 'That's the same school Adrian goes to. I thought Beth looked slightly familiar. I've probably seen her going in or coming out of school. She'll be in the year above Adrian.'

'Well, that'll make life easier for you,' Jessie said. 'One school run to do.'

'Yes, indeed.'

'When I collected Beth from school today I informed the school secretary that she'll be staying with you for a little while.'

'Thank you,' I said. 'So Beth and Derek live quite close?'

'About three-quarters of a mile away,' Jessie confirmed. 'Well, goodnight. I'll be in touch, and thank you.'

'You're welcome.'

I saw Jessie out and closed the front door. Returning to the sitting room, I found Adrian and Paula now sitting either side of Beth. Adrian was still turning the pages of his book but was also giving a little commentary on the pictures, while Paula, having felt brave enough to leave her brother's side, was snuggled close to Beth and holding her hand. I was pleased my children were making Beth welcome.

'Jessie has just told me that you go to Orchard School,' I said, smiling at Beth. 'That's Adrian's school too.'

Beth gave a small nod, while Adrian turned to her and said: 'I recognized you when you first came in.' Then, looking at me, he said: 'We don't really know each other. Beth's in another class.'

'Still, it's nice you are both in the same school,' I said.

'My teacher is Miss Willow,' Beth said quietly to Adrian.

'And mine is Mr Andrews,' Adrian said. 'He's OK, but he shouts sometimes.'

As Adrian and Beth began talking about school, I thought it was a piece of good fortune that Beth lived locally, as one school run would certainly make my life easier. A more experienced foster carer would have realized that having a child's family live so close, far from being a bonus, could actually cause problems.

Chapter Two

Mr Sleep Bear

I usually put the children to bed in ascending order of age – the youngest first – as younger children generally need more sleep. But tonight, as it was past the bedtimes of all three children, I took them upstairs together. I'd already placed Beth's case in her room and had taken out her pyjamas, towel and wash bag. I would unpack the rest of her case the following day when I had more time. I now asked Beth and Adrian to change into their pyjamas while I got Paula, who was very tired, ready for bed. I switched on the light in Beth's room and checked she had everything she needed and then left her to change; Adrian was already in his bedroom and knew what to do.

In the bathroom, I washed Paula's face and hands and then helped her into her pyjamas. I took her round to the toilet. She was so tired she wanted 'a carry' from the toilet to her bed. I tucked her in, gave her a big kiss and said goodnight.

'Night-night, Mummy,' she yawned, her little arms encircling my neck. 'Luv you.'

I hugged her hard. 'I love you too, precious. Lots and lots. Sleep tight.'

By the time I left the room, she was nearly asleep.

I checked on Adrian who, now changed, was in the bathroom having a wash and brushing his teeth. 'Straight into bed when you've finished,' I said. 'I'll be in to say goodnight in a few minutes.' He sometimes 'got lost' on his way from the bathroom to his bedroom and ended up downstairs playing, but I think even he was tired tonight, and he nodded.

I continued to Beth's room. The door was pushed to but not shut. I gave a brief knock before I went in. Although Beth was only seven, I'd be giving her the same privacy I gave all the children. Nowadays foster carers draw up a 'safer caring policy', which includes privacy and is designed to keep all family members feeling safe and secure, but back then such matters were left to the carer's common sense, and common sense told me that even quite young children liked some degree of privacy.

Beth had changed into her pyjamas and had also taken her clean school uniform out of her case ready for the following morning. It was laid neatly on the end of her bed.

'Well done,' I said, impressed. 'You've got your uniform ready.'

'I always do it at home,' she said quietly. 'But I don't know where these go.' Her brow creased. She was holding her dirty washing: underwear, socks and the uniform she'd presumably been wearing that day and had packed in her case. 'At home I put them in the washing machine, but I don't know where that is here.'

'You don't have to worry about that,' I said, relieving her of the clothes. 'I'll see to it here. I'll put them in the laundry basket and wash them tomorrow. Come on, let's go round to the bathroom and then get you into bed. Everything will seem much better in the morning.' Beth looked very sad and worried.

She gave a little careworn sigh and then picked up her towel and wash bag. 'I hope I've remembered everything,' she said anxiously. 'I didn't have much time to pack. Jessie was in a hurry.'

'Beth, love, try not to worry,' I said, touching her arm reassuringly. 'If you've forgotten anything, I'm sure I'll have a spare here you can use. And if not, we'll ask your social worker to collect it from home. OK?'

She nodded, although she didn't look much happier. I thought she appeared to shoulder a lot of responsibility at home for a child of her age. She looked permanently worried, although given her father was in hospital that was hardly surprising.

In the bathroom, Beth saw our towels hanging on the towel rail and immediately draped hers over, although a lot more neatly than ours. At the sink I showed her which tap was hot and which was cold. She gave a little nod. Not knowing how good her self-care skills were, I stayed in the bathroom to see if she needed any help. It soon became obvious that she didn't. Unscrewing the cap on the toothpaste, she squirted a carefully measured amount of paste onto her toothbrush and then returned the cap to the tube, screwing it into place. She put the tube back into her wash bag and then methodically brushed her teeth and rinsed thoroughly. Once she'd finished she placed her toothbrush in the beaker with ours and then turned on the hot and cold water taps, mixing the water in the basin to the right temperature and testing it with her fingers before washing her face and hands.

'Good girl,' I said, even more impressed.

'It's too late for a bath, isn't it?' Beth asked, glancing at me in the mirror.

'Yes. Just have a hands-and-face wash now. You can have a bath tomorrow when we're in a better routine. Missing one bath won't hurt.'

'That's what my daddy says,' Beth said, smiling weakly. 'I hope they're looking after him in hospital.'

'They will be, love,' I reassured her.

I waited while Beth carefully patted her face and hands dry and then returned her towel, neatly folded, to the towel rail.

'Good girl,' I said again.

We went round the landing towards Beth's room and she said she'd use the toilet before she went to bed, as she did at home. While Beth was in the toilet I popped into Adrian's room to say goodnight and remind him to switch off his lamp. 'Night, love,' I said, tucking him in and kissing his forehead. 'Love you. Sleep tight. And thanks for your help with Beth.'

'She's all right, for a girl,' Adrian said, which, coming from a six-year-old boy, was a compliment. 'Love you too,' he said. 'Will Dad be coming home at the weekend?'

'Yes, I hope so.'

'Good, I miss him.'

'I know you do.'

I gave Adrian another kiss and came out of his bedroom. Beth had finished in the toilet and I went with her into her bedroom. I'd already closed the curtains, and with the Cinderella duvet cover, pillowcase and Disney wall posters, I thought the room looked warm and inviting. Although it obviously wasn't as good as being at home.

I dimmed the lights and drew back the duvet ready for Beth to get in, but she stayed where she was and made no move to get into bed.

'Is there anything else you need?' I asked gently.

Beth shook her head.

'OK, love, into bed then. It's very late and you must be tired.'

I waited, but still Beth didn't make any move towards the bed. 'It's bound to seem a bit strange sleeping here on the first night,' I said. 'But I can leave the door open and the light on if you like.'

'No, it's not that,' she said, her face clouding.

'What is it then, love? Can you tell me?'

'I'm not used to sleeping alone.'

'Oh, I see. Do you have a cuddly toy in your case that you usually sleep with?' I thought this was likely, as many children sleep with a 'cuddly' toy for comfort so they don't feel alone at night. I hadn't seen a soft toy in Beth's case when I'd taken out her nightwear, but then I hadn't searched further down in the case.

'No, I don't have a soft toy,' Beth said. 'I don't need one at home. I cuddle up to my daddy.'

'Oh, I see. Your daddy cuddles you until you fall asleep?' I said, remembering I'd done this with Adrian when he'd been little, as had John, and that I still did so with Paula sometimes. I could certainly cuddle Beth until she fell asleep, but she needed to get into bed first.

Beth looked at me seriously and fiddled with the sleeve of her pyjamas. 'No,' she said, after a moment. 'I sleep with my daddy, in his bed.'

'Oh,' I said again. 'Not every night, surely?' For this seemed rather unusual to me for a girl of Beth's age.

Beth nodded, almost sheepishly.

'Don't you have a bed and bedroom of your own?' I asked. It was possible they didn't have a second bedroom.

'Yes, I have a bedroom,' Beth said. 'But I don't sleep in it. I don't like sleeping by myself. I like sleeping with my daddy and he likes me sleeping with him. Can I sleep with you? I don't want to be alone.'

The safer caring policy for foster carers now advises that foster children should never sleep in a carer's bed, and babies and children under two – who can share a carer's bedroom – must have their own cot or bed. But then there was no safer caring policy so, as usual, I had to rely on my common sense. I wasn't comfortable with having a seven-year-old who wasn't a relative sleeping in my bed, apart from it not being fair on Adrian and Paula, who slept in their own beds. I also thought that Beth's father might not like the arrangement, possibly feeling I was trying to usurp his position as parent. Obviously I didn't want Beth to be upset, so I needed to find a solution.

'Beth, love,' I said gently as I perched on the edge of the bed. 'I can't really let you sleep in my bed. But I will stay with you and cuddle you until you fall asleep. I'll leave your bedroom door open and the landing light is always on. If you wake in the night you can call out and I'll come round straight away.'

Beth looked at me, unconvinced. But she needed to get into bed and off to sleep, so I thought I might have to be firm. 'Come on, in you get,' I said, patting her bed encouragingly. 'I'll stay with you until you're asleep.'

Reluctantly, Beth climbed into bed and I pulled the duvet up to her chin. I then lay on the bed beside her, on top of the duvet, and put my arm around her to cuddle her.

'How's that?' I said.

'My daddy strokes my forehead,' Beth said. 'Like this.' She lightly trailed her fingers over her forehead.

Many children like having their forehead caressed when they are finding it difficult to go to sleep. It's soothing.

'All right, close your eyes, and I'll stroke your forehead,' I said. 'It won't be the same as when your daddy does it, but I'll try my best.'

Beth finally closed her eyes and I began gently stroking her forehead. Ten minutes later she was still awake, and her eyes opened. 'The light's too bright,' she said. 'It's dark in my daddy's room.'

Although I'd dimmed the bedroom light, I got off the bed and switched it off completely, but I left the door slightly ajar so I could see by the light of the landing. I returned to Beth's bed, lay down and began stroking her forehead again, but ten minutes later her eyes shot open again.

'It's not the same,' she said fretfully. 'My daddy's under the covers with me. I can feel him nice and warm when he cuddles up.'

Apart from not feeling wholly comfortable doing this for Beth, I knew that if I began this routine it was going to be difficult to break it later. I didn't know how long Beth would be staying with me, but I knew I needed to create a practical working routine. I couldn't spend every evening tucked up in bed with Beth; I had things to do. Then I had a flash of inspiration and I remembered Mr Sleep Bear. Mr Sleep Bear, as I'd named him, was dressed in blue-stripped pyjamas and had been given to Adrian by my mother when he'd been very small. One evening, when Adrian hadn't been able to go to sleep, I'd tucked the bear into his bed and told him that now he had Mr Sleep Bear with him – who was also very tired – he would go straight to sleep. And he did. After that, whenever Adrian hadn't been able to go to sleep, Mr Sleep Bear came to the rescue. Adrian had outgrown the bear some years before and Paula had never used him, having a number of soft toys of her own that she took to bed with her.

'I know,' I said, climbing off the bed. 'I've got just the person to help you go to sleep.' Beth looked at me, concerned, as well she might. 'It's nothing to worry about. I'm going to fetch Mr Sleep Bear. He's a very special bear who will send you off to sleep. Stay in bed and I'll get him. He's in my bedroom.'

Leaving Beth in bed, I went quickly round the landing to my bedroom and took Mr Sleep Bear from the ottoman where I stored Adrian's outgrown toys. It was now after ten o'clock and I was tired and still had some clearing up to do. Please work your magic on Beth, I thought as I carried the bear round the landing and into Beth's room. She was propped up in bed now, wide awake, and looking at me inquisitively.

Mr Sleep Bear

'This is Mr Sleep Bear,' I said, sitting him on the bed. 'He's very soft and cuddly and he helps children get to sleep. When he's in your bed you'll find you will fall asleep very quickly. He can stay with you all night. And if you do wake up, just cuddle up to him and you'll go straight back to sleep,' I emphasized. Clearly the child had to believe in the magic to make it work. 'Now, lie down, good girl, and we'll get you off to sleep.'

Beth lay on her back and I raised the duvet to her chin, then tucked Mr Sleep Bear in beside her.

'Will you lie with me until Mr Sleep Bear makes me go to sleep?' Beth asked.

'Yes, of course, love.'

I lay beside Beth and she turned onto her side, away from me and facing Mr Sleep Bear. Looping her arms around the bear she drew him to her. 'Close your eyes,' I encouraged, 'and you'll soon feel very sleepy.' I certainly did!

I began stroking Beth's forehead while she cuddled Mr Sleep Bear. It was only a few minutes before her breathing deepened and her face relaxed in sleep. I stopped stroking her forehead and waited a moment to make sure she was in a deep sleep. Then I carefully got off the bed and tiptoed out of her bedroom, leaving the door ajar so I would hear her if she did wake and call out.

I was feeling rather pleased with myself as I went downstairs. Beth was asleep, and tomorrow I'd start what promised to be a relatively easy routine with only one school to go to. In the kitchen, I let Toscha out for her evening run and then set about the washing-up. My feeling of well-being continued. Beth seemed a very pleasant child who'd been well brought up, and I was sure she'd get along well with Adrian and Paula. I liked Beth, and the only problem I could foresee was that she was going to miss her father dreadfully. But, of course, I hadn't spotted the warning signs. That was to come later.

Chapter Three
The Photographs

Beth slept through the night and I woke her for school just after I'd woken Adrian.

'Well done, love,' I said. 'You did sleep well.'

'It was Mr Sleep Bear,' she said, yawning and stretching. 'He made me sleep.' I smiled. She looked far more relaxed after a good night's sleep, but naturally as soon as she woke her thoughts turned to her father. 'Do you think my daddy will come home today?' she asked, sitting upright in bed.

'I don't think so,' I said gently as I opened the curtains. 'Jessie will tell us when she has any news, but I think your daddy will stay in hospital for a few days, at least.'

'I hope I can see my daddy soon. I miss him,' Beth said, climbing out of bed.

'I know you do, love, and Jessie said you can see him as soon as he is well enough to have visitors.'

'What are visitors?' Beth asked.

'People who go and see a person. You can have visitors in hospital or at home.'

'We don't have visitors,' Beth said quite adamantly. 'It's just me and my daddy.' So I thought that the two of them appeared to be very alone in the world, with no relatives or friends who visited, but I didn't comment.

The Photographs

I left Beth to get dressed, then I checked that Adrian was out of bed and that it was all right for Beth to be using Mr Sleep Bear, as the bear had originally been his, and he said it was fine. I helped Paula wash and dress and then we went downstairs where I fed Toscha and made Paula breakfast and myself a mug of coffee. Adrian and Beth knew they had to come down for breakfast as soon as they were ready. Beth was down first and she wanted cereal and toast, 'like I have with daddy', she said. Paula was already seated on her booster seat at the table eating porridge and Beth sat beside her. Adrian joined us a couple of minutes later and I was pleased I'd asked him if it was all right for Beth to use Mr Sleep Bear as, impressed by the bear's magic powers, Beth talked about him quite a bit over breakfast. So much so that Paula wanted a Mr Sleep Bear too. Whoops, I thought. We only have one.

'You have Mr Snuggles and Flopsy and Mopsy to help you sleep,' I reminded Paula, naming some of the favourite soft toys she took to bed.

'And Balo,' she said with a smile.

'Yes, that's right.' Crisis averted.

It was only natural that Beth would want to talk about her father. They were close and she was worried about him and missed him, and her talk soon left Mr Sleep Bear and returned to her father. 'Will my daddy have breakfast in the hospital?' she asked.

'Yes, definitely,' I said. 'And lunch and dinner, and cups of tea in between.'

'Will my daddy get dressed or stay in his pyjamas?' Having never been in hospital it was a sensible question to ask.

'He may stay in his pyjamas to begin with,' I said. 'Then, when he's feeling a bit better, I expect he'll get dressed.' Clearly I didn't know if this was so, but it seemed a reasonable supposition.

'I don't think my daddy took his pyjamas with him,' Beth said, now looking at me anxiously.

'Don't worry. I'm sure your social worker will have thought of that. But if your daddy hasn't got his things with him, then the hospital will give him what he needs until someone can take his things in.' Although, of course, if Derek was as alone in the world as Beth had suggested, there may not be anyone to take in what he needed. I made a mental note to ask Jessie about this when she telephoned.

Beth's talk of her daddy continued during the whole of breakfast, when we went upstairs to brush our teeth, in the hall while we put on our coats and shoes and in the car on the way to school. Beth's questions and comments about her father's welfare were intermingled with little reminiscences of what they did together: 'Daddy and me cook our meals together ... I like to help my daddy ... I make him cups of tea ... Daddy and me sit on the sofa and watch television ... My daddy takes me to school ... My daddy helps me with my reading ... I love my daddy so much ...' and so on and so on.

I'd noticed that Adrian had gone quiet in the car and I was pretty sure I knew the reason why. Beth's continual talk of her father was reinforcing to Adrian that he didn't see his own daddy as much as he would have liked. While I'd gone to great lengths to reassure Adrian that his father working away couldn't be helped and that he loved him very much, there was no doubt that Adrian missed him more than he admitted. Paula, that much younger, hadn't known any different and was used to her father not being there during the week. But Adrian could remember a time when John had returned home every evening after work and they'd spent time together, similar to Beth's descriptions. As I parked the car near the school and we climbed out, I tried to change the subject, but it didn't work and Beth continued with her reminiscing. 'My daddy calls me his little princess,' she announced proudly.

'That's nice, love,' I said. I threw Adrian a reassuring smile, but he looked away.

We entered the playground and Adrian ran off to play with his friends as he usually did. There were ten minutes before the klaxon sounded for the start of school and I waited in the playground with Beth beside me and Paula in her pushchair. I said hello to some of the other mothers I knew and then a woman with a similar-aged child to Beth came over. I'd seen her before in the playground at the start and end of school, although I didn't know her personally.

'Hi,' she said pleasantly. 'My daughter, Jenni, is a friend of Beth's. They're in the same class.' I smiled and nodded as the two girls smiled shyly at each other. 'I understand Beth's daddy isn't well,' the mother continued. 'Jenni said Beth is living with you?'

'Yes, just for a short while, until her daddy is better,' I confirmed.

'Jenni would like Beth to come and play. We don't live far from them. She could stay for tea. We've asked Beth before, but her father wouldn't let her. I think he's over-possessive.'

Not knowing the woman or the reasons for Derek's decision not to let Beth go to Jenni's house, I wasn't about to agree – either that Derek was over-possessive or that Beth could go to tea. Derek had clearly had his reasons for not letting Beth go, and it wasn't for me to overturn his decision.

'That's very kind of you,' I said. 'I'll ask Beth's father if it's OK and then we'll arrange something.' Which seemed a fair reply to me.

'Yeah, sure,' she said, with a small shrug, and went off to talk to another mother. Her daughter followed. I hoped I hadn't offended her.

'Would you like to play at Jenni's house if your father agrees?'
I now asked Beth.

'I play with Jenni at school,' Beth said.

'Yes, I know, that's nice, but Jenni's mother is asking if you'd
like to go and play at her house. I'll need to ask your dad first.'

'My daddy will say no,' Beth said evenly. 'He doesn't want me
going there.'

Parents of young children have the responsibility for deciding
whom their children associate and play with outside of school.
Derek – for whatever reason – had decided that Beth shouldn't
see Jenni and Beth had accepted that. As Beth's foster carer, it
wasn't for me to question his decision. That was until Beth
added: 'I can't play with children when I'm not at school. At
home I play with my daddy.'

I looked at Beth carefully. 'Do you ever have friends back to
your home to play?'

'No,' Beth said.

'Have you ever been to a friend's house to play?'

'No,' Beth said again.

I was now thinking that Jenni's mother may have been right
when she'd said that Beth's father was over-possessive, but I also
knew it was not for me to criticize. Beth's social worker had said
that Derek had been doing a good job of raising his daughter,
and there was nothing to suggest Beth wasn't happy at home –
far from it; she doted on her father.

The klaxon sounded and Adrian – now back to his normal,
happy self – ran over to say goodbye. He gave Paula and me a
quick kiss, called, 'See ya later!' to Beth and joined his friends
who were lining up ready to go into school.

'I'll wait here for you at the end of school,' I said to Beth.

We said goodbye and she walked over to where her class was
lining up and began chatting to some of the girls. Beth seemed a

sociable child and clearly had friends at school, it was just that she didn't socialize with them outside of school, as most children her age did.

I wasn't anticipating going into the school; there was no need. Jessie had informed the school that Beth was staying with me and the school already had my contact details from Adrian attending. The lines of children began filing into the building and I turned to leave. Then Miss Willow, Beth's teacher, ran over. 'I understand Beth is staying with you?' she said, arriving at my side a little out of breath.

'Yes, that's right, until her father is better.'

'Do you think we could have a chat this afternoon after school?' she asked.

'Yes, of course,' I said.

'Thank you. See you later.' She ran back to her class to lead them into the building. Whatever was all that about? I wondered.

I returned home, cleared up the breakfast things and then spent some time playing with Paula and looking at picture books with her. Paula still had a little nap mid-morning and while she slept I took the opportunity to unpack the rest of Beth's case. It was a very large suitcase and was taking up space in her room. I'd briefly opened it the evening before when I'd taken out Beth's nightwear and wash bag, and Beth had also done some unpacking that morning after breakfast. I now began removing the rest of her clothes, hanging and folding them in the wardrobe and drawers. Although I didn't take much notice of what I was unpacking, there seemed to be a lot of flimsy, frilly clothes more suitable for summer than the middle of winter.

Having taken out the clothes, I now found a towel stretched over the remaining items that felt hard to the touch. I lifted the towel to find lots of framed photographs hastily wrapped in newspaper. Foster children often bring a couple of photographs of their family with them; indeed, I encourage them do so as they take comfort in seeing pictures of their family when they can't be with them. I usually frame the photographs and set them on the shelves in their room so they can see them from the bed at night. However, Beth's photographs were already framed, and there were a lot of them. I was up to ten and still counting. Little wonder the case had been heavy, I mused. I guessed she'd stripped their living room of photographs, for the frames were lacquered wood and more like the ones you'd find displayed in a living room than in a child's bedroom. I removed the newspaper from each picture and set them to one side. All of them so far were of Beth and her father, and I could now put a face to Derek. I already knew he was nearly fifty, and I now saw that he was of average height and build, with grey hair and blue-grey eyes. I wondered if I'd find a photograph of Beth's mother, but they were all of Beth and her father.

Having emptied the case, I took it through to my room where I heaved it up and on top of my wardrobe, out of the way. I returned to Beth's room and set about arranging the photographs on the bookshelves. There were fifteen photographs in all, of various sizes, some portrait shape and some landscape. Beth and her father were posing for the camera and smiling in all of them, and they had clearly enjoyed many days out. The photographs included shots of them on the beach, at the zoo, the funfair, the castle and a museum, as well as at home. The last one was taken at Disneyland. Lucky girl, I thought. Beth was dressed up as a fairy-tale princess and her father was dressed as the handsome prince. I arranged the photographs over three shelves and stepped back to admire my handiwork. I thought Beth would be pleased when she saw the display.

The Photographs

Yet as I stood there gazing at their photographs, I began to feel slightly uncomfortable. I couldn't say why, but all those pictures of Beth and her father with their arms around each other, and smiling at each other or into the camera, unsettled me. Then Paula woke from her nap and, shaking off my feeling of disquiet, I went into her room to get her up.

That afternoon Jessie telephoned. She said she'd spoken to a nurse on Derek's ward and he'd had a comfortable night. She asked me to tell Beth. Jessie also said it was too early to say how long Derek would be in hospital or when Beth could see him, but asked me to telephone the hospital over the weekend so that Beth could talk to her father.

'Yes, of course,' I said, and I wrote down the telephone number of the hospital, which Jessie now gave to me.

'Derek's on Ward 3,' Jessie added. 'He's very anxious about Beth, so hearing from her should help. Could you telephone Saturday and Sunday, please?'

'Yes. It will help reassure Beth too,' I said. 'They're very close and she's naturally worried about him, although I've reassured her he's being well looked after.'

'Thank you. Does Beth have everything she needs with her?'

'I think so. I unpacked her case this morning. She seems to have everything with her.'

'Tell me about it!' Jessie said. 'I had to stop her from bringing more. What have you done with all those photographs?'

'I've put them on the shelves in her bedroom. Which reminds me, Beth was worried that her daddy didn't have his pyjamas and wash things with him in hospital. I said I'd ask you.'

'Reassure her he has everything he needs,' Jessie said. 'Marianne took them in, but best not tell Beth that.'

'Marianne?' I queried.

'She was Derek's long-term girlfriend,' Jessie said. 'Ex now – their relationship has finished. But he still phones her if he needs help. She has a key to his flat.'

'Oh, I see,' I said. 'That's kind of her.'

'Yes, it is. I take it Beth hasn't mentioned Marianne?'

'No. I got the impression that Beth and her father were very alone in the world.'

'Yes, they are now,' Jessie said pointedly, but didn't say any more.

Chapter Four

Inappropriate

That afternoon, I was wondering when I should go in to school to see Miss Willow, when Adrian came into the playground, where I was waiting, with a message. 'Miss Willow says to tell you that she and Beth are in her classroom, and I'm to take you up.' He seemed a little proud of the responsibility.

'Thank you, love,' I said.

The other children were now coming out of school so I folded the pushchair and then left it out of the way in the porch of the main entrance.

'Am I going to school now?' Paula asked as Adrian took her hand.

'No, sis, you're too small,' he laughed.

'We're going into school for a little while,' I explained to Paula. 'So I can see Beth's teacher.'

'I'm going to big school now!' Paula declared.

Beth's classroom was on the first floor and Adrian and I took Paula by the hand and we went up the stairs together, with Paula counting the steps – as far as she could – as she did at home. We arrived on the landing and Miss Willow and Beth came out of their classroom.

'Hello,' Miss Willow said, coming forward to greet us. 'Thank you for coming in.'

'How's my daddy?' Beth immediately asked me.

'He's doing well,' I said. 'Your social worker telephoned. I'll explain later.' For I didn't want to delay Miss Willow.

'I thought Beth and Adrian could wait in the library,' Miss Willow said.

'Yes. I'll bring Paula in with me,' I said.

'We'll come down when we've finished,' Miss Willow said to Adrian and Beth.

'Yes, Miss,' they chimed respectfully. Adrian and Beth went downstairs where the library was situated.

Taking Paula's hand, I followed Miss Willow into her classroom.

'Thank you for coming,' she said again. 'Do sit down.' Then to Paula: 'Would you like to do some crayoning?'

Paula gave a shy nod. 'I am sure she would,' I said.

Miss Willow took some paper and crayons from one of the cupboards and set them on the table, then she drew up two extra chairs for Paula and me. Beth liked Miss Willow, and I could see why. She was a warm, friendly person. I guessed she was in her late twenties; she was fashionably but smartly dressed and had long brown hair. I knew she'd joined the school the year before, and playground gossip said she was an excellent teacher. I was quietly hoping that Adrian would be in her class when he went up a year in September.

'I won't keep you long,' she said apologetically. 'But I thought it would be a good idea if we had a chat, as Beth is living with you. I take it you don't know yet how long Derek will be in hospital?'

'No. When Jessie, their social worker, phoned she said he'd had a comfortable night, but that was all.'

'And you don't know Derek personally?' Miss Willow now asked.

'No. I've never met him, although I've probably seen him from a distance in the playground at the start and end of school.'

Miss Willow gave a small, thoughtful nod. 'It's no secret he's a single parent. Beth has never known her mother.'

'So I understand,' I said.

She paused again. 'Has Beth said much to you about her father? I know she's only just arrived, but I wondered if she'd talked about him?'

'She talks about him non-stop,' I said, smiling. 'They're obviously very close and she misses him a lot.'

'Yes,' Miss Willow said, and paused again as though collecting her thoughts.

I glanced at Paula, who was concentrating on her drawing. 'That's nice. Good girl,' I said encouragingly.

'I'd be grateful if you would keep what I'm going to say to yourself,' Miss Willow continued, her expression now serious.

'Yes, of course.' I met her gaze.

'The deputy head is aware I've asked to see you. We've been worried about Beth for some time. Not academically – she's doing very well with her work – but with regards to her home life.' Miss Willow paused again. 'To put it bluntly, we have concerns that Beth's relationship with her father is far too insular for a girl her age. It's claustrophobic, and stifling her social development. Beth's not allowed to attend school outings – there is always an excuse – and I know from the other children she's not allowed to go to birthday parties or play with friends outside of school. Beth talks a lot about her father. Her whole life seems to revolve around him, and his around her. There was a woman in Derek's life, but they parted some months ago. The situation deteriorated after that. Beth's father became ill and Beth became his carer. I was so worried by some of the things Beth was telling me that I spoke to the deputy head, and she alerted the social services. Has Beth said anything to you about …' Miss Willow paused, searching for the right words '… anything that you think is inappropriate?'

I held her gaze. 'Beth's only been with me a short while,' I said. 'She talks about her father a lot, and she's brought lots of photographs with her, but she hasn't really said anything inappropriate.'

Miss Willow gave a small half-nod. 'I understand. If you do think of anything, would you let her social worker know, please?'

'Yes, of course,' I said, puzzled and concerned. I wasn't sure exactly what I was being asked and had the feeling I wasn't being told the full story; perhaps confidentiality stopped Miss Willow from saying more.

'Hopefully the situation will improve now Derek is receiving medical help,' Miss Willow added.

'Yes,' I said.

'Don't get me wrong,' Miss Willow added. 'Beth's a good kid. And I know she'll be very well looked after staying with you.'

'Thank you.'

I helped Paula down from her chair and folded her drawing to take with us. I said goodbye and we left the classroom. Holding Paula's hand we counted down the steps but I was preoccupied and concerned by what Miss Willow had said. 'Inappropriate' was the word she'd used. Had Beth said anything inappropriate? Not really, although I remembered I'd felt uncomfortable with the idea of her sleeping snuggled up in my bed as she did with her father. Was that because it was inappropriate? I didn't know. What Miss Willow had said had taken me by surprise; I'd been expecting a chat about Beth's progress at school. I realized she must have spoken to Jessie about her concerns, although Jessie hadn't mentioned them to me.

* * *

30

Inappropriate

When we arrived home I told Beth that Jessie had telephoned the hospital and had spoken to a nurse who had said that her daddy had slept well. I also told Beth that she could telephone her father over the weekend. She was delighted. When she went into her bedroom she was pleased with the way I'd displayed her photographs, although she spent a few minutes rearranging them. Beth talked about her daddy over dinner, but with John due home the following evening for the weekend Adrian didn't appear to feel it so much. 'You'll meet my daddy tomorrow,' he said happily to Beth.

'You'll meet my daddy tomorrow,' Paula repeated.

That night, when I went into Beth's room to say goodnight, she said, 'I don't need Mr Sleep Bear any more. I've got my daddy with me.'

I was puzzled for a moment until Beth lifted the duvet to reveal the largest of the framed photographs nestled in bed beside her.

I smiled. 'I see,' I said. 'But the frame is very hard. It might hurt you if you lie on it in the night.' I was also concerned that the glass could break and cut her if she rolled over onto it in her sleep.

'I'll put him under my pillow,' Beth said. 'That's what I did when my daddy was in hospital before.'

'Oh, when was that?' I asked. I wasn't aware Derek had been in hospital before.

'About a year ago, I think,' Beth said, kissing the photograph and then sliding it under her pillow. 'He had to have an operation on his tummy. It was called ernie. When he came home he wasn't allowed to lift anything heavy.'

'That would be a hernia,' I said. 'So who looked after you while your daddy was in hospital?'

'Marianne,' she said, pulling a face. 'She stays at our flat sometimes. She's horrible. I hate her.' It was the first time I'd seen

Beth scowl. 'She loved my daddy, but he didn't love her. He sent her away. It's much, much better with just the two of us. I love my daddy and he loves me.'

'I know, love.'

The following evening, Friday, John returned home for the weekend. As soon as Adrian and Paula heard his key in the front door they rushed down the hall with shouts of 'Daddy! Daddy's home!'

I stayed in the living room where I was listening to Beth read as John let himself in and then hugged and kissed Adrian and Paula. 'We're in here!' I called from the living room.

John came into the living room, an arm around Adrian and Paula, and I kissed him and introduced Beth. John knew that Beth was staying; I'd told him when he'd telephoned the evening before. John was as committed to fostering as I was, but now he was working away he could only help at weekends.

'Hi, Beth,' he said. 'How are you settling in?'

'My daddy's ill in hospital,' Beth said. 'I miss him.'

'I'm sure you do,' John said. 'But the doctors will make him better.'

John sat on the sofa with Adrian beside him and Paula on his lap, making a fuss of the children and generally catching up on their news. Beth was sitting beside me and I saw her expression change and grow gloomy. I could guess why. Now that John was home, the children's situation was reversed: Adrian and Paula had their daddy with them, which highlighted that Beth's father was absent. I would try to make it up to her by giving her extra attention.

John ate his dinner with Adrian and Paula seated at the table watching him, while I read Beth a story in the living room. Once John had eaten we played a game together and then I suggested to Beth that she might like to come and help me put Paula to bed. I thought it would give her something to focus on and it would also be nice for Adrian to have some one-to-one time with his father. But Beth didn't want to come. She said she wanted to stay in the living room, so I left her with John and Adrian. Twenty minutes or so later when I came down to tell John that Paula was in bed and ready for a goodnight kiss, Beth was on the sofa snuggled into John's side. Adrian, sitting upright, was on the other side of him. Both children were gazing at the book John had open on his lap and was reading from. I told John that Paula was ready for her goodnight kiss and Beth said to John: 'Do you have to go?' Taking hold of his arm she snuggled closer into his side.

John hesitated.

'Yes, he does,' I said.

'I won't be long,' John said, and gently moved Beth away.

I'd discovered early on in fostering that it was very important (but not always easy) to get the balance right between the attention we gave our own children and those we fostered, to ensure that everyone felt loved, cherished and special.

That night, as I tucked Beth into bed, she asked if John could give her a goodnight kiss, as he had with Paula. 'Yes, of course,' I said without hesitation. I called to John, who was in Adrian's room.

John came into Beth's bedroom, said goodnight and gave her a kiss on her forehead.

'Thank you,' she said sweetly.

'You're welcome,' John said, and I could tell he thought that Beth was as sweet and uncomplicated as I did.

* * *

That weekend was bitterly cold and on Saturday we mainly stayed indoors. The children played – sometimes together, sometimes separately and sometimes with John or me. I thought that early afternoon was probably a good time for Beth to telephone her father, so after lunch I left John, Adrian and Paula in the living room and I took Beth to use the telephone in the main bedroom where it would be quieter. Beth perched on the edge of my bed and waited as I dialled the number for the hospital and then asked for Ward 3. Once I was through to the ward I gave my name, explained who I was and that Beth would like to speak to her father, Derek.

'Just a minute,' the nurse said. The telephone clunked as it was set down. There was a wait of a minute or so and then the telephone was picked up and a male voice said: 'Hello, Beth, is that you?'

'Derek, it's Cathy,' I said. 'Beth's foster carer. Beth is here beside me.'

'Oh, thank you so much,' Derek said. 'Thank you for phoning. That is kind of you. I can't begin to tell you how much I'm missing Beth.' Softly spoken, his voice broke. I could hear the emotion in his voice and my eyes immediately filled.

'I'll put her on now,' I said. I passed the telephone to Beth.

'Hello, Daddy,' Beth said in a small voice. 'When are you coming home?'

'Soon, baby,' I heard him say. 'As soon as I can, my princess. But Daddy's not well right now. I have to get better first.'

'How long until you get better, Daddy?' Beth asked. 'I miss you so much.'

'I miss you too, princess. Every minute of the day. Have you been to school?'

'Yes, Cathy took me.'

'Good. Thank her for me.'

Inappropriate

Beth lowered the telephone and, looking at me with round, sad eyes, said: 'My daddy says thank you.'

'That's OK,' I said, loud enough for Derek to hear.

'How long before you can come home, Daddy?' Beth asked again.

'Soon, princess. As soon as I'm better,' Derek said.

'What's the matter with you, Daddy?' Beth now asked.

Derek fell silent and I thought it was a difficult question to answer – to explain mental health to a young child.

'Things have been getting on top of me,' he said after a moment, his voice trembling. 'I keep crying. You saw me. That was wrong. It made you cry too.'

'I know. I don't like seeing you cry, Daddy. It makes me upset. I wish you were here with me and I could make you better.'

It went quiet again, and then Beth said: 'Don't cry, Daddy. Please don't cry.'

I heard a stifled sob on the other end of the telephone and then Beth passed the telephone to me. 'Daddy wants to speak to you.'

I took the phone. I could hear Derek's muffled sobs. 'It's Cathy,' I said gently. 'Try not to upset yourself. Beth's fine. I'm looking after her.'

'I know you are,' he said, his voice catching. 'But I can't talk to her right now. Hearing her little voice is too upsetting for me. Can you telephone me tomorrow, please? I promise I won't cry.'

I swallowed hard; the poor dear man, I thought. 'Yes, of course we'll telephone tomorrow. Is this time all right for you?'

'Any time is good,' Derek said, his voice faltering again. 'Thank you. Please give Beth my love. I'll be all right tomorrow, I promise.' Unable to say any more, he hung up and the line went dead.

I replaced the receiver and looked at Beth. Her eyes glistened and her bottom lip trembled. I took her in my arms and held her. 'Daddy is a bit upset,' I said. 'But he'll be all right soon. He said to tell you he loves you lots and we're to telephone again tomorrow.'

'I love him too,' Beth said. 'So, so much.'

Sometimes, fostering can break your heart.

I cuddled Beth until she felt better, then I reassured her that her daddy was being well looked after and we'd speak to him again tomorrow. We then went downstairs to join John, Adrian and Paula, who were covering the table with paper ready to do some painting. Beth sat at the table next to John and was soon joining in, and for the rest of the day she wouldn't leave John's side. She followed him like a shadow. Clearly missing her own father, she was taking some comfort in John as a father figure, and it crossed my mind that when John left on Monday for another week working away, Adrian and Paula wouldn't be the only ones missing him – Beth would too. I also thought it was really nice that Adrian and Paula were able to share their father's attention so easily with Beth, and I felt very proud of them. They didn't complain and I recognized how lucky I was that my children were so understanding and accommodating of the children we fostered. It takes the commitment of the whole family to successfully foster.

At bedtime Beth wanted John to kiss her goodnight as he had done the previous night. Paula was already asleep in bed and John was in Adrian's room helping him complete a large jigsaw puzzle that was spread out all over the floor. This had been a work in progress since Christmas, when the puzzle had been given to Adrian. I called to John from Beth's room that Beth would like him to say goodnight and he came in. At the same time Adrian called out: 'Mum! Come and see my puzzle. We've nearly finished.'

Leaving John in Beth's room, I went into Adrian's room where I admired the puzzle. It had over a thousand pieces and there were only about two dozen left to be fitted.

'Fantastic!' I said. 'You have done well.'

'I'm not going to break it up when it's done,' Adrian said excitedly. 'Dad said we can glue it on a big board and then he'll hang it on my bedroom wall.'

'Sounds good to me,' I said, and congratulated him again on completing the puzzle.

I came out and retuned to Beth's room and was slightly surprised to see John sprawled on Beth's bed with his arms around her. He looked up at me as I entered. 'Beth wanted a cuddle like her daddy gives her,' he said innocently.

'She's got the photograph of her father under her pillow,' I said with a feeling of unease. 'And Mr Sleep Bear.'

Perhaps John heard something in my voice, for, giving Beth a quick kiss on the forehead, he climbed off the bed and returned to Adrian's room to complete the puzzle. John hadn't done anything wrong, but seeing him lying on the bed beside Beth hadn't seemed quite right. Miss Willow's words had come back to me, and the term 'inappropriate'. It was a word I would soon be learning a lot about.

Chapter Five

Marianne

Sunday was another bitterly cold day so we decided to go to the cinema in the afternoon for the three o'clock showing of a newly released Walt Disney film. After lunch – at about half past one – I took Beth upstairs to my room to telephone her father, leaving Adrian and Paula with their father in the living room. Beth perched beside me on the bed while I dialled the number of the hospital, and once the call was connected to the ward Derek came to the telephone very quickly. As soon as he spoke I knew he was in better spirits. His voice was lighter and sounded more alive.

'Thank you so much for calling. I'm sorry about yesterday,' he said.

'There's no need to apologize,' I said. 'I'm glad you're feeling a bit better. I'll put Beth on now.'

'Thank you, Cathy.'

I passed the telephone to Beth, who was smiling. 'Hello, Daddy. How are you?'

'I'm doing all right,' I heard Derek say. 'So, how's my little princess?'

'I'm all right too,' Beth said brightly. 'We're going to the cinema this afternoon and I'm going to have popcorn and an ice cream.'

Marianne

I was pleased that Beth was being positive rather than telling her father that she was missing him, as she had done the day before. I'd had a little chat with her that morning when I'd explained that I thought it would help her father if she kept their conversation happy and told him nice things, so he wouldn't worry so much about her. Clearly she'd taken on board what I'd said, for she was now describing the games we'd been playing and the paintings she'd done for him, which she said she would give him when she next saw him.

I relaxed, and drawing my legs onto the bed I rested against the headboard, prepared for a long telephone conversation. Presently, Beth did likewise and propped herself beside me on the bed. It crossed my mind that I could leave her talking to her father while I got on with something else, but then I thought that Derek might want to speak to me, and if Beth became upset I wanted to be on hand to comfort her. With us both relaxed back against the bedhead, Beth continued chatting gaily to her father, now answering his questions about her clothes. 'Are you wearing the blue dress I bought you last month? The one with the bow at the back.'

'No,' Beth said. 'I'm wearing my new pink dress.'

'Good. I like you in that,' Derek said.

'I know you do, Daddy, that's why I chose it.' Beth grinned.

Beth liked her dresses, preferring them to jeans or jogging bottoms, and spent some time choosing which one to wear when she wasn't in school uniform.

'I like to look nice for you, Daddy,' Beth said, tweaking the flex of the telephone.

'But I can't see you,' Derek joked.

'I know, but you can think of me in my pink dress, can't you?'

'Yes, I can,' Derek agreed. 'If I close my eyes I can picture you in your pink dress with your hair flowing over your shoulders like a real princess: Daddy's princess.'

'And you're my prince!' Beth exclaimed. 'And we'll live happily ever after in a magical fairy-tale castle, just you and me.'

Beth also liked her fairy-tale stories and I'd read her quite a few, as she'd told me her father did at home.

'So, what are you going to see at the cinema?' Derek now asked.

Beth told him. 'John is coming,' Beth added. 'He's staying for the weekend.'

'Who's John?' Derek queried.

'Cathy's husband,' Beth said. 'He's helping Cathy look after me.'

It went quiet on the other end of the telephone, and then Derek said: 'Please don't say that, my princess, or you'll make your daddy sad. There's only one man in your life and that's me, your daddy.'

'I know, I'm only kidding!' Beth exclaimed quickly. 'Please don't be sad, Daddy. I think about you all the time, even at night. I have to sleep by myself here and I miss you lots. I wanted to sleep with Cathy, but she wouldn't let me. I have your photo under my pillow, but it's not the same as being with you.'

'It'll have to do for now,' Derek said flatly. 'Remember, you never sleep with anyone else, only your daddy. Remember that.'

'I will,' Beth said.

I suddenly realized that the conversation seemed to have taken on a different direction, and one that I wasn't feeling wholly at ease with. I had the same feeling as I'd had when I'd looked at all the framed photographs of Beth and her father, although I still couldn't identify what it was that was making me feel uncomfortable. I looked at Beth, who was again tweaking the telephone flex. She looked serious as she continued to reassure her father.

'Of course I won't sleep with anyone else,' she said. 'I only ever sleep with you. You're my handsome prince and always will be.'

'Thank you, princess. I love you.'

'I love you too, Daddy. You're not sad any more, are you?'

'No.'

Beth then asked her father what he'd been doing that day and he said watching television. They chatted for about five minutes more, during which time Derek told her about the hospital routine and Beth asked questions, and then he said he had to go. They blew each other lots of kisses and said I love you before they said goodbye, then Derek asked to speak to me. Beth handed me the telephone and went downstairs to join John, Adrian and Paula.

'I was wondering when you will next phone,' Derek said.

'I'm not sure,' I said. 'The social worker just said Saturday and Sunday.'

'I want Beth to call every evening.'

'I suppose that's all right,' I said, unsure.

'Good. We have dinner here at six o'clock, so can you telephone me at seven. I'll be ready and waiting by the telephone then.'

'Yes, all right, seven o'clock,' I confirmed, hoping I was doing the right thing.

'Thank you,' Derek said. 'Give Beth my love and tell her I'll speak to her tomorrow.'

We said goodbye and I went downstairs, where I told Beth what her father had said. She was, of course, delighted she'd be speaking to her father every evening. 'I miss my daddy,' she said to us all.

'Of course you do,' John said. 'That's only natural.'

* * *

That evening, when all the children were in bed, and after a pleasant afternoon at the cinema, John and I sat together in the living room, talking.

'Adrian misses you a lot more than he says,' I said. 'I hope you won't have to work away for much longer.'

'I hope so too,' John said with a small shrug. 'But you know I have to go where the company sends me. I don't have much choice in the matter.'

'Perhaps you could telephone a bit more during the week?' I suggested. 'Beth will be speaking to her father every evening and it will be nice for Adrian and Paula to speak to you.'

'I'll try, but it's not always possible,' John said. 'Sometimes we don't finish work until very late.'

'I understand,' I said. I hoped Adrian and Paula did too.

My thoughts returned to Beth and her father, as they had been doing on and off for most of the afternoon, and I now voiced my concerns to John. I needed his opinion.

'I know you haven't seen that much of Beth,' I said thoughtfully, 'but from what you have seen, do you get the impression that her relationship with her father is a little too intense? They obviously love each other, but is it too much?' I didn't know how else to phrase it.

John looked at me oddly. 'No. Whatever makes you say that?'

'Well, Beth talks about her father non-stop, and you've seen all those photographs in her room. She isn't allowed to play with children outside of school, and her teacher said she thought their relationship could be stifling Beth's social development. Then, this afternoon, when they were on the telephone, their conversation made me feel a bit uncomfortable.' I stopped, unable to find the exact words I needed to express my instinct.

John was still looking at me. 'No, I don't think there is anything wrong in Beth and her father loving each other,' he said. 'I'd hope that if I was in hospital Adrian and Paula would talk about me a lot. I think her teacher should concentrate on teaching rather than trying to cause trouble.'

Which surprised me, as John was usually more supportive when I aired my concerns, so I let the matter drop. I didn't want any ill feeling. John would be leaving again in the morning.

Later I telephoned my parents as I usually did on a Sunday evening if I hadn't seen them over the weekend. Then John left the living room to re-pack his suitcase ready for an early start the following morning. I put any thoughts of Beth and her father out of my mind. John's comments had half convinced me there was nothing wrong. It was midnight before we were both in bed and when I woke it was to the sound of the front door closing as John let himself out. I looked at my bedside clock; it was 6.15 a.m. As I turned over I saw John had left a note on the pillow: *Hope I didn't disturb you. I'll try to telephone the kids more. Have a good week. John x.* I was pleased.

I stayed in bed for another quarter of an hour and then showered and dressed before waking the children ready for school. We fell into our weekday routine and Beth was downstairs first for breakfast, having washed and made her bed. Adrian needed a couple of reminders before he appeared, but as always, with a lot of chivvying along, we left the house on time. As we arrived in the school playground, Beth remembered that her class had swimming the following day and she hadn't packed her swimming costume in her case.

'Marianne must have it,' Beth grumbled. 'She still does our washing sometimes.'

'Don't worry,' I said, thinking that it was nice of Marianne to do their washing. 'I'll buy you another costume.' Although where I'd find one in the middle of winter, I'd no idea.

The klaxon sounded for the start of school and Beth said goodbye and joined her class. Adrian, who'd been playing with his friends, ran over, kissed Paula and me goodbye and then joined his class. Paula and I returned home. I intended to have a coffee before setting off for the shops, but fifteen minutes after arriving home the telephone rang, and when I answered a female voice I didn't recognize said: 'Hello. Is that Cathy?'

'Speaking,' I said.

'Hi, my name is Marianne. I'm Derek's friend.'

'Hello,' I said, surprised, and wondering how Marianne had my telephone number.

'Jessie gave me your number,' Marianne clarified. 'I have Beth's swimming costume and she'll need it tomorrow. I thought I could drop it off to you in my lunch hour. The offices where I work are not far from you.'

'Thank you very much indeed,' I said. 'That's great. I was about to go into town and try to buy Beth a new costume.'

'No need,' she said. 'It's washed and ready. I can be with you at twelve-thirty, if that's OK?'

'Perfect,' I said, grateful. 'I hope it's not too much trouble.'

'Not at all.'

'Thank you so much.'

'I just need your house number. I have the name of your road.'

I told Marianne the number of my house and, thanking her again, said goodbye and hung up. What a lovely lady, I thought. How very kind and considerate. I would, of course, invite her in for a coffee if she had the time. I wondered why Beth didn't like Marianne; she seemed very pleasant to me. With no need to dash into town, I now played with Paula and then, while she had her nap, I tidied the living room and made a sandwich lunch ready for when she woke at twelve.

We had just finished eating when the doorbell rang. 'That'll be Marianne,' I said to Paula as she clambered down from her chair. Always a bit cautious of strangers, she held my hand as we went to answer the door.

'Hello, Marianne?' I smiled at the lady.

'Yes. Nice to meet you.' She handed me a carrier bag. 'Beth's swimming costume and also a doll she's fond of, and a few of her favourite fairy-tale stories. I wasn't sure what you had here.'

'Thank you,' I said. 'That's nice of you. Would you like to come in?'

Marianne glanced at her watch and hesitated but didn't immediately say no.

'I could make you a quick coffee?' I offered.

'I'm not intruding, am I?'

'No.' I smiled. 'There's just Paula and me at home. Do come in.'

'And Beth's at school?' Marianne hesitated again. 'She wouldn't want to see me.'

'Yes, she's at school,' I confirmed.

Marianne came in and said hello to Paula, who hid in my skirt.

'She's a bit shy with anyone new,' I said. 'Come through and have a seat in the living room. Would you like a tea or coffee?'

'A coffee would be lovely, thank you.'

'Milk and sugar?'

'Just milk, please. Thank you.'

I showed Marianne into the living room and Paula came with me to make the coffee. Marianne was an attractive woman who I guessed was a few years younger than Derek – in her mid-forties. She was smartly dressed for the office in a black pencil skirt and light-grey jumper. She clearly looked after herself; her hair was cut in a stylish bob and her lacquered nails were without a chip. I glanced at my own nails as I made the coffee and thought that I should really make an effort to lacquer them, but somehow I never had the time, unless I was going out for a special occasion. I set the two cups of coffee on the tray, added a few biscuits on a plate and carried the tray into the living room with Paula beside me. I placed the tray on the coffee table and handed Marianne a cup and saucer and offered her the plate of biscuits.

'Thank you so much,' she said appreciatively.

'Thank you,' Paula said, helping herself.

Marianne smiled. 'How old is she?'

'She'll be three in April.'

'I'm guessing your son is about Beth's age?' Marianne asked, glancing at Adrian's most recent school photograph on the wall.

'Yes, he's a year younger than Beth,' I said. 'Coincidentally, they both go to the same school.'

'That explains it,' Marianne said. 'I thought you looked familiar when you answered the door. I drop Beth off at school sometimes on my way into work, when Derek is on an early shift. I've probably seen you in the playground.'

'Very likely. I'm there every day. What does Derek do?'

'He works in the warehouse at –' and she named a large electrical store on the edge of town.

'And you work locally?' I asked, making conversation.

'Yes, at Gilford Accountants on the high street. I'm a bookkeeper. Not very exciting, but it pays the bills. I've been doing the job a long while.'

'Thank you so much for bringing Beth's swimming costume,' I said as we sipped our coffee. 'Beth did very well in remembering to pack most of what she needed.'

'Yes, she would,' Marianne said. 'She's very self-sufficient.' Her comment should have sounded like a compliment, but it didn't. 'So how is Beth?' Marianne now asked, setting her cup in her saucer and looking at me. 'I visited Derek at the hospital yesterday evening and he said she'd phoned.'

'Beth's fine,' I said. 'She's obviously missing her dad a lot, but I think it helped speaking to him on the phone. We're ringing him again tonight. Derek has asked us to telephone every evening.'

'He would,' Marianne said bluntly.

I looked at her as the words hung heavily in the air, but Marianne didn't elaborate, so I took a chance and shifted the conversation to a slightly more personal level. 'Have you known Derek long?' I asked.

'Over ten years,' Marianne said 'I was friends with him and his wife when she was there.'

I nodded and looked at Paula, who had quietly helped herself to another biscuit. 'Two is enough,' I said. Paula grinned sheepishly.

'When his wife left,' Marianne said, 'Beth was only small. I stepped in and helped Derek when I could, juggling it around my work. Everything seemed fine when Beth was little and while I was just a friend of Derek's, although it's true that she was always a daddy's girl. But when our friendship grew into a relationship and I began staying some nights, Beth turned on me. The situation became intolerable, until Derek finally ended our relationship. He didn't have any choice really, with the way Beth was behaving.'

'But Beth's only a child,' I said. 'How could she be responsible?'

Marianne held my gaze. 'Beth can be very manipulative, especially when it comes to her father. But I blame him as much as her. It was the two of them against me. Their relationship really isn't healthy. Not at all.'

Chapter Six

My Concerns Grow

A chill ran down my spine as Marianne concentrated on the cup and saucer she held in her lap and continued. 'I expect that sounds like a horrible thing to say, but I'm not the only one who has concerns. Beth's teacher asked me why Beth wasn't allowed to go on any school outings. I had to explain that her father wouldn't let her and that Beth wasn't allowed to go anywhere without him, apart from school. Miss Willow thought he was far too possessive and I agreed. If it had been my decision, of course Beth would have been allowed to go on the outings, and to play with other children in the neighbourhood.'

'When you said their relationship wasn't healthy, what did you mean?' I asked.

Marianne frowned. 'It's difficult to explain. But Beth and her father are far too close, and not like a father and daughter should be. In many ways, Beth is more like a wife to him. She even sleeps in his bed.' Marianne looked at me. 'Sorry. I shouldn't have said that.'

'I know Beth sleeps in the same bed as her father,' I said. 'She told me on the first night she was here. She wanted to sleep in my bed, but I didn't think it was appropriate, or fair on Adrian and Paula.'

'Exactly!' Marianne said forcefully, meeting my gaze. 'So why is it that you and I think that, but Derek can't see it? How did you make Beth sleep in her own bed? She always kicked off something awful when I tried to make her. She has a nice room at home, but she won't use it.'

'On the first night I gave her a cuddly toy, which I said would help her sleep, and since then she's been sleeping with a photograph of her father under her pillow. It seems to work.'

Marianne gave a small half-hearted nod. 'Derek was never firm enough with Beth. He's petrified that she will leave him as her mother did. He worshipped Beth's mother and when she ran off with an old boyfriend he was devastated. In some ways he never got over it. I think he sees Beth's mother in Beth, and clings to her memory through her. I don't know, it's all so confusing.' Marianne toyed with the rim of her cup, deep in thought. I waited, for clearly she needed to say more.

'Beth would never let me sleep with her father,' Marianne said after a moment, looking up at me. 'If I stayed the night, I had to sleep in Beth's bed. It was like I was the child and she was his wife. She threw a tantrum if I didn't agree to this, or anything else connected with her father. She knows how to get what she wants. I know it sounds pathetic, but the two of them stopped letting me go in the kitchen to prepare meals. They started cooking together and they were all over each other, kissing and cuddling like a couple of lovebirds. If I tried to show Derek any affection, Beth would push me away or push herself between us, so he had to kiss and cuddle her. Derek thought it was funny and just laughed. I never knew if it was for my benefit – that they wanted to show me how close they were – or if they were always like that.' Marianne shook her head. 'I don't know. I still help them. Derek needs my help, and as long as I don't show him any affection Beth tolerates me.' Marianne stopped and looked at me, her brow creased in anguish and confusion. 'Sorry, I don't know why I'm dumping this lot on you,' she said.

'I can understand why you're so worried,' I said. 'None of this sounds right to me either. Have you discussed it with the social worker?'

'No. I thought about it. But I couldn't think of what to say. It made me sound pathetic, as though I was jealous – of a seven-year-old girl! Perhaps I am. I wouldn't mind some of the affection Derek shows Beth. But he doesn't need me emotionally. He has all he needs in Beth. Though I worry about her and what is really going on.'

I held her gaze as my stomach tightened. 'You don't think there could be anything more than kissing and cuddling, do you? I mean, you said their relationship isn't healthy, but you don't think there could be anything –'

'Sexual?' Marianne put in.

I nodded sombrely.

'I honestly don't know. And what's sexual and what isn't? Where do you draw the line? Some of their kissing and cuddling could be described as sexual. I don't think for one moment Derek would hurt Beth, but where will it stop? Beth will be a teenager one day, and then a mature woman. Will they become lovers?' Marianne fell silent.

Anxiety, and fear for Beth, gripped me. 'The social worker needs to know,' I said.

Marianne nodded.

'Shall I tell her what you've told me?'

'Yes, please. It'll sound better coming from you. It's a relief to share all this at last.' Marianne glanced at her wristwatch. 'I'm sorry, I must go. I'm late for work already. I don't want to lose my job on top of everything else.' She immediately stood and returned her cup and saucer to the tray. 'Thank you for listening and thanks for the coffee.'

'You're welcome.' I also stood.

Paula, who'd been playing on the floor with her toys, came to my side and slipped her hand into mine. The three of us walked in silence to the front door. Marianne paused before leaving and, turning to me, said anxiously: 'We are doing the right thing in telling the social worker, aren't we? Derek is very vulnerable and he isn't coping well.'

'Yes. Beth is a child who is also very vulnerable. She has to be protected. I'm sure the social worker will know what to do and will handle it sensitively.'

Marianne gave a resigned nod and, turning, went down the path and to her car. I closed the front door.

'Was that lady Beth's mummy?' Paula asked.

'No, love. She's a friend of Beth's daddy. She's been helping to look after Beth.' Paula had obviously heard Marianne and me discussing Beth, but at her age, thankfully, hadn't understood the content or implications of what we'd said.

It was with a very heavy heart that I took Paula into the living room, settled her with her toys on the floor and explained that I had an important telephone call to make and that I would use the telephone in the hall.

'OK, Mummy,' Paula said. 'I understand.'

I left the door to the living room ajar so that Paula could come out if she needed me. I returned down the hall and picked up the telephone on the hall table. I dialled the number of the social services and was put through to the children's services department. I gave my name, explained I was Beth's foster carer and asked to speak to Jessie. Jessie's colleague said that Jessie was out of the office on a home visit and wasn't expected back until much later that afternoon. I left my telephone number together with a message asking if Jessie would telephone me as soon as possible. The social worker then asked if it was an emergency and I said it wasn't, although I did need to speak to Jessie as soon as possible.

I replaced the receiver, went into the living room and checked on Paula, who was still amusing herself, then I took the tray containing the cups and saucers into the kitchen where, preoccupied with thoughts of Beth, I rinsed them out. I took the clean laundry upstairs where I distributed it into the drawers in the children's bedrooms. As I entered Beth's room, my gaze went to the rows of framed photographs on the shelves. I went closer and stood in front of them for a few moments, viewing them individually and also collectively. It was then I realized what it was about the photographs that made me feel so uncomfortable: it was the manner in which Beth and her father were posing. They either had their arms wrapped around each other and were gazing into each other's eyes or they had their heads together and were smiling at the camera. But in each of their poses they were more like a couple than father and daughter, or as Marianne had said – lovebirds. The more I looked at the photographs the more obvious it became. I thought of the photographs of Adrian and Paula with their father and I knew none of them were like this. Yet there was nothing overtly sexual in the pictures. Derek and Beth weren't touching inappropriately; it was the overall impression that was suggestive. Something definitely wasn't right.

My mouth went dry as I turned away from the photographs. I lay Beth's clothes on her bed and then reached under the pillow and slid out the photograph she slept with. It was a picture of Beth and her father on the beach. They were in their swimwear, kneeling on the sand and facing each other with their lips pursed as though blowing a kiss. It was the largest of the photographs and I now realized the most intimate. I wondered who had taken it and whether they had seen anything odd in the pose of this father and daughter. I returned the photograph to beneath the pillow, put Beth's clothes away and then came out of her room.

By the time I left for school Jessie hadn't returned my telephone call, so I telephoned again at five o'clock. A colleague said that Jessie had been delayed and she wasn't expected to return to the office that day. She said she'd leave a message for her to telephone me first thing in the morning.

When I told Beth that Marianne had brought her swimming costume, she pulled a face.

'I thought it was nice of Marianne to go out of her way to help us,' I said to Beth. 'It saved me a trip into town.'

'I'd rather have a new costume,' Beth grumbled. 'Daddy would have bought me a new one.'

'Really?' I said lightly, ignoring her ill humour. I continued with the preparations for dinner.

Beth was soon over her grumpiness and was excited by the prospect of telephoning her daddy at seven o'clock, and every evening. Over dinner she talked about little else. I watched her closely as we ate. With Marianne's words still fresh in my mind, everything Beth said about her father and her mannerisms when she spoke of him took on a more sinister tone. *Daddy kisses my feet and it makes me laugh*, Beth declared, giggling. *Daddy likes brushing my hair at bedtime until it shines. Daddy and me go to bed at the same time and he cuddles up to me.* Even *I'm Daddy's little princess* now had an uncomfortable ring to it. Yet Beth clearly loved her father as he did her. Their relationship, as Marianne had said, was confusing, and the concerns were difficult to identify and put into words.

* * *

As seven o'clock approached I steeled myself to make the telephone call to Derek, for I really didn't want to talk to him. Beth had been reminding me for the last hour that it was nearly time to telephone her daddy. Adrian was in the living room reading, and seven o'clock was usually the time I started Paula's bath and bedtime routine. That night, however, I bathed Paula early and then put her into bed with some toys and told her I'd read her a story after Beth had telephoned her father.

'I understand, Mummy,' she said sweetly.

'Good girl.'

Beth was already in my bedroom, sprawled out on the bed and waiting for me to make the call. I sat on the edge of the bed, hoping against hope that Derek wouldn't be able to come to the phone. I dialled the hospital and was put through to the ward. True to his word, Derek was ready and waiting and came to the telephone as soon as the nurse called him.

'Hello, Cathy,' he said brightly. 'How are you?' Ridiculously, I was surprised that his voice sounded normal.

'Good evening, Derek,' I said evenly. 'I'll put Beth on.'

'Before you do, can I have a quick word please?'

'Yes?'

'I just wanted to know if Beth was all right. You know, eating and sleeping well. She sounds all right on the phone, but obviously it's very worrying for me not to be with her.'

'I appreciate that,' I said. 'Beth is fine.' And I passed the telephone to her.

Impolite of me, yes, but my thoughts were in turmoil.

I sat on the edge of the bed as Beth talked to her father. They began by asking each other how they were and what they'd been doing. They said how much they were missing each other and blew kisses down the phone, which took on a new significance given what I now knew. Derek then began talking in a silly high-pitched voice to make Beth laugh, and they both giggled like children.

'Oh Daddy, you're teasing me again. Stop it.' Beth laughed.

More silly voices followed and then Derek asked Beth what she was wearing and she lowered her voice and fluttered her eyelids as she told him she'd changed out of her school uniform and into her blue dress with the bow, to please him – in a manner almost as if she were flirting. Then she said: 'Oh Daddy, I miss you and your warm cuddles so much.'

'I miss you too, princess,' Derek said. 'I miss holding you in my arms so very much. I can't wait until I'm home and can tuck you up in bed beside me again.' Which, in the light of what I now suspected, made me shudder.

I wasn't sure how much longer I could listen to all of this; they'd been on the telephone for nearly half an hour. Then Paula, who'd been waiting patiently in her bed, called out: 'Mummy, is it time for a story yet?'

'Yes, love,' I called back. 'I'll be with you soon.'

I waited while Derek finished telling Beth that he hoped he'd be home soon, and then I said to Beth: 'You need to say goodbye now.'

She looked at me, surprised.

'I'll explain,' I said, easing the telephone from her. 'Sorry,' I said to Derek. 'Can you say goodbye now, please? I need to end the call as my daughter is calling for me.'

'Can't you leave Beth to talk to me while you see to your daughter?' Derek asked.

Something told me I shouldn't leave Beth alone with her father, not even on the telephone. 'It's difficult,' I said to Derek. 'Beth is in my bedroom and my daughter is in her room.'

'Oh, OK,' he said reasonably. 'Can I say goodbye to Beth?'

'Yes, of course.'

I passed the telephone to Beth, who was glaring at me.

'Why is she telling you to go?' she asked her father. 'I can speak to you if I want.'

'You'd better do as she says as you're in her house,' Derek said.

And just for a moment I caught a glimpse of the 'them and us' situation Marianne had described, only now it was the two of them against me.

'And you'll telephone tomorrow?' Derek asked Beth.

'Of course I will, Daddy. I love you.'

There now followed a series of 'byes', 'miss yous' and 'love yous', with kisses blown in between, which seemed never-ending, so eventually I said, 'Bye, Derek,' loud enough for him to hear. Taking the telephone from Beth, I returned it to its cradle.

'You can't do that!' Beth said, rounding on me.

I looked at her, startled by her vehemence.

'It's nearly your bedtime,' I said.

'Not for much longer,' she grumbled, showing a different side to her. 'My daddy said he'll be home soon, and then I can go to bed whenever I want.'

I find that most negative or provocative comments are best ignored, so I set my face to a cheerful smile and asked Beth if she would like a drink before she started getting ready for bed. She didn't. She stomped round to her room and closed her bedroom door with a bang. I gave her time to cool down while I read Paula a story, and then, having said goodnight to Paula, I went to Beth's room and knocked on the door. I went in and told her it was time to have a wash and clean her teeth. She was calm now and clearly a little uncertain of me, possibly because, unlike her daddy, I hadn't done exactly as she had wanted. When Beth was ready for bed, I went into her room to say goodnight.

'Can I telephone my daddy tomorrow, please?' she asked politely.

'I'm not sure yet, love,' I said, honestly. 'I'll need to speak to your social worker first. Jessie said we were to telephone over the weekend, that was all, so I'll have to check if it's OK to phone every evening too.' In truth I thought that Jessie would stop telephone contact in the light of what I was going to tell her.

Beth accepted this and then asked for a hug and kiss goodnight, which I gave her. With a smile, she turned onto her side and, slipping her hand under the pillow, retrieved the photograph of her and her father on the beach. She gave his image a big kiss through the glass and then tucked the photograph under the pillow again. 'Night-night, Daddy,' she sighed. 'Night, Cathy.'

'Night, love,' I said. 'Sleep tight.'

I came out and drew the door to, leaving the landing light on. I felt sorry for Beth, and I didn't in any way hold her responsible for the relationship that appeared to have developed between her and her father. Derek was an adult and should have known better. He was responsible for overstepping the line from a healthy father-and-daughter relationship into something inappropriate and for his gratification, which I now believed it was. Beth was only a child – a child who had never known her mother's love. She didn't know it was wrong to reciprocate and return her father's inappropriate affection. I wondered if Derek's mental health had played a part, although I hadn't been told what was wrong with him. Until I could speak to Jessie I felt I carried the burden of what I knew, just as Marianne had.

After saying goodnight to Adrian and checking Paula was asleep, I went downstairs where I sat on the sofa and wrote some notes about the points I wanted to make when I spoke to Jessie the following day. Now, foster carers are encouraged to keep a daily log in respect of the children they foster, where they record any significant events as well as appointments for the child, but then logs hadn't been introduced, so as an aide-mémoire I made notes. When I'd finished, I let Toscha out for her evening run and then I had an early night. I was emotionally exhausted, but once in bed I found I couldn't sleep. Marianne's worries combined with my own concerns about the relationship between Beth and her father. I believed Marianne to be a genuine and honest person, and I thought she'd told me the truth. She'd never married or had children of her own, and it was clear to me she still thought a lot of Derek and Beth. I thought she would have made a good wife and stepmother, had she been given the chance. It said a lot of her that she continued to visit and support Derek and Beth despite the way she'd been treated by them.

After a restless night I woke feeling less refreshed than when I'd gone to bed, and I stumbled through the early-morning routine of showering, dressing and then waking the children ready for breakfast. We wrapped up warm that morning before leaving the house. The weather was freezing with a cruel north-easterly wind. We hurried to school and Paula and I were pleased when we were home again and in the warm. I made us a hot chocolate each and then I played with Paula, expecting Jessie to telephone at any moment. She still hadn't phoned by the time Paula had her morning nap, so once Paula was settled I returned to the living room and, with my notes on my lap, telephoned the children's services department. To my surprise, Jessie answered.

'Jessie, it's Cathy, Beth's carer,' I said. 'I left a message yesterday for you to telephone me.'

'Yes. Got it. It's on my list of to-dos.' She sounded rushed and stressed.

'Is it possible to talk to you now?' I asked. 'It is important.'

'Go on then, quickly. I'm due in a meeting soon.'

Quickly wasn't what I had in mind. I needed time to describe my concerns, but I went ahead anyway. It was a big mistake.

Chapter Seven
Guilty

'I'm worried about Beth,' I began. 'Marianne visited me yesterday. She brought Beth's swimming costume.'

'Yes, I know. I gave her your telephone number.'

'She told me some things about Beth and her father and the way they behave towards each other that are very worrying. I think you should know.'

'Like what?' Jessie asked. 'Marianne hasn't said anything to me.'

'No. She was going to, but she wasn't sure what to say. It seems that Derek behaves towards Beth in a manner that isn't appropriate.'

'Whatever do you mean?' Jessie asked, or rather demanded. 'Derek is in hospital.'

'No, before he went in, I mean. Marianne said the way he kisses and cuddles Beth isn't right. And Beth sleeps in his bed.'

'Lots of parents kiss and cuddle their children and let them sleep in their beds,' Jessie said. Which, of course, was true.

'But he's very possessive of her,' I continued. 'Beth's not allowed to play with children her own age away from school, or go to their birthday parties, or go on school outings. Miss Willow told me.'

'Yes, I know, and I've told Derek that Beth needs to start taking advantage of all aspects of the curriculum, including educational visits and after-school activities.'

I knew I wasn't handling this well, but I continued. 'Since Beth has been with me, I've noticed she talks constantly about her father. And she's brought fifteen framed photographs with her. All of her and her father.'

'That's nice,' Jessie said.

'But there's something not right about the photographs. Their poses are more like two adults than father and daughter.'

'I saw most of the photographs as Beth packed them. They seemed all right to me. They've got their clothes on. What's wrong with them?'

'It's the way they're cuddling and smiling at each other. It makes me feel uncomfortable.'

There was silence on the other end of the telephone and I could guess what Jessie was thinking. I knew I wasn't handling this correctly, but it was so difficult to put my concerns into words.

'Some of the things Beth and her father say to each other don't seem right,' I said. 'They are too lovey-dovey. And Marianne has to sleep in Beth's bed when she stays the night and Beth sleeps with her father.'

'Isn't that because Marianne's relationship with Derek has ended and is simply friendship again?' Jessie said. 'I guess she sleeps in Beth's bed or on the couch.' Which again was true.

I went to the next point in my notes. 'When my husband was here at the weekend, at bedtime Beth wanted him to lie on her bed and cuddle her like her father did.'

'And did he?'

'I told him not to.'

'So you dealt with the matter?'

'Yes. But there are other things.'

'Go on.'

'Beth is more like a wife to Derek than a daughter. She has a lot of responsibility. You saw it yourself when you took her home for her things before you brought her here. She was worried about the washing and the food in the fridge spoiling. I've had to reassure her that I take care of that sort of thing here. Add my concerns to Marianne's and Miss Willow's and there's definitely something not right,' I finished lamely.

There was a pause before Jessie asked: 'Are you suggesting that Derek is abusing his daughter?'

'No. Well, possibly. I don't know. But I think someone needs to look into it.'

There was another pause before Jessie said formally, 'Mrs Glass, I really don't think there is any cause for concern, but I'm planning on seeing Derek in hospital this evening if I can leave the office in time. I'll raise your concerns with him then and see what he has to say.'

'No, don't do that,' I blurted. 'I mean, I don't want you to say that I said these things.'

'How else am I to approach the matter? The poor man has a right to know what he is being accused of and to have the chance to defend himself.'

At that point I really regretted saying anything. 'But it's not just my view,' I said pathetically. 'Marianne and Beth's teacher have concerns too. And a parent in the playground came to me and said she thought Derek was over-possessive. Her daughter is a friend of Beth's, but she's not allowed to play with her or go to tea.'

'I hope Derek isn't becoming the subject of playground gossip,' Jessie said. 'Now, is there anything else? I'm running late.'

'No. I'm sorry.'

'I'll be in touch when I have any news. Derek is hoping to come out of hospital soon. That's one of the reasons I am going to see him – to talk about his discharge.'

Jessie said a quick goodbye and cut the call. I sat on the sofa, staring at the telephone, feeling a complete idiot, which is what I imagined Jessie probably thought of me too. Perhaps even a malicious idiot who was prone to idle gossip. I'd been so convinced that Derek's relationship with Beth was inappropriate – so too had Marianne and Miss Willow – but now I wasn't so sure. All the points I'd raised with Jessie had sounded feeble and unfounded, and she'd easily justified them all as normal behaviour. Could all three of us have been wrong? I thought it was possible. Then I realized I'd forgotten to ask Jessie if Beth should telephone her father in the evenings, although given Jessie's reaction to what I'd said I assumed the answer would be yes, for there was no reason not to telephone Derek; according to Jessie he'd done nothing wrong.

Paula woke a few minutes later and I went upstairs feeling anxious and wretched. I put on a cheerful face as I brought her downstairs and then played with her and read her some stories. But my heart wasn't in it. I was preoccupied and then I felt guilty for not giving her my full attention. I deeply regretted telephoning Jessie. I should have advised Marianne to telephone her, for I was now convinced she'd have made a better job of explaining her concerns. I wondered if Jessie would telephone Marianne and possibly Miss Willow to substantiate what I'd said, or possibly doubt my abilities as a foster carer. I felt a failure. I'd made a decision and it had been the wrong one.

* * *

Guilty

Beth was out before Adrian at the end of school and the first thing she asked was: 'Did you speak to my social worker? Can I telephone my daddy?'

'Yes,' I said.

'Goody!' she cried, and jumped for joy. 'I love my daddy!'

Adrian came out and I listened to his news on the way home, but my thoughts kept returning to the telephone contact I would have to initiate later. Jessie would have visited Derek by then and told him what I'd said. My stomach knotted and I had little appetite at dinner. Apart from it being very embarrassing to speak to Derek after what Jessie would have told him, I knew he had every right to be angry. I briefly considered writing down the number of the hospital and the ward and letting Beth make the call, but I wasn't that much of a coward. I tried consoling myself with the reminder that I'd done what I thought was right at the time and had only wanted to protect Beth. If Derek raised the matter, which I was sure he would, all I could do was apologize.

After dinner I gave Paula an early bath and settled her in bed with some toys, as I had done the evening before.

'Is Beth phoning her daddy again?' Paula asked.

'Yes, love. I think she'll be phoning him every evening while she's with us.'

'Can I telephone my daddy?' Paula asked.

'He's at work, love. He'll telephone if he can.' I felt for her and hoped John would phone.

Leaving Paula in bed with some toys, I went into my bedroom where Beth was sprawled on the bed, waiting for me, and looking forward to speaking to her daddy. She'd said a few times during the evening that she was hoping her daddy would tell her which day he would be coming home, so she was very excited. My stomach was churning. I sat on the edge of the bed and dialled the hospital and then asked for Ward 3. When I was put through to the ward I asked for Derek, expecting that, as before, he'd be ready and would come to the telephone straight away. But instead of calling Derek to the phone, the nurse who'd answered said to me, 'Hold the line, please.' I heard the telephone being set down and then there was a short silence before the nurse came back on the line and said: 'Derek is asleep.'

I was surprised. 'Are you sure?' I asked. 'It's seven o'clock and he's expecting his daughter to phone.'

'Just a minute,' the nurse said, and the telephone was set down again. I heard muffled voices in the background and then the telephone was picked up and the same nurse asked: 'Are you a relative?'

'No. I'm his daughter's foster carer.'

'Derek is asleep and shouldn't be woken,' she said. 'You'll need to speak to the social worker tomorrow.'

I hesitated, confused. 'I don't understand.'

'I'm sorry. As you are not a relative, I can't tell you any more. You'll have to speak to his social worker tomorrow.'

Aware something was wrong, Beth was no longer sprawling leisurely on the bed, but had sat upright and was looking at me, concerned.

'And he can't come to the telephone to talk to his daughter? Not just for a short while?' I asked.

'No. I'm sorry. He's asleep.'

There was nothing more I could say, so, thanking the nurse, I put down the telephone and turned to Beth. Her face was already crumpling. 'Why can't I speak to my daddy?' she asked, her voice trembling.

'Because he's asleep, love, and the nurse didn't want to wake him.'

'But he wanted to speak to me. He told me to phone. They should have woken him.'

'I'm sorry, love. I can't do any more. I only know what the nurse told me.'

'Can't we phone and try again?' Beth asked, her eyes filling. 'That nurse might be wrong. Can you speak to another nurse?'

'The nurse said your daddy was definitely asleep, pet,' I said, taking her hand in mine. 'Perhaps he's had a busy day.' But Beth didn't believe this any more than I did. 'I'll telephone Jessie tomorrow,' I said.

Beth burst into tears and I put my arms around her and comforted her. I felt sorry for her. She was so disappointed at not being able to speak to her father. I also felt guilty, for I was sure that in some way I was responsible for Derek 'being asleep' and not being able to come to the phone. It seemed too much of a coincidence that Derek hadn't been able to come to the phone after Jessie's visit.

I soothed Beth, and when she was feeling a bit better I gently dried her eyes. 'There, that's better,' I said. 'Now, why don't you go downstairs and play a game with Adrian, while I read Paula a story? I won't be long.'

'Can I come with you?' Beth sniffed.

'Yes, of course, if you want to.'

Beth nodded mournfully and I took her hand and we went round to Paula's room.

'Beth would like to listen to your story too, if that's all right?' I said to Paula.

'Yes. You can listen,' Paula said, patting the bed beside her. 'Have you spoken to your daddy?' she asked as Beth climbed onto the bed.

I saw Beth's bottom lip tremble. 'Not tonight,' I said. 'Her daddy was asleep.'

'Don't worry,' Paula said. 'I don't speak to my daddy much on the phone.' I could have wept. Perhaps I was feeling overly sensitive, but Paula's comment touched me deeply, and I dearly hoped John would remember his promise to telephone during the week.

There wasn't much room on Paula's single bed for the three of us, but we managed. Propped up against the headboard, I balanced precariously on the edge of the bed as I read Paula's favourite stories. Although the books were a little young for Beth, she seemed to enjoy them as much as Paula did. Also, I think she enjoyed the closeness and intimacy of the bedtime story. It's a lovely way for children to unwind at the end of the day.

'I'm going to ask my daddy to read me stories in bed when I go home,' Beth said.

'Can't your mummy read you stories?' Paula asked innocently.

'She doesn't live with us,' Beth said.

'My daddy doesn't live with us much either,' Paula agreed.

I didn't know whether to laugh or cry. I read the next story and continued reading for half an hour.

Later, when Beth was in her bed and I went to say goodnight, she was clearly still thinking of her father. 'Why didn't Daddy want to speak to me?' she asked.

My heart clenched, and I felt even guiltier. 'It wasn't that Daddy didn't want to speak to you,' I said. 'He was asleep.'

'But it was only seven o'clock,' Beth said. 'And he knew I was going to phone. He told me to phone every evening.'

'I know. But sometimes in hospital plans change at the last minute. It can't be helped. I'll telephone your social worker tomorrow and see what she says.'

Beth finally accepted this and I tucked her in and kissed her goodnight. She turned onto her side and, sliding the photograph of her father from under the pillow, kissed his image through the glass. 'Night, Daddy,' she whispered. 'I'll telephone tomorrow. Please be awake.'

She returned the photograph to under the pillow. I said goodnight again and came out.

I had another restless night thinking about Derek, what Jessie had said and the conversation I would have with Jessie the following day. Eventually I fell asleep in the early hours and it seemed I'd no sooner fallen asleep than the alarm was ringing. I tumbled out of bed and into the school-day routine: waking the children, helping Paula wash and dress and then making breakfast. It was another cold January day, with grey skies that stretched as far as the eye could see. We wrapped up warm in our coats, scarves and gloves and hurried to school. On the way home I stopped off at the local grocery store for milk and bread. Also shopping was a friend of mine, Kay, with her daughter Vicky; her children were a similar age to mine. We began chatting and presently Kay said, 'Cathy, rather than stand here talking, why don't you come back to my house for coffee, and the girls can play?' We did this from time to time – meeting at Kay's house or mine and sometimes with other friends and their children too.

'I'd love to,' I said. 'But I have to speak to Beth's social worker first thing about something urgent.' Kay knew I fostered, as did my other close friends.

'So why not come over later when you've spoken to the social worker? Say about eleven o'clock? How does that sound?' Although Paula often had a short nap at eleven o'clock, she was coming to the end of the time when she needed a daytime sleep.

'Thanks. That would be great,' I said. 'We'll see you later.'

'See you later,' the girls chimed, grinning at each other.

I bought the groceries I needed and went home. I wondered if Jessie would telephone me; the last time we'd spoken she'd said she would call if she had any news. I waited until just after ten o'clock and then I decided to telephone her. Settling Paula with some toys in the living room, I told her I was going to use the telephone in the hall so that I didn't disturb her, and that once I'd finished we'd get ready and go to Kay's, which pleased her.

I dialled the children's services and asked for Jessie's extension. She answered.

'It's Cathy, Beth's carer,' I said.

'I was going to telephone you later. How is Beth?'

'All right now, but she was upset last night when we phoned her father. He couldn't speak to her.'

'I know,' Jessie said.

'The nurse said he was asleep.'

'He was sedated,' Jessie said bluntly. 'They were putting him to bed as I left.'

'Oh dear,' I said. 'Can I ask you why he was sedated?'

'He was upset,' Jessie said, equally bluntly. 'When I told him of your concerns, he became very agitated and started shouting and crying. The doctor was called and said he would give him something to calm him down and help him sleep.'

'I'm so sorry,' I said. As I'd feared, I was responsible.

'It's not your fault,' Jessie said, which surprised me. 'Derek was in a fragile state to begin with. I told him I thought the allegations were unfounded and I had no reason to doubt his ability to parent Beth, but he still took it very badly. He feels there is a lot of prejudice against a man bringing up a daughter alone, and I think he could be right. He's overheard mothers discussing him in the playground. One even suggested that the reason his wife had disappeared was because he'd "done her in". Miss Willow had also spoken to him, so I'm afraid your comments were the final straw. I reassured him that as far as I'm concerned the matter is finished, but it didn't help. Hopefully he's recovered now.'

'I do hope so,' I said. I hesitated, then I dared to ask: 'Did you tell him what Marianne said?' From what Jessie had said, it seemed that she hadn't mentioned Marianne's worries to Derek, just mine.

'Yes. Derek admitted there was a problem between Marianne and Beth. He said they seemed to be jealous of each other and vied for his attention. It was going from bad to worse, which was why he ended his relationship with Marianne. He explained this to Marianne, but it appears she doesn't want to believe it.'

Put like that it all seemed so rational and reasonable. I felt an absolute fool – a vindictive fool who had caused a lot of trouble and set back Derek's recovery.

'I'm sorry,' I said. 'Will Derek be well enough for Beth to speak to him this evening?'

'Yes. I should think so. I'm going to telephone the hospital later and see how he is today. If you don't hear from me, assume he's all right and telephone as normal. But Cathy, I would appreciate it if you just made the call and then passed the telephone to Beth. I don't want you engaging in conversation with Derek. Understood?'

'Yes.'

'Also, I want Beth to see her father later in the week. The doctor agrees it will help his recovery. I was thinking of Friday after school. I was going to ask you to take Beth, but given the animosity between you and Derek I think it's better if I take her.'

'All right,' I agreed, feeling completely ineffectual.

'If I don't speak to you before, I'll collect Beth at about four o'clock on Friday, and return her after the visit.'

'Thank you,' I said. 'Shall I tell Beth she'll be seeing her father on Friday?'

'Yes. It will help cheer her up. Should help cheer up Derek too. Poor man, he was so upset. Inconsolable.'

Which compounded my feelings of guilt and wretchedness.

Chapter Eight
Wise Owl

Paula and I went to Kay's house as arranged at eleven o'clock and the two girls played while Kay and I talked over coffee. Kay soon realized I was preoccupied and it wasn't long before she asked: 'Is everything all right, Cathy? You don't seem your usual chatty self.'

'Sorry,' I said. 'I have a problem connected with the fostering. I made an error of judgement and caused someone a lot of upset.' Kay knew that confidentiality forbade me from discussing the details, as did my other friends and family.

'I'm sure you didn't mean to,' Kay said. 'I know how much fostering means to you, and how much you love it. All that time you invest in it. Anyone can make a mistake.'

'Thank you.' I smiled weakly. 'Unfortunately this was rather a large mistake and I've hurt someone a lot.'

We stayed for just over an hour and then Kay offered to make us some lunch, but I politely refused, saying I had things to do. In fact, I felt I was such poor company that it would be better for her if we went. 'Another time would be good,' I said. 'Or you could come to us. We can arrange something next week.'

'That'd be lovely,' Kay said. 'Try not to worry.'

'Thank you.'

We said goodbye, and I went home – to brood.

That afternoon, when Beth came out of school, she asked if I'd spoken to Jessie and if she could telephone her father.

'Yes, you can,' I said with a smile. I'd assumed that Jessie would have telephoned me by now if the call wasn't going ahead. 'Also, Jessie is going to take you to see your daddy after school on Friday.'

Beth's face lit up. 'Fantastic! I'm going to see my daddy. What was the matter with him last night?'

'He was asleep, like the nurse said,' I replied, which was close to the truth. I wouldn't normally explain sedation to a child Beth's age unless it was absolutely essential, as it would be upsetting for them.

I continued to worry about the distress I'd caused Derek by unjustly accusing him for the rest of the day. I was looking forward to the weekend, when John would be home and I could share my worries with him, for, as the saying goes, a problem shared is a problem halved. Just as we'd finished eating dinner, the telephone rang. I left the table and answered it in the living room. I was very pleased to hear John's voice.

'Hello, love. What a lovely surprise!' I said. 'Adrian and Paula will be so pleased you phoned. I'll call them now. And when you've finished talking to them I'd like a chat too. Adrian! Paula!' I called from the living room. 'Dad's on the phone.'

They came running and jumped onto the sofa and sat side by side. I handed the telephone to Adrian. 'You speak to Dad first and then pass the phone to Paula,' I said to Adrian. He nodded.

'Hi, Dad!' Adrian began with a broad grin. I could see how delighted he was that his father had made the time to call. Paula was grinning too.

I left Adrian and Paula to talk to their father and I returned to Beth, who was still sitting at the dining table, although she'd finished eating.

'When can I telephone my daddy?' she asked pensively.

'At seven o'clock, love. In forty-five minutes,' I said, glancing at the wall clock. 'Not long now.'

'Their daddy doesn't telephone much, does he?' Beth said.

'No, so I'm very pleased he's found the time to telephone now.'

'Why doesn't he phone them much?' Beth asked. 'Doesn't he want to speak to them?'

'That's not the reason,' I said, taken aback that Beth should think this. 'Their daddy is very busy at work. He phones when he can, and please don't say that to Adrian and Paula. They miss him enough already.'

'I miss my daddy too,' Beth said. 'Can I speak to their daddy?'

I hesitated. This was a small chance for Adrian and Paula to speak to their father, yet I didn't want to say no. 'When they've finished you can say a quick hello,' I said, 'but not for too long. You don't want to be late phoning your daddy, do you?'

'No,' Beth agreed. I awarded myself full marks for tact and diplomacy.

We could hear Adrian's voice floating through from the living room as Beth helped me clear the dishes. Adrian was answering his father's questions about school and then football club. Then, a little while later, I heard Paula's voice: 'Hello, Daddy. I've been playing at Kay's house today, with Vicky.' She began telling him her news. Then I could hear the two of them chatting, presumably holding the telephone between them, and then Adrian called: 'Mum! Dad wants to speak to you. He has to go soon.'

Beth came with me into the living room and Adrian handed me the phone. 'Hi, love,' I said to John. 'Beth would like to say a quick hello, if you have the time?'

'Sure. Put her on.'

I passed the telephone to Beth and, smiling, she said, 'Hi, I'm going to speak to my daddy soon. It's been nice talking to you. Goodbye.' Satisfied, she returned the telephone to me.

'How's work?' I now asked John. 'Still very busy?'

'Absolutely. But managing to keep on top of it.'

'Good. I'm so pleased you found the time to phone and speak to the children. I wanted to discuss something with you, but if you're in a hurry it can wait.'

'Is it urgent?' John asked. 'I haven't eaten yet.'

'No. You go for your dinner. It can wait until the weekend.'

There was a short pause before John said, 'I'm afraid I won't be able to make it home this weekend. Sorry, but it's unavoidable.'

'Oh,' I said, taken aback and very disappointed. John always came home at the weekends unless he was working abroad, which wasn't often. 'Oh, I see. Why?' I asked. The children were watching me, aware something was wrong.

'Inundated with work, I'm afraid,' John said.

'And you can't bring the work home with you?' I suggested. Which he had done before.

'No, not this time, I'm afraid. I'm needed on site.'

'I see,' I said again. 'Will you be able to phone over the week-end? We'll all miss you.'

'I'll try,' John said. I heard a noise in the background, as though someone might be in the room, then John said, 'I have to go. They're waiting for me to go to dinner. It's another working meal, I'm afraid.'

'Oh dear, I am sorry,' I sympathized. 'I hope it doesn't run on too late. Do try and find some time to relax over the weekend or you'll be exhausted.'

John gave a small snort of laughter. 'Say goodbye to the kids for me. Bye, Cathy.'

'Bye. Love you.'

'And you.'

The line went dead and I replaced the received. The children were still looking at me and I tried to hide my disappointment.

'Dad's not coming home, is he?' Adrian said a little crossly.

'No. I'm afraid he can't make it this weekend. He has to work,' I said.

'He's always working,' Adrian said, cross and sad. 'Doesn't he want to come home and see us?'

'Of course he does, Adrian. You know that. Your dad has a lot of responsibility and sometimes he has to work away. Of course he comes home whenever he can.'

'I'm seeing my daddy on Friday,' Beth put in, which didn't help at all.

'I'm going to my room!' Adrian said. Jumping up from the sofa, he fled the room and ran upstairs, close to tears.

'Beth, I'd like you to stay here and look after Paula for a moment, please,' I said. 'I won't be long.'

Beth took Paula's hand. Their expressions were serious.

'Play a game or something,' I called as I left the living room.

Upstairs, Adrian's bedroom door was shut so I gave a brief knock and went in. Adrian was sitting on the floor, cross-legged and staring down. I went over, sat beside him and took his hand in mine.

'Adrian, love,' I began gently. 'I know how much you miss your dad. I miss him too, so does Paula. Your daddy loves you very much and I know he would come home if it was at all possible.'

'Why does he have to work away?' Adrian asked sadly, glancing up at me. 'Why can't he come home at night like he used to? Like other fathers do.'

'Do you remember I explained he was given a promotion at work?' I asked gently. 'He was pleased, because it showed he was doing a good job. It means he earns more money to look after us, but it also means he has to work away sometimes.'

'I'd rather he came home more and had less money,' Adrian said.

My heart went out to him. So would I, I thought, but I didn't say so. John was very career orientated and I had to respect that. He believed he'd made the right decision in accepting the promotion, and I supported him in it and would never undermine his decision by voicing my concerns.

'Dad shouldn't have to work away for too much longer,' I added.

'How long?' Adrian asked.

'If all goes well, he thought about six months,' I said. 'Which will mean he'll be home for the summer. You'll be able to play cricket and football with him in the evenings and at weekends like you used to.'

Adrian cheered up a little at this thought and managed a small nod.

'OK, love?' I asked.

'I guess.'

'Now, I can't really leave Paula any longer, and Beth needs to telephone her father, so can we continue our chat a little later?'

'Yes,' he said.

'Thank you. And believe me, I do know how much you miss your dad, but it shouldn't be for much longer.'

Adrian smiled and I kissed his forehead. 'You're not too old for hugs and kisses from your mum, are you?' I said.

Adrian laughed, aware of what was to come. He covered his head with his hands as I took him in my arms and began kissing him all over his face, head and neck, as I used to when he was little. He laughed and giggled and made 'ugh' noises, and jokingly tried to push me off. 'Ahh, help!' he cried. 'Someone save me!'

With a final shower of kisses and a big hug, I released him and stood. Still laughing, he wiped the sleeve of his jersey over his face as though wiping off the kisses, as boys of his age often do.

'I'll be back as soon as I've seen to the girls,' I said, also laughing.

I went downstairs to Beth and Paula, who were still in the living room, now sitting on the sofa next to each other with Beth — bless her — reading Paula a story. 'Thank you, love,' I said to Beth.

'Is it time to telephone my daddy?' Beth asked, closing the book.

'Yes. Come on.'

Indeed, it was one minute to seven and I daren't be late phoning Derek after all the upset I'd caused him. However, Paula wasn't washed and ready for bed yet, and that would take at least fifteen minutes. It then occurred to me that, as I wasn't allowed to speak to Derek — just to make the call — and there was no reason why Derek and Beth shouldn't be left alone, once Derek was on the phone I could leave Beth talking to him while I got Paula ready for bed.

Beth was already skipping up the stairs in eager anticipation of telephoning her father. Paula and I followed, counting the steps as we went. The three of us went into my bedroom, where Beth propped herself on the bed.

'Is she staying?' Beth asked me, referring to Paula.

'Just until I've got your father on the phone,' I said.

I dialled the number of the hospital and asked for Ward 3. When I was put through to the ward, I asked for Derek. The nurse called him and he came to the telephone straight away. 'Hello,' he said, sounding slightly subdued.

Without speaking, I passed the telephone to Beth. 'Hi, Daddy!' Beth cried, grinning. 'How are you?'

'I'm fine now,' I heard Derek say, perking up.

'Come on, love,' I said to Paula. 'Bath and bedtime.'

Leaving my bedroom door open so that I could hear Beth if she needed me, I took Paula into the bathroom, which was next door, and left that door slightly open too. As Beth spoke to her father, I ran Paula's bath, dropped in her plastic bath toys and then helped her undress and clamber in. I could hear Beth talking, but not her father's replies – I was too far away. They'd begun by saying how fantastic it was that they would be seeing each other on Friday, and Beth had asked him what games they could play in the hospital and how long she could stay.

Paula played with her toys in her bath and Adrian played in his room as I washed Paula. Beth's words floated in. They'd finished talking about her visit on Friday, and Beth was now telling her father what she was wearing. As usual, she'd changed out of her school uniform and into a dress as soon as we'd arrived home. She'd spent a considerable amount of time trying to decide which dress to wear.

'It's the lilac dress with little flowers on,' she said. 'The one with the lacy petticoat.'

Beth was then silent as Derek replied. Beth laughed and then said, 'Yes, I've brushed my hair. It's all shiny, but not as nice as when you do it. Will you brush my hair on Friday?'

Derek replied and Beth giggled. 'Of course I've got clean knickers on,' she exclaimed. 'Daddy, you are funny.'

Beth fell silent again for some time as Derek spoke, and then Beth cried, 'Yippee! I've wanted my ears pierced for ages. Can we buy those studs with the little diamonds? We both liked those.'

Clearly Derek had agreed to Beth having her ears pierced. Personally I thought she was too young, although I knew that many girls of her age had their ears pierced, and some boys did too. As Beth's father, it was Derek's decision as to whether she was old enough for ear-piercing, and if I thought that the ensuing discussion they had about going to the jewellers and choosing the earrings sounded more like a couple choosing an engagement ring, I pushed the thought from my mind. I'd been wrong; I wasn't going down that path again.

I finished bathing Paula and then helped her out of the bath while half listening to Beth. I wrapped Paula in a large, soft bath towel and while she began drying herself I let the water out of the bath and rinsed it out. I then helped Paula to dress in her clean pyjamas. Beth's voice had grown serious now and sounded quite authoritative. 'Tell the doctor I can look after you at home,' she said. 'You don't need to stay in hospital. Or shall I tell him when I see him on Friday?'

Derek said something, which I guessed was probably no, for Beth then said: 'OK. You tell the doctor. But make sure he knows I can look after you. It's just you and me, and we'll be fine. We don't need help.'

Paula and I went round the landing to her bedroom where she chose some storybooks for me to read. I lay beside her on the

bed and began reading the first picture book while Beth continued on the telephone. Paula's bedroom was further away from
my room than the bathroom was, so I couldn't hear what Beth
was saying. Only when she laughed or exclaimed loudly did I
hear her clearly: 'Oh Daddy! You are funny!' or similar.

Two picture books later, Beth suddenly appeared at Paula's
bedroom door. 'Daddy was tired, so we've said goodbye,' she
said, coming in.

'I'm sure he's very tired with all that talking.' I smiled. 'You've
been on the telephone for quite a while.'

'Can I share Paula's story like I did last night?' Beth asked.

'Yes, or I could read you a story of your own later, when I've
finished reading to Paula?' I suggested.

'I'd rather listen to Paula's story,' Beth said, clambering in
beside Paula, who was making room for her. Then, suddenly
remembering something, Beth exclaimed: 'Oh dear! I forgot to
tell my daddy I want him to read me bedtime stories when I go
home.'

'Never mind,' I said. 'You can tell him another time.'

'I'll tell my daddy when I see him on Friday,' Beth declared.

'My daddy isn't coming home on Friday,' Paula said, looking
at me with big sad eyes.

'No, but he will come home the next Friday,' I said, and kissed
her cheek.

I didn't want Paula upset by Beth talking about seeing her
father, so I quickly returned to the safety of the book: *Wise Owl
sat in his usual tree at the bottom of the garden. 'What's up, Mousey?'
Wise Owl asked, swooping down and landing silently beside him.
'Your whiskers are drooping and your tail's gone limp. There's something bothering you.'*

* * *

That evening at bedtime Beth was still very excited at the prospect of seeing her father on Friday – so excited, in fact, that she couldn't get off to sleep. She was in bed, snuggled on her side, and had gone through the ritual of kissing the photograph of her father, which she'd returned to beneath the pillow. I'd given her Mr Sleep Bear to help and I was now perched on the edge of the bed lightly stroking her forehead until she fell asleep. In the light coming from the landing I could see the bookshelves containing the framed photographs of Beth and her father. I thought how strange it was that a person's views could so easily be influenced and coloured by what they believed. I'd believed the photographs were inappropriate because I'd thought Derek's relationship with Beth was inappropriate. I'd seen things in the pictures that weren't there.

Or had I? Try as I might, as I ran my eyes over the pictures waiting for Beth to fall asleep, I couldn't help but think that Beth seemed older in the photographs – more sophisticated and mature – than she did in person. Which added weight to Marianne's comment that Beth and Derek were more like lovers than father and daughter. I turned away and concentrated on something else.

Chapter Nine

Sexualizing the Innocent

As Beth was looking forward to seeing her father on Friday, I was willing the day to come. I hoped that then her conversation – at present dominated by seeing her father – would be replaced by more general talk. Of course I was pleased that Beth was able to see her father, but her continuous chatter about her wonderful daddy wasn't helping Adrian and Paula. They were disappointed enough already that they wouldn't be seeing their father at the weekend. This seemed to be rubbing it in.

'I don't know what to wear when I see my daddy tomorrow,' Beth declared over dinner on Thursday evening.

'It might be a good idea to choose something this evening,' I suggested. 'Jessie will be collecting you at four o'clock tomorrow, so you won't have much time then.'

'Good idea,' Beth said. 'I'll choose my dress after dinner. Then I can tell my daddy what I'm going to wear when I talk to him tonight. I am phoning him tonight, aren't I?'

'Yes, love. You are,' I said.

'So I'll tell him what I'm going to wear then.'

'Will he want to know?' Adrian asked, glancing up. 'I don't think my dad is especially interested in what we wear.'

Good point, I thought. Meeting Adrian's gaze, I threw him a reassuring smile. Of course John liked the children to look smart, just as I did, especially if we were going out, but he wasn't interested in the detail. I doubted many men were.

'My daddy always wants to know what I'm wearing,' Beth persisted. 'Sometimes he chooses what I wear and sometimes we choose it together.'

Adrian returned to his dinner, which was far more interesting than Beth's talk of clothes, as she continued: 'Perhaps I'll wear my yellow dress. Or I could wear the blue one again. I've got a blue necklace and bracelet that go with the blue dress. I think I remembered to pack them.' And so it went on.

I smiled politely.

As soon as Beth had finished eating, she asked if she could leave the table to go to her room and choose her dress for the following day. I readily agreed. She slipped from her chair and skipped out of the room and upstairs.

'Can I go to my room and choose a dress?' Adrian said with a smile.

'You don't wear dresses, silly,' Paula said, not appreciating that he was joking.

'We have to be patient,' I said. 'Beth's very excited about seeing her father, which is only natural.'

'Can I have a blue dress like Beth's?' Paula asked.

'And me!' Adrian added. 'And a necklace and bracelet to match, please.'

I cleared away the dinner things and then went upstairs to see how Beth was getting on. Paula came with me. Beth's bedroom door was wide open and we went in. Her wardrobe was open and every drawer too, with most of the contents strewn across the bed, chair and floor. It looked like an upmarket bring-and-buy sale. Beth was standing in the middle of the room, surrounded by all the clothes and looking very fraught.

'I really can't decide what to wear!' she declared, close to tears.

I thought this had gone far enough. 'I think I'll decide which dress you wear,' I said. 'Then it won't cause you a problem.'

I thought she might object but instead she looked at me relieved. 'Yes, please, you choose,' she said.

'You've got lots of clothes,' Paula said as I began picking through them.

'Yes, and they've all got to be put away,' I pointed out.

I quickly singled out a dress; it was one of the few that were suitable for winter. Made from a warm pink-and-grey check material, it had long sleeves. 'This is perfect,' I said enthusiastically, holding it up.

Beth stood for a moment, hands on hips, considering the dress and then finally smiled. 'Yes,' she said.

I hoped Paula didn't pick up any grand ideas about what she should wear. I put the dress to one side and then began gathering together the other clothes. Beth helped, so too did Paula by collecting up the packets of children's lacy tights that were scattered across the floor. We finished just before seven o'clock and then the three of us went into my bedroom, where Beth propped herself on the bed ready to telephone her father. Once Derek was on the line I passed the telephone to Beth and, following our new routine, took Paula into the bathroom for her bath. I could hear Beth talking as I bathed Paula; she was telling her father of the problems she'd had trying to choose a dress, until I'd come to the rescue. She then described the dress I'd chosen and the matching necklace and bracelet she was thinking of wearing with it. I was only half listening as I was finding Beth's chatter about clothes tedious. Girls of her age should be thinking about more interesting things. Eventually I called out: 'Tell your daddy what you did at school today. And about your class assembly. I'm sure he'll be interested.' I thought that even Derek must be tiring of all the dress talk by now.

Beth did as I suggested, although I was too far away to hear Derek's reply. Then Beth asked him what he'd had for his dinner and if he had eaten it all.

Once Paula was ready for bed I took her into her room where she chose some books for me to read. I'd read one story when Beth joined us.

'Have you finished talking to your daddy?' Paula asked, making room for Beth beside her on the bed.

'Yes, and I'm seeing him tomorrow. I'm so happy.'

'This book is called *Grandma's Shopping*,' I said, opening the next picture book.

'I haven't got a grandma,' Beth said.

'I have,' Paula said. 'And a grandpa. They're very nice and they love us lots.'

I smiled. 'You'll meet them soon,' I said to Beth. And I began the story.

The following morning Beth was unusually quiet and hardly said a word at breakfast. I'd been expecting her to be very talkative about seeing her father that afternoon, so I was immediately concerned that something was troubling her. I also noticed she wasn't eating as well as she usually did.

'Are you all right, love?' I asked as she toyed with her cereal.

She set her spoon in her bowl and looked at me seriously. 'No. I'm very worried,' she said, frowning.

Adrian, Paula and I all looked at her, concerned.

'What are you worried about, love?' I asked, setting down my mug of coffee so that I could give her my full attention. 'Can you tell me? I might be able to help.'

Beth looked at me, clearly deep in thought, and frowned again. I wondered what on earth it could be that was troubling her. She usually voiced her concerns reasonably easily.

'I've been thinking,' she said with a heartfelt sigh. 'I don't want to wear the dress you chose. I want to wear my red one.'

'Is that what you're worrying about?' Adrian asked incredulously, taking the words right out of my mouth.

Beth nodded.

'Beth, love,' I said gently. 'Your daddy will love you whatever you wear. It's you he wants to see, not your dress.'

'But I want to look nice for him,' Beth persisted.

'And you will. Now finish your breakfast. We don't want to be late for school.'

'I don't want any more,' Beth said, pushing the bowl of half-eaten cereal away. 'I'm not hungry.'

'All right, leave what you don't want.'

Beth got down from the table and went upstairs to brush her teeth. I quickly drained the last of my coffee and went upstairs after her. I wanted to talk to her alone.

'Beth, love,' I said, going into the bathroom, 'are you sure there's nothing worrying you – apart from which dress to wear?' For it seemed incredible to me that choosing what to wear could cause a child this much consternation. I wondered if it was masking a more deep-seated problem that Beth was finding difficult to share. 'Your daddy is being well looked after in hospital,' I reassured her, wondering if this was the problem.

'I know he is,' Beth said. 'And I'm seeing him later, but I don't know what to wear.'

'You'd tell me if there was anything else worrying you, wouldn't you?' I asked. 'I'd do my best to help.'

'Yes,' Beth said. 'Thank you, but I'm fine.'

There was nothing more I could say.

* * *

The day passed quickly with a big shop at the supermarket, unpacking it all on our return, then general housework and playing with Paula. When I took Beth's clean laundry to her room I noticed she'd returned the grey-and-pink check dress to her wardrobe, but hadn't chosen anything in its place. There wouldn't be much time when we returned from school before Jessie collected Beth. I thought about choosing another dress for her and insisting she wore it, but I didn't want to upset her, and I wondered why Derek had let the situation get so out of hand. It must take them ages to get ready to leave the house when there was no school uniform to rely on. But then, from what I'd heard of their telephone conversations, Derek shared Beth's love of clothes and accessories. Oh well, I thought, it wouldn't do if we were all the same.

Beth was in very good spirits when she came out of school that afternoon and skipped over to me happily. 'I'm seeing my daddy soon!' she cried. 'I'm so happy. And I know what I'm going to wear.'

'Good,' Adrian said as we made our way to the car. 'Dare I ask what it is?'

'I'm not telling you,' Beth teased. 'You'll have to wait and see. It'll be a big surprise.'

'I can't wait,' Adrian said dryly. I wondered how much attention she'd paid to her lessons that day and how much time she'd spent thinking about what she was going to wear. Whatever would she be like as a teenager? I thought with a smile.

Once home, Beth quickly took off her coat and shoes, then went straight up to her room to change. 'Remember, Jessie will be here in fifteen minutes,' I called after her. 'Do you want some help?'

'No. I'll be ready on time,' she replied.

I went into the kitchen to begin the preparation for dinner. I assumed Beth would eat when she returned from seeing her father. As I worked, I kept one eye on the clock. At five minutes to four, with no sign of Beth, and Jessie due in five minutes, I left what I was doing and went upstairs. Beth's bedroom door was closed, so I knocked. 'It's Cathy. Are you ready, Beth? Jessie will be here soon.'

'I'm ready,' Beth called from inside. 'You can come in.'

'Good girl,' I said.

I opened her bedroom door, took a step in and stopped. Good grief! I thought but didn't say. 'Oh. Is that what you're wearing?' I asked, trying to hide my shock.

Beth grinned, pleased. 'Yes. Do you like it?'

I could see how pleased she was with herself. Not only did I not like the dress she was wearing, but also it wasn't suitable for a child, the cold weather or hospital visiting. It was very short, made from bright-red glossy satin and had puffed sleeves and a big lace collar. I remembered seeing the dress when I'd unpacked Beth's case, but I'd assumed it was for 'dressing up' in at home. Beth was also wearing black lacy tights and children's high-heeled shoes, which again I'd assumed were for dressing up. However, what concerned me even more was what Beth had put on her face.

'Are you wearing make-up?' I asked, aghast.

Beth nodded and turned to admire her handiwork in the mirror. 'I did a good job, didn't I?'

I stared at her reflection in the mirror: bright-blue eye shadow, navy mascara and red lipstick. Normally I didn't let young girls wear make-up unless it was part of playing at home, nor did I let them dress provocatively, which was the only word to describe Beth's appearance. It sexualizes the innocent. She looked like a child prostitute and I shuddered at the thought. But what could I say? Beth was so happy. I didn't want to hurt her feelings and ruin her evening, and Jessie was expected any minute.

'Usually my daddy helps me put on my make-up,' Beth said, again admiring her face in the mirror. 'But I did it all by myself this time.'

'Your father puts make-up on you?' I asked, shocked.

'Yes. He says he has a steady hand and can do it better than me.'

I shifted my gaze from Beth to the photographs on the shelves. 'Were you wearing make-up in those photographs?' I asked.

'Yes, daddy did it for me.'

Which explained why Beth looked that much older in the photographs.

'Where did you get the make-up from?' I now asked, for I was sure I would have remembered seeing it when I'd unpacked.

'It was in my drawer at school,' Beth said, finally turning from the mirror. 'I took it in to show my friends – they're not allowed make-up. Then I forgot it. I remembered today and I put it in my coat pocket so I wouldn't forget it.'

The doorbell rang. 'That'll be Jessie,' I said. There wasn't time for Beth to change.

'Mum! Doorbell!' Adrian yelled from the living room.

'Yes, I heard!' I returned.

We went downstairs, with Beth clutching the banister rail and tottering on her high heels. I opened the front door. 'I'm sorry,' I said to Jessie. 'Beth got herself ready.'

Beth appeared beside me.

'Oh gosh! You are dressed up,' Jessie exclaimed, seeming more impressed than shocked.

'I wanted her to wear a warmer dress,' I explained. 'And I'm afraid I didn't know about the make-up.'

'Daddy bought it for me,' Beth said proudly.

Jessie nodded, apparently not sharing my concerns. 'Get your coat on then,' Jessie said. 'Daddy will be waiting.'

I took Beth's coat from the hall stand and helped her into it. 'Be careful on those heels,' I said as she tottered unsteadily over the doorstep. 'Have a nice time.'

'I should have her back soon after six,' Jessie called. 'It's a twenty-minute drive each way and an hour visiting.'

'Thank you,' I said.

'Can't we stay longer?' Beth said as they went down the path.

'We'll see,' I heard Jessie say. Then they disappeared onto the pavement and to Jessie's car.

I closed the front door. Adrian and Paula appeared in the hall from the living room. 'Has Beth gone?' Paula asked. 'I didn't say goodbye.'

'They were in a rush,' I said. 'You'll see her later. She'll be back before your bedtime. And Adrian,' I said, 'when Beth comes home please don't say anything about what she is wearing.'

'Why not?' he asked.

'Let's just say it's not what I would have chosen, but I don't want her upset.'

'Sure, Mum, I promise I won't say a word.'

'Good boy.'

Chapter Ten

Calm Before the Storm

True to his promise, Adrian didn't say a word when at six fifteen I answered the front door and Beth stepped in. I heard him gasp in amazement and then, clamping his hand over his mouth to stifle a laugh, he ran upstairs to his room. Beth thankfully didn't see, while Paula, standing beside me, stared at Beth open-mouthed.

'You look like a lady,' Paula said.

A lady of the night, I thought, for Beth's lipstick had smudged and her mascara had run, creating black rings around her eyes.

'Did you have a nice time?' I asked Beth kindly as she began taking off her coat.

'We played lots of games,' she said. 'There were some strange people there, but they were friendly. Daddy bought me two chocolate bars from the trolley that came round.'

I smiled. 'Are you coming in?' I asked Jessie, who was still standing in the porch. 'I could make you a coffee.'

'No, I must be getting home,' Jessie said, although she didn't immediately say goodbye or turn to leave.

'Sure?' I asked. 'I could make it a quick coffee.' I would also have liked some feedback on how the contact had gone.

'No, thank you,' Jessie said. She took a breath as though she was about to ask me something, but changed her mind.

'Will Beth be visiting her father again soon?' I asked. I thought that next time I would be better prepared in respect of her clothes and make-up.

'Yes, I would think so, although it will depend on when Derek is discharged.' Jessie hesitated again and then said: 'I'll telephone you when I have any details.'

'And the evening went well?' I asked.

'They enjoyed themselves,' she said.

Jessie threw me a quick smile, said goodbye and returned down the garden path. I closed the front door. I thought she seemed a bit preoccupied, but I didn't give it any more thought. It was Friday – the end of the working week – and she was probably very tired.

Before I gave Beth her dinner I persuaded her to go to the bathroom and wash off her make-up. She did so, and without being asked also changed out of her dress and into her nightwear. She said she didn't want to spoil her dress by dropping her dinner down it. Beth was very sensible when it came to such matters, more like a woman than a child. Once she'd finished eating, she asked me if it was time to phone her daddy. It was nearly seven o'clock, but I'd assumed that, having just seen her father, she wouldn't telephone him again until the following evening.

'Daddy wants me to phone,' she added.

Jessie hadn't said not to telephone, so at seven o'clock Beth, Paula and I went upstairs and into my bedroom where I dialled the hospital and then passed the telephone to Beth. Paula and I went into the bathroom where I bathed her as Beth talked to her father. Beth was still very excited from seeing him and chatted gaily about the games they'd played – snakes and ladders, draughts, cards and some games I wasn't familiar with. I heard her tell him that she didn't like the lady who'd kept making funny noises, but the men were friendly. I guessed that contact had taken place either on the ward or in a common room where other patients had been present. As with the previous evenings, when Beth had finished talking to her father she joined Paula for a bedtime story in her room. She was still in very good spirits. But later, when it was her bedtime, she grew sad.

'I miss my daddy so much,' she said, climbing into bed.

'I know you do, love. But you can telephone him again tomorrow, and I'm sure he'll be better before too long.'

'I sat on his lap and gave him lots of cuddles,' she said with a small wistful smile.

'You both had a good time then,' I said.

'We did,' Beth said. 'Another man wanted me to sit on his lap, but Jessie said not to.'

'Was Jessie with you and Daddy the whole time?' I asked out of interest.

'Yes, but she went to get a coffee. I wish I could stay with my daddy in hospital. His bed is big enough for two.'

I smiled. 'I'm sure he'll be well enough to go home soon,' I reassured her again, and then I gave her a big hug. 'You're going to meet my parents on Sunday,' I said, trying to divert her attention. 'We're going to visit them. They live in the country.'

Beth brightened up a little. 'Is it a special occasion?' she asked.

'Yes, I suppose it is.'

'I'll wear my red dress then, with my lacy tights and high-heeled shoes.'

Oh dear, I thought. I walked right into that one. 'You'll need something a bit warmer and more practical,' I said diplomatically. 'We usually go to the park or for a walk in the woods when we visit. I'll help you choose something to wear.'

'OK,' Beth said easily and snuggled down into the bed.

'And Beth, love,' I said, 'I don't want you wearing any make-up while you're staying with me. I know your father doesn't mind, but I don't like it.' I thought it best to deal with the matter now.

'Why don't you like it?' Beth asked.

'I don't like make-up on children,' I said. 'I think children are beautiful enough already. They don't need make-up.'

Beth considered this for a moment. 'Will Paula wear make-up when she's older?'

'Not until she is much, much older – a teenager, and then only a little if she really wants to. Now, off to sleep, love,' I said, adjusting the duvet. 'You've had a busy day. You can have a lie-in tomorrow. It's Saturday and there's no school.'

Beth smiled. 'Daddy and me have a lie-in at the weekends. We stay in bed and have big cuddles. Then he makes us breakfast and we have it in bed. Do you do that here?'

'Not usually,' I said, and serving the children breakfast in bed wasn't something I wanted to start. 'But when you go home I'm sure you'll have breakfast in bed again.'

Beth nodded and, turning onto her side, slid the photograph of her father from beneath the pillow. She kissed it goodnight and then returned it to under her pillow. I tucked Mr Sleep Bear in beside her.

'Sleep tight,' I said, giving her a kiss.

'I will.' Beth smiled.

I came out, leaving Beth's bedroom door slightly ajar, as she liked it. I checked on Adrian and Paula who, also tired at the end of the week, were sound asleep. I went downstairs, made myself a cup of tea and then sat in the living room. The house seemed very quiet – uncannily quiet for a Friday evening. I couldn't remember the last time I'd spent one alone. John was usually home by now and we always had plenty to talk about, especially if he'd been working away. Sometimes we opened a bottle of wine and enjoyed a glass each as we sat chatting and exchanging our news. Now it was just Toscha and me, and I suddenly felt very alone. As if sensing my feelings, Toscha jumped down from where she was curled on her favourite chair and onto my lap. I stroked her soft fur as she circled, before settling into a ball and purring gently.

I stroked her and sipped my tea and wondered what John was doing. I guessed he'd probably finished another working dinner by now and had returned to his hotel room and might be watching television. I thought he was probably feeling lonely too and that he might telephone. John didn't like living in hotels. He'd said more than once that hotels were great for holidays, but quickly lost their appeal if you were incarcerated in them every evening after work. I knew he would have come home if it had been at all possible. I also worried that he was working too hard. At home he could relax and unwind over the weekend so that he could start the new week refreshed. Now he would lurch from one working week into the next. Poor John, I thought, alone in his hotel room and wishing he was at home with me, just as I was wishing he was sitting beside me on the sofa. I considered opening a bottle of wine, but decided it wouldn't be the same without John.

Typical of many young children, having been given the opportunity of a lie-in, on Saturday morning Adrian, Paula and Beth were awake even earlier than on a school day. Wanting to make the most of every minute of the weekend, they were all out of their beds and playing by seven o'clock. They stayed in their dressing gowns, playing in their bedrooms, while I showered and dressed. Then I made us all a cooked breakfast. As we sat at the table enjoying eggs, bacon, sausage and tomatoes, Beth told

Adrian and Paula that she had a cooked breakfast at the weekends too, and that her daddy brought it to her in bed.

'You have breakfast in bed every weekend?' Adrian asked.

Beth nodded.

'Don't you go getting any ideas,' I said to Adrian with a smile. 'The only time you have breakfast in bed is on your birthday or if you're ill.'

'Not keen anyway,' he said, pulling a face. 'All those toast crumbs, it's like sand in the bed.'

I laughed.

'My daddy brings my breakfast on a tray,' Beth said, 'so I don't get crumbs in the bed. And if I spill my juice, he doesn't mind, he just changes the sheets.'

Derek was clearly a very indulgent and tolerant father, although I wasn't sure it was right to spoil a child so much; she could grow up to be self-centred and expecting to be pampered all the time. I supposed it was different if you just had one child. If you had more than one then you treated them all the same and time simply didn't allow for pampering them all to the extent that Beth's father pampered her.

The morning was cold again but bright, so after breakfast I suggested that once they were dressed we could go to the park for a while. The children were enthusiastic and helped clear away the breakfast things, and then we went upstairs to get ready. I intended to choose something appropriate for Beth to wear. Adrian lived in joggers or jeans at the weekend and knew what to wear. Paula came with me into Beth's room, where I opened her wardrobe door and took out two tracksuits that I remembered unpacking, but which she'd never worn.

'Can't I wear a dress?' Beth asked.

'They're not really practical for playing in the park on a cold day,' I said. 'These are perfect, and they look brand new.'

'They are,' Beth said. 'I haven't worn them.'

'They're both lovely. Which one would you like to wear today?' I asked. 'The blue or pink?' I held up the tracksuits and Beth looked from one to the other.

'The pink one,' she said at last.

'Excellent choice,' I said. 'And you can wear the blue one when we visit my parents tomorrow.' Which neatly solved that problem too.

I took out warm socks and a vest for Beth as she took some pants from her drawer. All Beth's clothes were in very good condition and many of them seemed brand new. I thought that Derek must spend a lot on clothes for Beth, perhaps indulging her wishes in this as he did in other things. I left Beth to get ready and went with Paula to help her wash and dress. Half an hour later we were all downstairs and in the hall, wrapped up warm in our coats, scarves and gloves, ready to go to the park. Adrian was bringing his football and I'd asked Beth if she wanted to take a ball or skipping rope or a scooter to the park, but she didn't. She added that she didn't often go to the park as parks were for children. I didn't state the obvious and I was pleased Adrian didn't either.

Outside the weather was crisp and cold and quite beautiful. The wintry sun shone from a clear blue sky, causing the remaining frost to sparkle like magic. We walked to our local park where Beth and Adrian ran off to the play equipment – swings, seesaw, roundabout – while I took Paula to the area for younger children and helped her on and off the little rocking horse and then the baby swings, which she loved, although I wasn't allowed to call them 'baby swings'. 'They're big-girl swings,' she said indignantly. 'Just smaller.' Which is what I'd told her before.

We were in the park for over an hour. I'd taken my camera with me and I took plenty of photographs of the children playing. When my hands and feet grew cold and the children's noses glowed red, I suggested we return home for a hot chocolate. The children asked for one last swing and then we left.

As we stepped into the hall I saw that the light on the answerphone was flashing, showing a message had been recorded. I pressed play and John's voice came through. The children paused from taking off their coats. 'Hi, kids, sorry I missed you. I expect you're out shopping with your mother. Enjoy the rest of your weekend. I'll try to telephone during the week. Be good. See you next weekend. Love Dad.'

The line went dead and the answerphone clicked off. I could tell from Adrian's and Paula's expressions that they were pleased to hear their father's voice, but sad that they'd missed his call. 'Perhaps he'll telephone again later today,' Adrian said hopefully.

'Perhaps, or next week as he said,' I suggested.

We finished taking off our coats and shoes and I made us a hot chocolate. Then, after lunch, I covered the table with old newspaper and arranged paints and water in the centre. I gave the children an apron, paintbrush and a stack of plain paper each and they painted lots of wonderful pictures: of cats, dogs, themselves, each other, birds, fish and swirling geometric designs. Eventually we ran out of space to dry any more pictures and we cleared away the paints and got out the play dough. When they tired of modelling the dough they helped me make some biscuits to take with us to Nana and Grandpa's the following day. We had dinner and then watched a film on television. When Beth telephoned her father that evening she told him about all the things she'd done. I thought he must be relieved and pleased that Beth was enjoying herself and not upset and pining for him. I also thought it was a pity I couldn't talk to Derek, as I usually did with the parents of children I fostered. I could have reassured him that Beth was doing well and he shouldn't worry. But after I'd upset him with the unfounded allegations, Jessie had said that I shouldn't speak to him, and I had to accept that.

Sunday was grey and overcast to begin with. A thick blanket of cloud stretched as far as the eye could see, but as I drove to my parents' (with Beth uncomplaining in her blue tracksuit), the sun came out, which caused Adrian to burst into song:

> *The sun has got his hat on,*
> *Hip-hip-hip-hooray!*
> *The sun has got his hat on,*
> *He's coming out today.*

'That's Grandpa's song,' Paula said.

'Grandpa sings it, yes,' I said. 'And you know the words too.'

'So do I!' Beth said and began singing.

All three children sang the chorus about six times. None of us knew any more of the verses; I don't think my father did either.

'I know other nursery rhymes,' Paula said when they'd exhausted this one. She began singing, 'Mary, Mary, quite contrary, how does your garden grow?'

Beth joined in and when they'd finished Adrian began a rousing chorus of 'The Grand Old Duke of York', which we all joined in with, laughing. We headed down the motorway singing and laughing and only stopped as I pulled into the driveway of my parents' house. My parents must have been looking out for us, for as I cut the engine their front door opened and they came out to greet us. I let the children out of the car and then introduced Beth to Mum and Dad.

'Hello, love,' Mum said, welcoming her. She hugged and kissed us all, while Dad hugged and kissed Paula and me and then shook hands with Adrian and Beth. My parents have a gift for making new children feel at home.

Once inside we presented Mum with the biscuits and then I went with her into the kitchen to help make coffee for the adults and pour juice for the children, while everyone else went into the sitting room. We set the drinks and a plate of the biscuits on a tray and I carried it into the sitting room. Mum told everyone to help themselves. Paula had already found a place on Grandpa's lap and was looking very comfortable. Beth and Adrian sat in easy chairs to have their drinks and biscuits, and when they'd finished Adrian showed Beth the toy box, which had been Mum's idea so that I didn't have to keep packing bags of toys to bring with us to keep the children amused. She'd added to it over the years, so there were toys for boys and girls of most ages. The two of them began doing a jigsaw puzzle together, while Paula stayed snuggled on her grandpa's lap. Mum and I sat together on the sofa and chatted as delicious smells drifted in from the kitchen.

'Dinner won't be long,' she said. 'Grandpa and I thought you might like to go for a walk after we've eaten.'

'Can we go to the dark woods?' Adrian asked eagerly, glancing up from the puzzle.

'Yes, if you'd like to,' Mum said.

'I would!' my father put in.

Adrian grinned. 'The woods are very spooky,' he told Beth. 'And they're very dark – that's why I call them the dark woods. You can hide and jump out at people. They are full of scary monsters.'

'I don't like the woods,' Paula said, snuggling closer to Grandpa.

'We'll stay together,' my father reassured her. 'You can hold my hand, like you did last time. There aren't any monsters.'

Once we'd eaten – a full roast with all the trimmings – my father suggested we went for our walk while the sun was out and then return for pudding later. We all helped clear away the dirty dishes, and then put on our coats and shoes.

The Great Woods, as they are really called, are about three miles from my parents' house and too far for the children to walk, so we took both cars. We parked in the small visitors' car park; there were only two other cars. The Great Woods are more popular in summer and some visitors take picnics. My father opened the wooden gate that led to the track that ran through and around the woods. The woods are very atmospheric or, as Adrian said, 'spooky', because of the hundreds of very tall pine trees growing close together. Not much light comes through the branches, even in summer, and now in winter it was very dark in places. The density of the trees also magnifies the slightest sound in an otherwise eerily quiet wood, so that a twig crunching or bracken snapping makes you jump. It was easy to see how some of the locals believed The Great Woods were haunted.

'Remember, you must be able to see us at all times,' I called as Adrian and Beth ran ahead. This was a rule I'd started after one of our visits when Adrian had become too adventurous and had got lost for a couple of minutes. I think it had scared him as much as it had us, so I knew he would do as I'd asked, and Beth was keeping very close to him.

The rest of us followed in the direction Adrian and Beth had gone – along the single track flanked by trees and bracken. Every so often they'd disappear from view and then spring out from their hiding place, making grizzly noises to scare us. Dad always warned Paula when we were about to be scared, so that when they did spring out she wasn't too frightened; indeed, she often laughed. It was great fun. The track took about forty-five minutes to walk and then we returned to my parents' house and enjoyed Mum's wonderful homemade apple crumble with lashings of custard. As Beth had to telephone her father at seven, we left at six. My parents stood on the doorstep, waving and blowing kisses until we were out of sight.

'They're very nice people,' Beth said. 'I've had a lovely day.'

'Good, love. I'm pleased,' I said. 'We've all enjoyed ourselves.'

The children were quiet on the way home, exhausted from their day out. That evening when Beth spoke to her father I heard her telling him all about the great time she'd had at Nana and Grandpa's, including a description of our walk in the scary woods. Beth then asked her father why she didn't have a Nana and Grandpa. I couldn't hear Derek's reply as I was in the bathroom helping Paula, but I knew from Jessie that Derek's father was in a care home and that he had no contact with his ex-wife's family.

That evening, once all the children were tucked up in bed and asleep, I sat in the living room with a cup of tea feeling a lot more positive than I had the evening before. Although John hadn't been able to come home for the weekend, we'd made the best of it. The children had enjoyed themselves and hadn't missed their fathers too much, and I'd enjoyed the time I'd spent with them and the day at my parents'. In the weeks that followed, I came to view that weekend as a small oasis of calm before the storm hit and life changed irrevocably for us all, forever.

Chapter Eleven

Ignorance

On Monday morning I was standing in the playground with Paula waiting for school to start when Jenni's mother approached me. I hadn't got back to her about Beth going to her house for tea and I was rather hoping that the invitation had been forgotten. Beth hadn't been asking to go – indeed, she hadn't mentioned it at all – and given the upset I'd already caused Derek I was reluctant to ask him for permission and risk upsetting him further.

'Hi. You remember me?' Jenni's mother asked with a smile.

'Yes, of course,' I said, returning her smile. 'Beth often talks about Jenni and the games they've played during their lunch break.' However, Beth also talked of other children, so I'd formed the impression that perhaps Jenni wasn't the special friend her mother thought her to be, but more one of a group of friends. I was now anticipating another invitation for Beth to go to tea, but instead Jenni's mother asked quite brusquely, 'Is he still in hospital, then?'

'Derek? Yes, he is at present. But he should be home soon.'

'Aren't they keeping him in?' she now asked. I was starting to feel uncomfortable with the bluntness of her questions. Thankfully Beth and Jenni were standing to one side and talking to Paula, so I doubted they could hear.

'He should be discharged soon,' I confirmed, not wanting to get drawn into a discussion about Derek.

She raised her eyes upwards in exasperation. 'It's not right, is it?' she said. 'I mean, a man like him bringing up a girl alone. Bad enough before he went loopy, but now! Don't you think something should be done about it? I do!'

As a foster carer I was used to deflecting personal questions about the children I fostered. I was also used to hearing derogatory comments, but never before had I heard something so blatantly prejudiced and cruel.

'Done about it?' I queried, trying to kerb the hostility in my tone. 'Whatever do you mean?'

'Well, he's not all there, is he?' Jenni's mother said. 'That's why he's been locked up. He shouldn't be in charge of a child. It's not right.'

I was quietly seething. 'Derek certainly is "all there",' I said. 'And by all accounts he's done a very good job of raising his daughter alone. I doubt I would have coped as well.'

'So why is he in the funny farm, then?' Jenni's mother persisted.

I thought there was nothing to be gained by continuing this conversation with someone expressing such bigoted views, and it wouldn't be long before Beth and Jenni overheard. 'I'm sorry,' I said tightly. 'I really can't discuss Derek with you, but I think some sympathy wouldn't go amiss. The poor man is in hospital.'

'Exactly,' Jenni's mother said. 'A mental hospital!'

I turned away and pretended to adjust the zipper on Paula's coat as a displacement for what I really wanted to say. For a moment I thought she was going to say something else about Derek or mental illness – something probably just as disparaging as her previous comments – but instead she said to her daughter, 'Come along, Jenni.'

Ignorance

'But I want to stay and talk to Beth,' Jenni moaned.

I kept my head down and concentrated on Paula's zipper.

'Do as you're told,' Jenni's mother said firmly, and taking her daughter by the hand she led her away.

I straightened and watched her cross the playground to stand with another mother and her child. She immediately began talking animatedly to the other woman, gesticulating with her hands. I could tell from her body language she was annoyed and I could easily guess with whom. Shortly, both women looked over at me and I knew I was the subject of playground gossip just as Derek had been.

The klaxon sounded for the start of school and I said goodbye to Adrian and Beth. 'Have a good day,' I called after them.

They waved as they ran to join their classes.

I drove home, angry with Jenni's mother and her heartless attitude. There is so much ignorance and prejudice surrounding mental illness; I hoped she didn't express her venomous thoughts to her daughter, as it could affect her friendship with Beth.

My hope was short-lived.

That afternoon, when Beth came out of school, she was quieter than usual. I asked her a few times during the rest of the day if she was all right and she nodded and said she was. She perked up a bit to speak to her father but at seven o'clock, it was only at bedtime, when I asked Beth again if she was worrying about anything, that she said, 'I don't think I'm going to be friends with Jenni any more.'

'Oh? Why is that?' I asked.

'She said some nasty things about my daddy. They upset me and I wanted to cry, but I didn't.'

'What sort of things?' I asked gently. 'Can you tell me?'

Beth was sitting up in bed and I perched on the edge, facing her, and took her hand.

'Jenni said my daddy has something wrong in his head and he has been locked up,' Beth said, her little face very sad. 'Jenni said he shouldn't be allowed to look after me because he's a nutter.'

I knew where that had come from. You couldn't blame Jenni. At her age she was just repeating what she'd heard at home. Beth's eyes had filled and she was now looking at me for reassurance.

'What Jenni said was very rude and also utter rubbish,' I said forcefully. 'You visited your daddy last Friday. You saw he was in a hospital, being made better. He wasn't locked up, was he?'

Beth shook her head. 'No,' she said quietly. 'I should have told Jenni that, but I was too upset. I just walked away.'

'Sometimes children say things they don't understand,' I said. 'I think that's what Jenni did. But it was probably best you didn't get into an argument and just walked away. That's what I would have done.'

'My daddy tells me not to argue,' Beth said sadly.

'He's right,' I said.

'Will I be allowed to live with my daddy again?' Beth now asked.

'Yes, of course, love. As soon as he is well and has left hospital.'

Beth paused thoughtfully and then asked, 'What is the matter with my daddy? I know he's ill, but how is he ill? What's the matter with him?'

Beth had asked her father this question on the telephone when she'd first arrived, and he'd told her that things had been getting on top of him, and then he'd burst into tears and had had to cut short the call. Jessie had never told me exactly what was wrong with Derek, but from what I knew I'd assumed he'd had a mental breakdown.

'Sometimes adults can become very unhappy,' I said to Beth. 'It's called depression. Things start to get on top of them, sometimes little things upset them, and they keep crying. So they go to the doctors or the hospital and the doctors make them well again.'

'When I was at home my daddy kept crying,' Beth said. 'I tried to make him better, but it made him cry even more. Was it my fault he kept crying?'

'No. Definitely not. It was part of his illness.'

'He used to get very tired too,' Beth said. 'And sometimes he got angry and shouted at me for no reason. He never shouted before. Is that part of his illness?'

'Yes, love, it would have been.'

'And not sleeping?' Beth now asked, clearly relieved at finally being able to discuss this. 'Daddy used to come to bed with me and then get up when he thought I was asleep. I'd wait for him to come back to bed, but sometimes he didn't so I'd go and look for him. He was sitting in a chair with his head in his hands, or sometimes he was just walking up and down. If I asked him what was the matter, he'd start crying again.'

I nodded and soothed her hand. The poor child had coped with so much, watching her father's breakdown. Thank goodness, I thought, that Derek had sought help when he had and not left it any longer – for both their sakes.

'Crying easily was part of your daddy's illness,' I said gently. 'But the doctors are making him better. When you saw him last Friday he wasn't crying, was he?'

'No,' Beth said, brightening a little. 'He was laughing and joking and cuddling me like he used to.'

'There you are!' I said.

'But why did Jenni say those horrible things if they aren't true?' Beth asked.

'She didn't understand what she was saying,' I said. 'I'm sure she didn't mean to hurt you. Tomorrow I'll come into school and see your teacher and ask her to explain to Jenni that what she said was upsetting.' While I didn't think Jenni was being intentionally malicious, the matter needed to be dealt with.

'Oh no, please don't do that!' Beth cried, her eyes widening in alarm. 'I don't want you going into school and getting Jenni into trouble. I want us to be friends again.'

'She won't get into trouble,' I said. I knew Miss Willow would handle the matter sensitively and tactfully. 'Suppose Jenni says something else horrible? I don't want you being upset and hurting.'

'I'll tell her not to be horrid,' Beth persisted. 'I can stand up for myself, but I don't want you to go into school.'

I hesitated; my instinct was to go in, but I was swayed by the forcefulness of Beth's request not to. 'If you really don't want me to, I won't,' I said. 'But I want you to promise me that if Jenni says anything else that upsets you, you'll tell me. I don't want you worrying. I'm here to help you.'

Beth look relieved and finally smiled. 'I promise I'll tell you,' she said. 'But I'm sure it will be OK. Thank you for helping me. I wish I had a mummy like you.'

It's the little comments that are totally unexpected that often take my breath away and make me well up. Beth's comment about having a mummy like me did just that. I felt my eyes mist and a lump rise to my throat.

'That was a lovely thing to say,' I said.

'It's true,' Beth said. 'If I had you for a mummy I'd be so happy.'

And not for the first time I wondered why Beth hadn't let Marianne be her mummy. From what I'd seen of Marianne I was sure she'd have made a very loving and caring stepmother. It was such a pity.

True to my word, I didn't go into school to see Miss Willow on Tuesday morning, despite still feeling it was the proper course of action. However, on Tuesday evening I had reason to reverse my decision. I'd said goodnight to Beth, Paula was asleep and I went into Adrian's room to say goodnight to him. He was sitting up in bed reading a book, as he often did last thing at night.

'Time to switch off your light and go to sleep,' I said.

He closed his book and looked at me seriously. 'OK,' he said. 'But first I need to tell you something.' Adrian didn't share his worries easily and often internalized them, so I knew whatever he wanted to say must be important and worrying him considerably.

I sat on the edge of his bed and looked at him. 'Yes, love? What is it?' I was thinking it was probably about missing his father, but what he said gave me even greater cause for concern.

'Mum, I think you need to know that some of the kids at school are saying things about Beth's father.'

My heart sank. 'What sort of things?'

'They're saying her dad is a head case and calling him a nutter. That he's barmy and has been locked up.'

'Who said this?'

'I don't know which kids, but you know Oliver in my class?' I nodded. 'His sister is in Beth's class and she told him that some of the kids in her class are saying these things and calling Beth's dad names.'

I felt a mixture of anger and deep sadness and regretted not going into school that morning. 'Thank you for telling me, love,' I said. 'I'll go in and see Miss Willow first thing in the morning.

She'll know how to deal with it. Did Oliver tell you anything else?'

Adrian shook his head. 'Not really. Only that they were saying these things behind Beth's back.'

'What did you say to Oliver?'

'I told him Beth was staying with us while her dad was in hospital.'

'Good. That was a sensible reply.'

'I feel sorry for Beth,' Adrian added, looking sad. 'I wouldn't like it if kids said things about my dad behind my back.'

'No,' I agreed. 'And the things they were saying were very hurtful, but please don't worry. You did the right thing in telling me and I'll deal with it tomorrow.'

Reassured, Adrian turned off his light, ready to sleep.

The following morning when I woke Beth I told her I'd decided I would go into school and have a quick chat with her teacher before school started. I thought it was better she knew.

'But Jenni hasn't said any more nasty things,' Beth protested, immediately guessing why I wanted to speak to Miss Willow.

'I know, but I feel I should speak to your teacher anyway. I won't mention Jenni by name. I'll just say a child in the class.' I thought that Beth was probably unaware that other children, apart from Jenni, were calling her father names, as Adrian had said it was going on behind Beth's back. I wasn't about to tell her and upset her further.

Beth pouted as though she was going to cry. 'Beth, love,' I said. 'Sometimes adults know what is best for children and have to make decisions for them that they don't fully understand. I'm sure your daddy would want me to go into school and speak to your teacher if I was worried about you.'

Ignorance

At the mention of her father being in agreement, Beth looked at me thoughtfully and then gave a small, reluctant nod. 'All right, but please don't tell on Jenni.'

'I won't,' I said.

Once in the school playground I left Beth and Adrian playing with their friends while I took Paula into school with me. I'd told Beth and Adrian that if the klaxon sounded while I was in school then they should go in with their classes as they normally did. I was feeling slightly nervous and apprehensive about approaching Miss Willow and kept running through what I wanted to say. The school secretary-cum-receptionist was in the office and said good morning. I asked her if it was possible for me to speak with Miss Willow and she glanced at the wall clock.

'Just a quick word,' I added.

'I should think so,' she said. 'She's usually in her classroom at this time. Go on up. You know where it is.'

'Thank you.'

I took Paula's hand and headed for the staircase to the first floor, aware that parents (and carers) were asked to make appointments to see teachers rather than just turning up, but I hadn't wanted to leave this any longer. I hoped Miss Willow would understand. On the landing I saw the door to Miss Willow's classroom was open and as we approached I could see her standing at the front of the room writing on a wall chart. She looked up. 'Hello. How are you both?' she said, slightly surprised. 'Have you come to see me?'

'Yes, please, if you can spare five minutes.'

'Certainly. Come in.'

She put down the marker pen she'd been using to write on the chart and drew out three children's chairs from under the front table. We sat down.

'I won't keep you long,' I said. 'I know how busy you must be, but I need to talk to you about something quite urgent.' Her face immediately grew serious. 'I thought you should know that some of the children in the class have been calling Beth's father names.'

'What!' Miss Willow said, horrified. 'What sort of names? I certainly wasn't aware of this.'

'It seems that some of the children have been calling her father "a nutter" and similar derogatory names. One child said it to Beth, and some others have been saying it behind her back.'

'That's dreadful,' Miss Willow said, truly appalled. 'Who is responsible?'

'Beth doesn't want to get anyone into trouble,' I said. 'And there is more than one person involved.'

Miss Willow shook her head. 'I'm so sorry. I'll deal with it immediately. I really had no idea this was going on. Poor Beth.'

'Thank you. I was wondering if perhaps you could speak to the whole class? Perhaps about name calling in general and how hurtful it can be, rather than mentioning Beth specifically.'

'Absolutely. Of course,' Miss Willow agreed. 'And I'll explain that people go into hospital for all sorts of reasons. Sometimes it's because they are physically ill and sometimes it's because they're very unhappy and need help. There seems to be a lot of ignorance surrounding mental health.'

'Yes,' I agreed, relieved. 'That would be perfect. Thank you. I am grateful.'

'No need. I should have picked this up sooner. I'm usually more tuned into bullying, which is what this is.'

Aware that school was due to start soon, I made a move to go.

'How is Beth?' Miss Willow asked.

'She's doing very well,' I said. 'She saw her father last Friday and I expect she'll see him again this Friday. I understand he's making a good recovery and should be discharged soon.'

'And Beth will be returning to live with him?' she now asked.

'Yes, as far as I know.'

'Despite the concerns you and I raised with her social worker?'

'Well, yes,' I said, a little taken aback. 'Didn't Jessie tell you that the concerns were completely unfounded? I felt dreadful because I caused Derek so much distress.'

Miss Willow studied me carefully for a moment and then said something rather odd. 'I wouldn't feel too bad. Jessie did tell me the outcome, but the file's not closed yet.' The klaxon sounded for the start of school and Miss Willow stood. 'I'll walk you downstairs,' she said. 'I have to go into the playground to bring my class in.'

The three of us went out of the classroom. 'Does Beth know why you've come to see me?' Miss Willow asked as we walked.

'Yes. She wasn't altogether happy about it, but I felt it was best.'

'Absolutely. I'm very grateful you told me, and please be reassured I'll deal with the matter today.'

'Thank you,' I said again.

We arrived in reception and went out of the main door. We said goodbye and Miss Willow went over to her class, where Beth was already standing in line. Beth saw us and gave a little wave and Paula and I waved back. Adrian was also lining up in his class, but he was too busy chatting to his friends to see us. As Paula and I left the playground and began towards the car, I felt relieved and vindicated for going in to see Miss Willow. She had taken the matter seriously and would deal with it sensitively, for, as she'd said, name calling was a form of bullying, although I doubted the children involved would have thought of it as such.

I stopped off at the local shop on the way home for a few essentials, and then the rest of the day disappeared in household duties and playing with Paula. Paula would be three in April and would start nursery – mornings only – in September. I thought she was ready for the extra stimulation and socializing that nursery would bring. Once she was settled I was planning on looking for a part-time job that would fit in with school and fostering – possibly administration work, which I'd done before.

Although the day was cold, it was dry and the sun was out, so I decided to walk to school to collect Adrian and Beth, but I took the pushchair just in case Paula tired. As we waited in the playground I chatted to some other mothers. I saw Jenni's mother and her friend standing some distance from me, but she didn't look over. The klaxon sounded and when Beth and Adrian came out they were both in good spirits and Beth looked relieved, so I thought that whatever Miss Willow had said must have been exactly right. However, on the way home Beth asked, 'Why was my social worker in school?'

'I didn't know she was,' I said, surprised. 'Did she speak to you?'

'No. I was in class. I saw her through the classroom window.'

'Perhaps she went into school about another child,' I suggested, which seemed a reasonable possibility.

Beth gave a small shrug and then began hopscotching the paving stones as we walked. Adrian and Paula joined in, so our progress home was slow but fun. Even I had a quick hopscotch, which made them all laugh.

I thought no more of Beth's comment about seeing Jessie in school and the rest of the afternoon and evening continued as usual, with dinner, Adrian and Beth doing their homework, a few games and then the bath and bedtime routine. Beth telephoned her father at seven o'clock while I bathed Paula and they talked mainly about what she would wear when she visited him the following day, although I intended to have a say in that. I hadn't heard from Jessie that week so I'd assumed the arrangements for Beth visiting her father would be the same as the previous week, which from their conversation is what Beth and Derek appeared to assume too. They were naturally looking forward to seeing each other, but it wasn't to be.

The following morning, when I returned home from taking Adrian and Beth to school, Jessie telephoned, and what she said was not only devastating for Beth, but also made no sense at all.

Chapter Twelve

Very Upset

'**B**eth won't be visiting her father this evening,' Jessie said evenly. 'Would you tell her, please?'

'Yes, but why? What's the matter? Is Derek unwell? Beth will be so disappointed.'

There was a pause before Jessie replied. 'Reassure Beth that her father is well, but tell her my manager and I have made the decision to cancel her visit. I'll explain the reasons why when I see her. That's all you need to say.'

An uncomfortable tightness settled in my stomach. 'Is there something wrong?' I asked, all manner of thoughts flashing through my mind.

'I'm not in a position to say any more at present,' Jessie said flatly. 'I need to make some more enquiries. Did Beth telephone her father yesterday?'

'Yes. She does every evening.'

'How long does the call last?'

'At least thirty minutes. Sometimes longer.'

'And what do they talk about?'

I was being questioned, but why? I felt my heart starting to race. 'I can't hear much of their conversation,' I said. 'Beth uses the telephone in my bedroom while I bath Paula. From what I've heard they talk a lot about what Beth wears – she always changes into a dress when she arrives home from school. They tell each other that they miss each other and sometimes Beth tells her father about school, but not often.'

There was a pause, as though Jessie might be writing down what I was saying. 'Can you hear Derek's replies?' she asked.

'Not from the bathroom. No. I used to sit on the bed next to Beth, and I could hear his replies then.'

'So why did you stop sitting with Beth while she telephoned her father?'

'After you told me you didn't have any concerns about their relationship, I didn't think there was any need to. Also, I have to get Paula ready for bed. Derek and Beth talk for some time and if I waited until they'd finished Paula would go to bed late every evening.'

There was another pause before Jessie asked, 'Does Derek call Beth his little princess?'

'Yes. It's a term they both use quite a lot,' I said, not understanding why she was asking 'Beth often says, "I'm Daddy's little princess." I'm sorry, have I done something wrong?'

'No,' Jessie said flatly, then added, 'Beth isn't to telephone her father until further notice.'

'What? Not at all?' I asked, shocked.

'Not for the time being.'

'She'll be so upset,' I said. 'She looks forward to the telephone calls, and on top of having her visit cancelled she'll be devastated.'

'I appreciate that,' Jessie said. 'But I'm afraid it can't be helped. I'll let you know if and when telephone contact can resume, but it won't be for a while, so don't give her false hopes, please.'

I was struggling to make sense of what I was being told, and so too would Beth. She was being stopped from seeing and speaking to her father for no obvious reason. 'And you can't tell me any more?' I asked.

'Not at present,' Jessie said. 'Is there anything more you can tell me about Beth's telephone calls to her father? Why does she use the telephone in your bedroom?'

'Because Adrian is usually watching television in the living room at that time. So it saves him being interrupted, and it also gives Beth some privacy. It's a routine we've got into.'

There was another small pause, then Jessie asked, 'Is there anything else you can tell me about Beth?'

It would have helped if I'd known in what connection she meant. 'Not really. She's been coping well. There was an incident of bullying at school, but I saw Miss Willow and she dealt with it. Beth saw you in school yesterday.'

'Did she?' Jessie said without surprise. She didn't elaborate. 'I'll arrange an appointment to see you when I know more. Thank you for your time.' She wound up the conversation and said goodbye.

I slowly replaced the handset and stayed where I was on the sofa. Whatever was going on? What had happened to end contact so abruptly? What could I tell Beth?

Paula looked over from where she was playing on the living-room floor. 'Was that about Beth?' she asked.

'Yes, love, it was.'

'You look worried, Mummy,' she said sweetly. Then standing, she came and sat beside me on the sofa. I put my arm around her and held her close. We were both silent for a while. Paula seemed to appreciate the enormity of what I'd just been told and that I needed time to think.

Suddenly my thoughts were interrupted by the telephone ringing. I reached over and picked up the handset. As I did it crossed my mind that perhaps it might be Jessie able to give me the reason for her decision, or possibly even saying the decision had been reversed and Beth could telephone and see her father as planned. But it wasn't Jessie.

'Is that Cathy?' a slightly familiar female voice asked.

'Yes. Speaking.'

'It's Marianne, Derek's friend.'

'Oh. Hello.'

'I hope I haven't interrupted anything, but I need to speak to you urgently.'

'Yes, go ahead.'

'Derek phoned me a little while ago and he's very distraught. He says he's been stopped from seeing Beth and speaking to her on the phone. He didn't seem to understand why. He said something about a meeting. I've tried to telephone the social worker, but she's not available. I wondered if you knew what had happened?' Marianne spoke quickly and I could hear the anxiety in her voice.

'I don't know,' I said. 'Jessie has just telephoned me, but all she said was that Beth wouldn't be seeing her father this evening and she wasn't to telephone him until further notice. She didn't say why.' I wondered if I should tell her about the questions Jessie had asked me about Beth and her father, or that Jessie had been into Beth's school, but decided it was confidential and if Jessie wanted her to know she'd tell her.

'Jessie didn't give you a reason?' Marianne asked.

'No. She just asked me to tell Beth. She's going to be so upset.'

Marianne gave a heartfelt sigh. 'I don't know what's going on. I've told Derek I'll go to the hospital as soon as I finish work. I can't do anything now, I'm at work. He said something about a meeting he'd had to attend yesterday with Jessie and the psychologist, but I couldn't understand what that had to do with anything. He was too upset to explain. Do you know anything about the meeting?'

'No. Jessie didn't mention it,' I replied honestly.

Marianne sighed again. 'OK. Thank you. Sorry to have troubled you, but I didn't know who else to call. I'll try to get hold of Jessie again later.'

'Marianne, I'm very worried too,' I said. 'If you find out anything from Jessie could you tell me, please? It's going to be difficult enough anyway telling Beth she's not seeing her father, and without a good reason I really don't know what to tell her.'

'Yes, of course I will.'

She said a quick goodbye and I replaced the handset. So not even Derek understood the reason why contact had been stopped.

Paula looked up at me. 'Was that about Beth too?' she asked quietly.

'Yes, love. It was.'

'Oh dear, poor Beth.' Paula sympathized, appreciating something was badly wrong but not knowing what.

Marianne didn't telephone back that day so I assumed that she hadn't learned any more from Jessie. As the afternoon drew on and the end of school approached, my anxiety grew at the prospect of having to tell Beth she wouldn't be seeing or phoning her father. I took the car to school, hoping that Beth wouldn't mention her father until we were at least in the car or – better still – home, where I could talk to her in private. Paula and I waited in the playground and, as usual for a Friday afternoon, as soon as the klaxon sounded the children bounded out, excited by the start of the weekend. Beth was out before Adrian and ran to my side, beaming. The first thing she said was, 'I'm seeing my daddy tonight!'

Paula looked at me, aware I had something important to say to Beth.

'Beth, love,' I said gently, bending towards her. 'I'm afraid there's been a change of plan.'

Beth's face immediately lost its happy, carefree expression and she scowled at me. 'I'm not seeing my daddy, am I?'

'No, not tonight, love. I'm sorry. I'll explain when we get home.'

She glared at me, a mixture of disappointment and anger. Then she stamped her foot hard in rage. 'I want to see my daddy!' she shouted.

Paula jumped in fright and some of the other children and mothers standing nearby looked over.

I placed my hand reassuringly on Beth's shoulder. 'I'm sorry, love,' I said again. 'Jessie phoned. I'll tell you what she said when we get home.'

'Tell me now!' Beth demanded, stamping her foot again.

'No, love, when we get home,' I said evenly.

'You can't stop me seeing my daddy!' she shouted. 'No one can!' Even I was starting to feel embarrassed, and Paula was looking scared.

'Losing your temper won't help,' I said, keeping my voice calm. 'I'll tell you what I know when we get home, not here.'

'Hate you!' Beth hissed. 'Hate you all.' She folded her arms across her chest, her face set in anger and she turned her back on us.

I hadn't seen Beth this angry. Paula was obviously frightened by her outburst and slipped her hand into mine. Adrian came out of school and, seeing Beth's expression, asked her lightly, 'What's up with you?'

'Shut up!' she shouted.

He frowned.

'That's enough, Beth,' I said. 'I know you're upset, but being rude won't help.'

'Can we go now, Mum?' Adrian asked, clearly embarrassed and wanting to be away from the playground.

'Yes. Come on,' I said.

Paula kept her hand firmly in mine as we began across the playground. Adrian went a little in front and Beth lagged behind. I could see she was putting distance between us and a couple of times I glanced over my shoulder to make sure she wasn't getting too far behind. She still had her arms crossed and was staring down as she walked, a fierce expression marring her usually pretty features. We went out of the school gates and along the pavement towards the car, with Beth walking some distance behind us. Even when we arrived at the car she stood a little away and glared at me when I looked at her.

'Come on. In you get,' I said to all three children as I opened the rear door.

Adrian slid in first, then Paula and finally Beth. I checked their seatbelts as I usually did, but as I checked Beth's she roughly pushed my hand away. I thought it best to ignore her small act of aggression and closed the rear door, which automatically child-locked. No one spoke in the car during the ten-minute drive home, but I could see their faces in the rear-view mirror. Adrian and Paula were looking ahead with very worried expressions, while Beth was staring out of her side window, still very angry.

I parked on our driveway, got out and opened the rear door for the children. Adrian clambered out first, followed by Paula and then Beth, who stomped past me and up to the front door.

'Don't worry,' I said quietly to Adrian and Paula. 'She'll be all right soon.' I could see how much Beth's anger was upsetting them.

Very Upset

I unlocked the front door and Beth shot in first. Kicking off her shoes, she threw her coat on the floor and then stamped upstairs to her bedroom where she slammed the door.

'What was all that about?' Adrian now asked, relieved we were home.

'Beth can't see her father tonight,' I said. 'Understandably she's upset. Can you look after Paula for a moment, please, while I go up and talk to her?'

'Can we have the television on?' Adrian asked.

'Yes, of course. Until dinner time.'

I helped Paula out of her coat and shoes, took off my own, and then Adrian took Paula through to the living room. I went upstairs to Beth's room, where I gave a perfunctory knock on her door before going in. She was lying on her side on the bed clutching the framed photograph of her father to her chest.

'Get out!' she cried as I entered. 'I hate you all. I want my daddy!'

'I know you do, love,' I said gently. I went over and perched tentatively on the edge of the bed. I didn't want to be within striking distance if Beth lashed out, which I thought she might do while she was so angry.

'Why won't you let me see my daddy?' she demanded, glaring at me.

'It's not my decision,' I said. 'Jessie phoned me this morning and said she and her manager had made the decision that you weren't to go to the hospital or telephone your father again until she tells us.' There was no easy way to say it.

'What? I can't telephone him?' Beth asked, sitting up so quickly that I started. Her eyes blazed.

'I'm afraid not,' I said. 'I don't know – Jessie didn't say – but there must be a good reason.'

'I can't telephone him at all?' Beth asked, her voice rising slightly in disbelief.

'Not for now. Not until Jessie tells us to.'

'But that's not fair!' Beth cried, clutching the photograph. Then her anger turned inwards and on herself. 'I bet it's my fault I can't see him,' she said. 'I've done something. It's all my fault!' Tears sprang to her eyes.

'No, it's not,' I said. 'It's not your fault at all.'

'It must be!' she cried. 'I love my daddy and he loves me. I must have done something really bad for them to stop me seeing him.' Like many children in care who can't see their parents, Beth felt she was to blame.

I moved closer and took her hand. She didn't resist. 'Beth, love,' I said gently. 'Sometimes social workers have to make difficult decisions, and they can't always tell us straight away the reason for their decision. We're going to have to be patient and brave, until Jessie can tell us what the problem is. Hopefully it won't be long.'

Beth looked at me, all anger gone, now replaced by sorrow. 'Perhaps my daddy doesn't love me any more,' she said pitifully. 'Perhaps he loves someone else, not me.'

With the photograph still held close to her chest, she laid her head against my shoulder and began sobbing quietly. I put my arms around her and drew her to me. 'Of course your daddy loves you,' I said. 'And deep down you know that. It wasn't his decision not to see you. He's very upset too.'

'You don't know that,' Beth sobbed. 'You don't know he was upset. Perhaps he told Jessie he didn't want to see me any more.' I could appreciate why Beth felt so rejected, and with no reason for the cessation of contact it was difficult for me to reassure her. I decided I had no choice but to tell her about Marianne's telephone call, to prove to her that it wasn't her father's decision and that he too was upset at not seeing her. 'Marianne telephoned me this morning,' I began.

Beth raised her head from my shoulder and looked at me, her eyes wet from crying. 'Why?'

'She asked me if I knew why you weren't seeing your daddy. He telephoned her earlier because he was upset at not being able to see you. He wanted to see you very much.'

'Did he really?' Beth asked.

'Yes, love. I wouldn't make it up. He phoned Marianne, and then she phoned me.'

'But if my daddy wants to see me and I want to see him, why can't we see each other?' Beth asked.

'I honestly don't know. Marianne and your father don't know either. Jessie said she'd tell us when she knows more. But it may not be for some time. I know it's upsetting for you, but there's nothing we can do for now and I think we should try to make the most of the weekend.' I decided not to tell Beth that Jessie had said she was making further enquiries, as it begged the question about the nature of the enquires and Jessie hadn't told me.

'So I can't phone my daddy at all over the weekend?' Beth asked, her face clouding again.

'No, love, I'm afraid not.'

Her face crumpled and I put my arms around her and held her close. I felt so very sorry for her and impotent to help. As I cuddled and soothed her, I heard a key go into the lock in the front door downstairs and then the door open. For a moment I wondered who was letting themselves in, and then I realized.

'John's home,' I said to Beth. 'Let's dry your eyes and go downstairs.' I thought John's entrance was well timed. It should help distract Beth from her disappointment and also cheer up Adrian and Paula, who were naturally worried about Beth.

Adrian and Paula had heard their father come in and had rushed down the hall to greet him with shouts of 'Daddy! Daddy's home!'

'Hi, love,' I called to John from Beth's room. 'I'm with Beth. We'll be down in a minute.' I'm not sure whether John heard me, for he was making such a fuss of the children. I could hear him telling them how much he'd missed them.

'OK?' I asked Beth. 'Do you feel you can come down now?' She gave a small nod. 'Good girl.'

She slid the photograph of her father under the pillow. I held her hand and we went downstairs. John, Adrian and Paula were still in the hall hugging each other. 'Hi. How are you two?' John said, looking up as Beth and I arrived at the bottom of the stairs.

'We're good,' I said. Beth managed a weak smile.

I went over and kissed John's cheek; I couldn't give him a bigger kiss or a hug as he was fully occupied hugging Adrian and Paula. I thought it would be nice if the three of them had some time alone, as they hadn't seen each other for two weeks. I also thought that watching their joyful reunion might upset Beth even more.

'Would you like to come and help me make John a cup of tea,' I suggested to her. 'I could do with your help, and I'm sure he'd like a cup of tea.'

'Yes, please. I'm gasping,' John said.

Beth was happy to come with me, and John shoulder-lifted Adrian and Paula into the living room amid squeals of laughter and delight. Here was another example of the careful balancing act that was required between the needs of one's own children and the looked-after child, so that everyone had their fair share of attention and no one felt compromised or left out. Later, we'd all be together, but for now it was right that Adrian and Paula enjoyed their father's attention.

Very Upset

Beth was meticulous in setting a cup and saucer on the tray for John and then arranging biscuits on a plate, and while this little activity distracted her from her upset, my thoughts were still with Derek. Marianne had said she was going to the hospital after work and I guessed she would be there now. I wondered how Derek was and if Marianne had found out the reason why he wasn't allowed to see or speak to Beth. Surely Jessie had told Derek the reason, even if he'd been too upset to tell Marianne when he'd telephoned her? It crossed my mind, but only for a second, that the reason might have something to do with the concerns Marianne, Miss Willow and I had previously raised. But I dismissed the thought. Jessie had said those concerns had been proved unfounded, so it couldn't be that.

Chapter Thirteen

Two-Parent Family

John enjoyed the tea and biscuits Beth carefully carried into the living room on the tray and handed to him. Adrian and Paula had calmed down a little from the excitement of having their father home and were seated on the sofa either side of him, telling him their news. Beth and I sat in the easy chairs and joined in the conversation. There was a joyous, festive atmosphere to our talk that evening – the upside of having a partner working away is that their homecoming becomes a celebration and the whole family is merry. Even Toscha was purring and rubbing herself around John's legs. After a while I left John with the children and went into the kitchen to make dinner. I'd chosen some of John's favourite dishes to cook: chicken casserole with creamed potatoes, peas and sweetcorn, followed by apple crumble and cream. These were also favourites with Adrian and Paula and most of the children I fostered, including Beth.

Beth was quieter than usual during the meal and didn't mention her father, other than to tell John that she wasn't allowed to see him or telephone him. I motioned to John that I'd explain later as I hadn't had a chance to speak to him on his own.

After dinner we played some games – snap first, mainly for Paula, and then Uno for Adrian and Beth. Adrian had taught Beth how to play Uno and they both enjoyed the game, as did

John and I. Paula helped play my hand, as the rules of Uno were a bit beyond her at her age. As it was Friday and we didn't have to be up early for school the following morning, the children stayed up later than usual. Occupied with the games, Beth temporarily forgot her sadness and seemed to take comfort in having John there – indeed, she wouldn't leave him alone. If I felt slightly uncomfortable about the way she was always touching him – rubbing his arm or running her fingers through his hair – I dismissed it. She was missing her father, that was all.

Just after eight o'clock, when I saw Paula begin to yawn and rub her eyes, I said, 'Bedtime, love. Say goodnight.' She went round everyone saying goodnight and offering her cheek for kissing.

The bedtime routine was easier with John home and only half the work for me. While I took Paula to bed he kept Adrian and Beth amused, then, once Paula was in bed, John and I swapped places, and he spent time saying goodnight to Paula while I continued playing games with Adrian and Beth. Then at nine o'clock John saw Adrian into bed while I went with Beth.

Beth became sad again at bedtime, so I sat with her and stroked her forehead until she fell asleep. By nine-thirty all three children were in bed and asleep and John and I went into the living room. I was looking forward to a kiss and a cuddle and to catching up on our news. John suggested he open a bottle of wine and he went into the kitchen to pour us a glass each. Just as he did, the telephone rang and I quickly answered it in the living room, hoping the ringing hadn't woken the children. I thought it might be an old friend telephoning for a chat, in which case I'd explain that John had just returned from working away and I'd phone back another time.

However, it wasn't an old friend.

'Cathy,' Marianne began as soon as I answered. 'I've just returned from seeing Derek at the hospital. I've been there for over three hours. I thought you'd want to know what happened. Are you OK to talk?'

She sounded very stressed and I could hardly say no. 'How is Derek?' I asked.

'Not good, which is why I stayed so long. All the worry has really set back his recovery, and of course I feel partly responsible.'

'Why do you feel responsible?' I asked, a sinking feeling settling in the pit of my stomach. I could hear John moving around in the kitchen as he took the wine glasses from the cabinet.

'There was a meeting at the hospital earlier this week,' Marianne continued. 'Derek had to attend. I'm not sure which day it was – he was unclear. Jessie was there; so too was a nurse from his ward and the psychologist. They talked about Derek and Beth's home life, and some of the things I told you – about the way Derek and Beth behave towards each other – came up.'

'Oh,' I said.

'I'm not blaming you,' Marianne said quickly. 'I agreed you should tell Jessie. But the way it was said made it sound as though I was accusing Derek of child abuse, which I certainly wasn't. They also talked about the things you'd told Jessie – about some photographs and other stuff. Miss Willow was mentioned too.'

'But I don't understand,' I said as soon as Marianne paused. 'Why now? I thought all that had been dealt with when I first brought it up. Jessie told me that there were no grounds for concern. Indeed, she made me feel I was being malicious for suggesting anything was wrong. So why has all this come up now?' John returned to the living room carrying a glass of wine in each hand, which he set on the coffee table within reach, and then sat beside me on the sofa, waiting for me to finish on the telephone.

'I don't know,' Marianne said. 'Each time Derek started to tell me what Jessie had said he became upset and started crying. It's possible it had something to do with Beth's visit last Friday. I believe Jessie took her to the hospital?'

'Yes, that's right,' I said. 'But Jessie didn't say anything was wrong when she brought Beth home. Although, come to think of it, I remember she seemed a bit preoccupied. But Beth hasn't said anything went wrong with her visit; in fact, she said she'd had a good time. Oh dear,' I said, suddenly remembering something, 'I hope it hasn't got anything to do with what Beth was wearing. She got herself ready and chose clothes that weren't suitable. She also put on a lot of make-up, but there wasn't time to do anything about it.'

'I doubt that's got anything to do with it,' Marianne said. 'Beth's always dressing up, and Derek didn't mention that. What he did say, though – which sounded odd to me – was that Jessie had stopped Beth from sitting on some of the other male patients' laps and also from playing kiss chase. I've no idea what all that was about, and Derek didn't seem to know.'

'I've no idea,' I agreed, puzzled and concerned. 'Beth didn't mention that to me.' John gave a small sigh and picking up the newspaper opened it to the first page.

'Marianne,' I said, 'I'm going to have to go soon. My husband has just returned home from work. Can we speak another time?'

'Yes, sure, although that's all, really. I take it Jessie hasn't telephoned you with any more information?'

'No.'

'I'll telephone her on Monday,' Marianne said, 'and see if she's willing to tell me what's going on. This is Derek's worst

nightmare. He was paranoid before about losing Beth, and now
…' Marianne left the sentence unfinished. 'I would never have
said anything if I thought this could have happened.'

I chose my reply very carefully. 'I think we all have a duty to
report genuine concerns about children,' I said. 'I don't think
you, I or Miss Willow did anything wrong in voicing our
worries. It was up to Jessie and the social services to act as they
saw fit. You shouldn't blame yourself.'

'I suppose you're right,' Marianne said. 'It's all so confusing. I
really don't understand what's going on.'

'It's very confusing for Beth too,' I said.

'Yes. Poor kid. I'll let you go now. I'll be visiting Derek again
over the weekend and I'll telephone you if I have any more news.'

'Thank you.'

We said goodbye and I hung up. John looked at me. 'Problems?' he asked, closing the newspaper and putting it to one side.

'Yes.'

'So tell me.' Which I did. And being able to share my worries
helped.

We had a good day on Saturday. Adrian and Paula were
delighted to have their father home and that he was able to spend
time playing with them. Beth put on a brave face and didn't need
much encouragement to join in the games. Indeed, as with the
evening before, she took comfort in having John there and
constantly sought out his attention. A few times during the day
she came to me and quietly made a comment about her father,
showing he was never far from her mind. 'I wonder what my
daddy is doing,' or 'I hope Daddy is all right.' I reassured her as
best I could. I didn't tell her that Marianne had telephoned the
previous evening, for she hadn't really said anything positive that
might help Beth, and given Beth's previous animosity towards

Two-Parent Family

Marianne I didn't think it was wise to tell Beth that Marianne had visited her father in hospital when she had been stopped from seeing him. However, I did tell Beth that if Jessie didn't telephone me on Monday then I would telephone her on Tuesday to see if she had any news, which was all I could say, really, and seemed to reassure her.

At seven o'clock – the time Beth would normally have been telephoning her father – she left John's side and, snuggling up to me on the sofa, whispered, 'Can't we telephone my daddy without Jessie knowing? I won't tell anyone.'

We were all in the living room watching some television and I replied quietly so as not to disturb the others. 'No, love. As your foster carer I have to do what your social worker tells me or I'll get into trouble.'

Beth thought for a moment. 'What if I phoned my daddy without telling you? You could write the telephone number on a piece of paper and leave it lying around. Then I could find it. I could go upstairs and phone, and you wouldn't know anything about it.'

I had to smile, but my heart went out to Beth; she was missing her father so much. 'Then I'd be in trouble for leaving the telephone number lying around and not supervising you properly,' I said, giving her a hug. 'I'm afraid we will have to wait until next week when I can talk to Jessie.'

She pulled a face, but accepted what I'd said and returned to John, while I strengthened my resolve to try to find out what was going on. Beth needed to know why she wasn't in contact with her father, and I shouldn't have to rely on second-hand information from Marianne.

On Sunday John suggested we go to Moorlands, which was a small zoo about a forty-five-minute drive away. The children loved the idea and by 10.30 a.m. we were all in our winter coats and piling into John's car. I appreciated that John had taken the initiative and suggested the outing. While he was working away all the initiatives and responsibility fell to me, but now he was home we were a proper two-parent family again, doing things together and sharing the responsibility. I'm sure the children appreciated it too.

Adrian remembered going to the zoo two years before, when Paula had been a baby. Beth hadn't been before and said more than once that she'd ask her father to bring her when he was well again. I smiled an acknowledgement but didn't say anything. In the light of recent developments I found that I was being guarded in what I said to Beth about her seeing her father. With so little information and then Marianne's comments, I'd no idea if or when Beth would see her father again.

John and I walked around the zoo holding hands as the children darted from one animal enclosure to the next. He appeared relaxed and was in a playful mood and I was reminded of our courtship, which can sometimes become lost with all the commitments a family and a responsible job bring. We took plenty of photographs of the children and the animals and I told Beth I'd have an extra set printed for her.

'I'll show them to my daddy,' she said, smiling at John.

We had lunch at the zoo's café, then saw the remaining animals and left at 3 p.m. Although the zoo was only small, we'd had a nice day, and when we arrived home the children drew pictures of the animals, while I made dinner and John watched the sport on television. Beth had wanted to watch sport with John, but I persuaded her to join Adrian and Paula – it seemed more apt, and I knew John liked to watch his sport in peace. After dinner I began the bath and bedtime routine earlier than I had the previous two days, in preparation for having to be up for school the following morning. When Paula was in bed I went downstairs to tell John she was ready for her goodnight kiss, but as I walked into the living room Adrian and Beth looked sombre.

'Is everyone all right?' I asked.

'I've just had to tell them that I've got to go soon,' John said.

'What, tonight?' I asked, surprised. 'I thought you'd be leaving in the morning.' Which is what he had been doing when he worked away.

'Unfortunately not,' John said. 'I have an early start tomorrow, beginning with an eight o'clock breakfast meeting. I need to get settled in at the hotel tonight.'

I felt as disappointed as Adrian and Beth looked. 'Oh dear,' I said. 'Well, I suppose it can't be helped.'

'I'm afraid not,' John said.

He stood and went upstairs to say goodnight to Paula while I stayed with Adrian and Beth. The room was quiet. I think we were all surprised by the abruptness of his departure, and I wondered why he hadn't mentioned it before. When John returned downstairs he stayed in the hall and called out, 'Are you all coming to see me off then?'

I went with Adrian and Beth into the hall where John was putting on his coat, his suitcase on the floor beside him. He must have packed it earlier while I'd been clearing up the dinner dishes.

'Bye, kids,' he said, hugging Adrian and then Beth. Beth clung to him and smothered his face in kisses.

I eased her away and John kissed my cheek, gave Adrian a high-five and then opened the front door. The cold night air rushed in. Paula, having heard the door open, called from upstairs, 'Is Daddy going?'

'Yes, love. I'll be up in a minute.'

The three of us watched John go down the path and to his car. He opened the rear door, put his suitcase on the back seat and then climbed into the front. We waved until he was out of sight, and I closed the front door.

'I wish he didn't have to work away,' Adrian said sadly.

'I know, love. But it won't be long until next weekend.'

'Will I see my daddy next Friday?' Beth asked, also looking sad.

'I'll ask Jessie,' I said. Which was the best I could offer.

Beth and Adrian returned to the living room while I went upstairs to resettle Paula. 'Has Daddy gone to work?' she asked.

'Yes, love, until next weekend.'

'Will you give me another cuddle?'

'Of course.'

I lay on the bed beside Paula and cuddled her until she turned over, ready for sleep. I gave her a kiss goodnight and then came out and went downstairs and into the living room where Adrian and Beth were looking at some books. They asked if I could read them some stories, which I was happy to do. Although they could both read, like most children they still liked to be read to sometimes, and since Beth's telephone contact had stopped she'd got out of the routine of going into Paula's room to listen to her story. I read the books they chose and we talked about the stories until it was time to begin their bath and bedtime routine.

Later, when all the children were in bed asleep, I sat alone in the living room, a single parent again, and watched the news on television. Toscha, sensing I needed company, jumped onto my lap and, purring, licked my chin, which made me smile. She spent some time curling herself into a ball and I stroked her luxuriously soft, silky fur. It was comforting. The weather forecast was now showing on the television, with the presenter saying the temperature was already dropping and icy rain was forecast during the night. Drivers should be aware of the treacherous road conditions and needed to take extra care. I hoped John made it to his hotel before the worst of the weather set in. I worried about him when he was away. He meant the world to me and I couldn't bear the thought of anything happening to him.

I went to bed at eleven o'clock but was awoken at two by Beth having a nightmare. I heard her shout out and, grabbing my dressing gown, I hurried round the landing and to her room. She was sitting upright in bed looking petrified, with tears on her cheeks. 'Oh, Cathy!' she cried, stretching out her arms to me. 'I thought my daddy was dead. I thought Jessie had phoned and said he was dead. He's not dead, is he?'

'No, love,' I said, holding her close. She gripped my arms. 'Your daddy is in hospital, getting better. He's not dead. You had a bad dream, that's all. It's gone now.'

'It was a very, very bad dream,' Beth said, breathless from shock. 'It was so real. I thought he really was dead, and I was all alone.'

'You're awake now, and your daddy is in hospital,' I said again. 'He's safe.'

Gradually her sobbing eased and she relaxed her grip on me. I persuaded her to lie down and I drew the duvet up to her chin.

'Can you stay with me and stroke my head until I'm asleep, like my daddy does?' she asked.

'Of course, love.'

I sat on the bed and in the half-light coming from the landing I gently stroked Beth's forehead until she fell asleep. I crept out of her room, quietly pulled her door to and returned to my room. I could see why Beth would have a dream about her father dying. With no information and all contact abruptly halted, it was like a bereavement to Beth, and her subconscious had dealt with it as such, in a dream.

The following morning when I opened my bedroom curtains I saw that a thick hoar frost had settled in the night. Coating the gardens and houses, it gave the outside world a magical fairy-tale quality. It was very pretty. As I woke the children and opened their curtains, I pointed it out so they too could appreci-ate the beautiful scene. Although the gritting lorries had been out on the main roads, they hadn't touched the side roads and I didn't want to risk driving. I left time for us to walk to school. The shrubbery we passed glistened white in the rising sun and the frosty spider webs hanging on the foliage were truly works of art.

In the playground it crossed my mind that perhaps I should go into school and see Miss Willow to update her – that Beth wasn't seeing her father – as well as possibly learning something new from her. I now thought it was very likely that Jessie's visit to the school had been in connection with Beth. However, I decided against going in. I thought I shouldn't make a habit of popping in without a prior appointment, and if Miss Willow had something to tell me then she'd ask to see me, as she had done on Beth's first day with me.

Once Adrian and Beth had gone into school, Paula and I returned home and I spent most of the morning listening out for the telephone, hoping it would be Jessie with good news, or at least news. The telephone rang only once and it was a friend of mine wanting to arrange to meet for coffee. If Jessie didn't phone then I'd call her the following day. That afternoon I took Paula to the mother and toddler group we usually attended two after-noons a week, and I switched on the answerphone before I left the house. The group met in the local community centre and it gave mothers of young children the chance to meet and talk to each other over a cup of tea, and their toddlers the chance to play with similar-aged children. It was also good preparation for children, like Paula, who would be starting nursery in a few months. At the end of the afternoon I went straight from the group to school to collect Adrian and Beth.

The first thing Beth asked when she came out was: 'Did you speak to my social worker? Can I telephone my daddy?'

'She hasn't phoned yet,' I said. 'But there's still time.'

Beth's face set in anger.

'If Jessie doesn't phone today, I'll phone her tomorrow,' I said. It had only been Friday when Jessie had telephoned, so I thought I should give her a day or so to make her enquiries and get back to me as she'd said she would.

Beth scowled at me and I ignored it. I could understand why she was angry. Thankfully she didn't make a scene and recovered quickly.

There were no messages on the answerphone when we arrived home. 'I'll telephone Jessie tomorrow,' I confirmed again to Beth. 'But please don't get your hopes up, love. We don't know what Jessie will say.' For I thought Beth was pinning too much on the phone call.

'Jessie might say I can telephone my daddy,' Beth said, undaunted.

'Or she might say you can't,' I said, being truthful. 'If she does say that, then I'll try to find out the reasons why.' Which I thought would help make any decision of Jessie's easier for Beth to accept. I was wrong.

Chapter Fourteen
The Meeting

The following day I gave Jessie until two o'clock to tele-phone me and then I telephoned her. 'It's Cathy Glass,' I said as she answered her extension. 'Beth's carer.'

'Yes, I know who you are,' she said. 'How can I help you?'

The question threw me, as I'd assumed she'd realize what I wanted. 'I was wondering if there was any news on Beth's father,' I said.

'He's still in hospital,' Jessie replied.

'Yes, I thought he must be. But do you know when Beth can start telephoning him again? She really misses him. And I haven't been able to give her a reason why she can't phone.'

'Did you tell her my manager and I had made the decision?'

'Yes. But it would be useful if I could tell her the reason for the decision.'

There was a short silence before Jessie said, 'I was going to telephone you later. I need you to come in to a meeting, here at the council offices.'

'Oh, I see,' I said, taken aback.

'I was thinking of Thursday at one o'clock,' Jessie said.

'How long will the meeting last?' I asked, thinking ahead. 'I'll need to leave by two forty-five to collect Adrian and Beth from school.' I'd also have to make arrangements to have Paula

looked after, but that wasn't Jessie's worry, that was for me to
sort out.

'It'll be about an hour, but best to have a contingency plan
ready just in case.'

'All right. Can you tell me what the meeting is about?' I
asked.

'Beth,' Jessie said.

Which I'd assumed. 'Can you tell me when she can start
phoning her father again? She knows I'm speaking to you today
and is hoping you'll be able to tell me.'

'No. It's something we'll address at the meeting on
Thursday.'

'Oh, I see,' I said. 'Can I tell her why she's not allowed to telephone her father?'

'Is Beth asking?'

'Yes.'

'Tell her I'll explain when I see her. I should be able to visit
her some time next week. I'll confirm a date and time when I
see you on Thursday. Was there anything else?'

'Err, no, I suppose not.'

'I'll see you on Thursday, then.'

I hadn't learned anything new – apart from that I had to attend
a meeting – and I was now even more confused (and worried),
as I knew Beth would be. If there's a problem, I'm a great
believer in knowing what the issues are and dealing with them.
It's impossible to deal with what you don't know. For me, ignorance is not bliss. It was Tuesday, and although the meeting on
Thursday was only two days away, it stretched before me, an
interminable distance to be got through before my questions
could be answered and some of this would hopefully make
sense.

When Beth came out of school that afternoon she ran up to me, her expression full of anticipation and hope. I didn't wait for the question I knew would come.

'I've spoken to Jessie,' I said straight away. Beth's eyes lit up. 'We're going to have to be patient. Jessie said to tell you she'd visit us next week and explain what is happening. In the meantime, we still can't telephone the hospital, I'm afraid. Sorry, love.'

Tears immediately sprang to Beth's eyes. 'Why can't I telephone my daddy?' she said, utterly deflated.

I touched her shoulder reassuringly. 'I honestly don't know, love. I asked Jessie, but she said she wanted to tell you when she saw you next week. I've got to go to a meeting on Thursday, so I may learn more then.'

'Can I go to the meeting?' Beth asked, wiping the back of her hand across her eyes.

'No, love. It's for adults only.'

'Will my daddy be there?'

Good question, I thought. Jessie hadn't said who would be attending, but I felt sure she would have told me if Derek was going to be present. 'No, I don't think so,' I said.

'If he is there will you tell him I love him very much and I miss him with all my heart.'

'Of course, love,' I said. I swallowed the lump that had risen in my throat.

That evening I telephoned my friend Kay. She was happy to look after Paula while I went to the meeting on Thursday, and also to meet Adrian and Beth if I wasn't in the playground at the end of school. Later, when Paula was in bed and Adrian was busy at the table putting the finishing touches to a model aeroplane he was making, Beth asked me if I would play snap with her. She produced a pack of cards from the cupboard where we kept our games and puzzles and we squatted on the floor of the living room. Beth began dealing the pack into two equal piles.

'I play snap with my daddy,' she said wistfully.

'That's nice,' I said. 'Did you play snap with him when you visited him at the hospital?'

'No,' she said.

'What games did you play?' I now asked, mindful of Marianne's comment that Jessie had stopped Beth from playing a game of kiss chase.

'I can't remember,' Beth said emphatically.

I didn't question her further. I wouldn't have raised the matter had Beth not mentioned playing snap with her father, but now I felt sure she wasn't telling me something. Her expression, the way she couldn't meet my eyes and the decisiveness of her denial suggested she could remember what she'd played with her father, but wasn't going to tell me.

On Wednesday evening John telephoned, and although he didn't have much time to talk it was lovely to hear from him – and, of course, Adrian and Paula were delighted to talk to their father. He also said a few words to Beth. But after he'd gone, Beth asked me, 'How come they can speak to their daddy but I can't speak to mine?'

While the two situations were obviously very different, I could appreciate how unfair it must appear to her, but there was little I could say beyond reassuring her that I hoped to learn more at the meeting on Thursday. Presently, Beth said she was going to her room and disappeared upstairs. I didn't go after her. She wasn't upset and I could hear her moving around in her room and her bedroom door was open, so I wasn't worried. Fifteen minutes later she came downstairs, having changed her dress to the one she'd worn the Friday before when she'd visited her father in hospital. She'd also applied similar lashings of thick make-up, including bright-red lipstick, mascara and scarlet eye shadow. She'd painted her nails luminous turquoise. Adrian took one look and burst into laughter, while Paula, remembering when Beth had been similarly dressed, innocently asked, 'Are you going to see your daddy tonight?'

'No. I'm not allowed to,' Beth said. 'But no one can stop me looking nice for my daddy. It makes me feel closer to him.'

It was pitiful and sad, and Adrian, now appreciating that she was striving to be closer to her father, stopped laughing. Beth spent the rest of the evening in her finery, flouncing around haughtily with an air of sophistication. I didn't like what she was wearing, but I didn't say anything. She looked much older with all the make-up, but not in a nice way. I was pleased when it was time for her bath and she could wash it all off. I used acetate on cotton wool to remove her nail varnish.

'When I get home from school tomorrow, I'm going to put it all on again,' Beth said to me, a little defiantly.

I let her comment go. I thought that if this made her feel closer to her father and lessened her sense of loss, then there was little harm in it. She wouldn't be going out like that while she was living with me. Although how her father could find this endearing – his little daughter all tarted up – I'd no idea.

On Thursday – the day of the meeting – I made an early lunch for Paula and me, and then at twelve fifteen I changed into a smart pair of black trousers and a cream blouse. I'd explained the arrangements to Paula – that she was going to play with Vicky for the afternoon, and I'd collect her from Kay's or I'd meet her in the playground, depending on when my meeting finished. I'd also told her that if I wasn't back in time Kay would collect Adrian and Beth from school when she collected her own son and look after everyone until I arrived.

'Yes, it's all right, Mummy, I understand,' Paula said sweetly, reaching up to kiss my cheek.

After I'd taken Paula to Kay's – about five minutes away – I continued to the council offices in town. I parked in one of the visitors' bays and went into reception. Jessie hadn't told me which room the meeting was to be held in, so I asked the receptionist. She checked on her list of scheduled meetings and told me Jessie had booked Room 3.

'It's on the first floor,' she said. 'Up the stairs and down the corridor on your left.'

I thanked her and, having signed the visitors' book, began up the wide balustraded staircase. I knew from the previous meetings I'd attended in the council offices that the meeting rooms on the first floor were small compared to the larger committee rooms on the second floor, so I assumed there wouldn't be many of us at the meeting. The door to Room 3 was closed, so I knocked and then gingerly pushed it open and went in. The room was empty, but I was five minutes early. It was hot and airless, but I knew better than to try and open a window. The building was old and most of the windows had either been jammed or painted shut, or, having been forced open, didn't close properly and remained draughty in winter. A small oblong table stood in the centre of the room with a chair at each side. Two more chairs were stacked in a corner. That was the only furniture in the room. I took off my coat and draped it over the back of a chair at the table and then sat and waited. I found the quiet rather pleasant after the busy morning I'd had. Paula had been very excited at the thought of playing with Vicky and had chatted gaily (and loudly) for most of the morning, planning the games she'd play with Vicky. Now all I could hear was the occasional creek of the radiator and the muted footsteps of those walking along the carpeted corridor outside the room.

At ten minutes past two, just as I was thinking of going down to reception to check I had the right room, the door opened and Jessie burst in carrying a pile of folders.

'Sorry to have kept you,' she said, flustered. 'It's been one of those mornings!'

I smiled. 'Don't worry,' I said.

She sat in the chair opposite and dumped the folders on the table in front of her, then hooked her shoulder bag over her chair. 'God, it's hot in here,' she said, glancing at the windows. 'I take it none of them open.'

'I daren't try,' I said. 'But I doubt it.'

Jessie laughed. The state of the windows in the building was a commonly shared joke. 'OK, let's make a start then,' she said. 'My manager is hoping to join us later. She's in a meeting.' She took her notepad from the top of the pile of folders and unclipped the pen.

'Is it just us and possibly your manager?' I asked.

'Yes. I needed you to come as I have to clarify some of the things you've told me. Let's start with the photographs. I'll see them for myself next week when I visit, but I want to hear what you have to say.'

I was taken aback. Why was she asking about the photographs now? I thought I was coming for a meeting, but it seemed it was more of an interview and I felt ill prepared.

'You mean the framed photographs that Beth has in her bedroom?' I asked.

'Yes, the ones she brought with her from home.'

'They are all of Beth and her father,' I said, not really understanding what Jessie wanted from me.

The Meeting

'Yes, I know,' Jessie said a little impatiently, pen poised over her notepad. 'You said you thought they were inappropriate. Can I have the details?'

I shifted in my chair. 'I'm sorry. I'm confused,' I said. 'I thought when I raised this with you before you said I was mistaken and there was no reason to be concerned about the photographs or any of the other issues.' I felt my cheeks flush hot.

'I didn't say you were mistaken,' Jessie said defensively, glancing up at me. 'But at the time we didn't have enough evidence to act.'

'And do you now?' I asked, with unease.

'Possibly. One of the reasons you are here is so I can gather evidence.' She met my gaze. There was a moment's silence as the obvious question hung in the air between us: what had changed to make her act now?

Jessie lowered her pen and sat back slightly in her chair. 'I'll explain,' she said. 'When I took Beth to see her father at the hospital, I stayed with them for most of the time – not because I had any concerns then, but because I wasn't sure if Beth would want to stay the whole hour, or if Derek would find her visit too upsetting and have to cut it short. As a result I was able to observe the way they respond to each other, and I was shocked. Some of their behaviour is simply not appropriate for a father and his daughter.'

I stared at Jessie and felt my pulse quicken.

'Beth flirts with her father,' Jessie continued. 'And he does nothing to stop it. In fact, he encourages her. She kisses and cuddles him in a manner that can only be described as provocative or seductive. He allowed her to go round giving kisses and cuddles to some of the other male patients. I stopped that. I also stopped Beth from organizing a game of kiss chase with the other men. She had no idea it was wrong. She gives her affection

147

far too freely and appears to be sexually aware beyond her years. She shows signs of sexualized behaviour. I arranged a meeting with the psychologist who's been treating Derek, and we've agreed that, combined with other concerns raised, there were grounds to act, which is why I stopped contact.'

I shivered despite the heat of the room. 'So you think Beth's been abused?' I asked.

'It's possible,' Jessie said.

'By Derek?'

'It's possible,' Jessie said again, and then looked down at her notepad. 'Can we start with the photographs,' she said.

A large knotted ball had settled in the pit of my stomach. I felt sick. Poor Beth, I thought. Whatever had she been through? And how long had it been going on? Yet while I felt dreadfully sorry for Beth, I also felt vindicated. I had spotted something was wrong, as had Marianne and Miss Willow, and I'd been right to contact Jessie and voice my concerns. Pity she hadn't believed me then, I thought.

I began by telling Jessie why the framed photographs made me feel uncomfortable: because of the way Beth and her father were posing, and because Beth was wearing make-up, which made her look much older. 'They look more like boyfriend and girlfriend than father and daughter.' I said. 'They're not touching sexually. It's more the overall impression. You'll see it for yourself when you visit next week. It's difficult to put into words, but there's an intimacy in the way they are looking at each other that isn't appropriate for a father and daughter.'

'And the photograph Beth keeps under her pillow?' Jessie asked. 'I heard her tell her father that she sleeps with his picture, so it feels like he's there in the bed with her.'

I nodded. 'It's the largest of the framed photographs and also the most intimate. She kisses it goodnight and then sleeps with it under her pillow. It appears to have been taken while they were on holiday. Beth and her father are in their swimwear. They're kneeling in the sand, facing each other, and have their lips pursed ready to kiss. I persuaded myself that there was nothing wrong with the photograph, or the others,' I added reflectively as Jessie wrote.

When she'd finished writing she looked up at me. 'Beth told her father you'd taken some photographs of her.'

'Yes, I have.'

'He's unhappy about that.'

'Why?' I asked, amazed. 'They're family photographs, in the park and on outings. I've given Beth a set.'

Jessie made a note. 'I'll need to see those photographs when I visit,' she said.

'Yes, of course,' I said with a stab of unease. I felt that I too was being investigated.

'Is there anything else you can tell me about the photographs that Beth brought from home?' Jessie asked.

'No, I don't think so,' I said. 'There's fifteen of them and I've arranged them on the shelves in her bedroom, but you know that already.'

Jessie nodded. 'Now to the telephone calls. I appreciate you stopped staying with Beth when she phoned her father, but can you tell me what you heard when you were present?'

If only I'd made some notes, I thought, as I tried to think back and remember. Having been reassured there was nothing wrong, I'd put the details from my mind. However, once I started to remember, the phone calls seemed even more significant now, in the light of Jessie's investigation.

'Beth sprawls on my bed to speak to her father, more like a teenager talking to her boyfriend than a little girl talking to her father,' I said. 'She smiles and laughs almost seductively, and twiddles the flex around her fingers. She changes out of her school uniform when she comes home and chooses a pretty dress to wear just to make the telephone call. She always told her father in great detail what she was wearing. He wanted to know everything – the dress, the petticoat and any accessories she was wearing. Beth often says she likes to look nice for her daddy, and he appears to encourage her. Sometimes, when she was describing what she was wearing, she'd lower her voice and flutter her eyelids in a sexy way. I remember once he asked her if she had clean knickers on, which made her laugh. It doesn't seem funny now.'

'No,' Jessie said sombrely. 'It certainly doesn't.'

I waited until Jessie had finished writing and then I continued. 'There was always a lot of giggling from them both,' I said. 'Derek used to tease Beth and sometimes he'd talk in a high-pitched voice to make her laugh. He called her his "little princess" or "Daddy's little princess". Beth often says, "I'm Daddy's little princess." Many of her dresses are very frilly, as though she's dressing up as a fairy-tale princess.'

'What Beth was wearing when I took her to the hospital wasn't appropriate,' Jessie said, looking at me. 'You know that?'

'Yes. I apologized at the time. Beth chose her own clothes and put on the make-up without me knowing. There wasn't time to do anything about it or you would have been late going to the hospital.'

Jessie nodded. 'Anything else you can tell me about their telephone calls?'

'They used to tell each other how much they missed each other, especially in bed at night. You know Beth sleeps with her father in his bed?'

'Yes,' Jessie said, her voice flat.

'They used to blow lots of kisses down the telephone and say they loved and missed each other, which sounded OK. But then

Derek would add something like, "I miss holding you in my arms and feeling your little warm body," or, "I can't wait until I'm home and can tuck you up in bed beside me again." None of which seemed right.'

I waited again until Jessie had finished writing. 'Anything else?' she asked.

'I don't think so. Not with the telephone calls, but there's the way Beth behaves towards my husband, John.'

'Go ahead,' Jessie said, concentrating on her notepad.

At that moment the door opened and a woman came in. 'Hello,' she said. 'Sorry I'm late.' I guessed it was Jessie's manager.

'Laura,' she said, introducing herself and pulling over a chair to sit down. 'I'm the team manager.'

'This is Cathy, Beth's carer,' Jessie said, introducing me.

I smiled at her. 'Hello.'

'Don't let me interrupt,' Laura said. 'Jessie can fill me in later.'

'Your husband, John?' Jessie said to me. 'You have concerns about the way Beth behaves towards him?'

'Yes, although I'd convinced myself there was nothing wrong. It's difficult to put into words, but Beth is very familiar towards him. Physical, tactile,' I said, searching for the right word. 'I'm sorry, this part of fostering is new to me. I haven't looked after a sexually abused child before.'

'We don't know for certain that Beth has been sexually abused,' Laura put in. 'Although the indicators are there.'

I nodded and continued. 'Beth is too "easy" with John, more so than my children would be with the daddy of one of their friends. She is very physical, touching, hugging and kissing him at any opportunity. At bedtime on the first weekend she was with us she asked him to lie on her bed and cuddle her like her father did. Although part of me said it was because she was missing her own father, it didn't seem right to me, so I stopped it, as you know.'

'Because it made you feel uneasy?' Jessie asked.

'Yes. Instinctively, I felt it wasn't right.'

'And now?' Laura asked. 'How does Beth behave towards your husband?'

'He wasn't able to come home the following weekend, but he did last weekend. To be honest she was the same towards him, although she didn't ask him to lie on her bed. I've established a bedtime routine where she has a story downstairs and then I take her up and she goes to sleep with a cuddly toy.'

'Good,' Laura said as Jessie wrote.

'Beth's always trying to get John's attention,' I said. 'Sometimes she even flirts with him.'

'Does Beth behave like this towards other males?' Laura asked. 'For example, towards your father, or your son.'

'Good grief, no!' I said, shocked. 'Adrian's only six, and my father is in his seventies.'

'So her behaviour is only directed towards your husband, who is in the role of father?'

'Yes, I suppose it is,' I said. 'Although I hadn't really thought about that before.'

Neither woman replied. Laura concentrated on the table as Jessie made a note. It was to be many weeks later before I found out the significance of Laura's questions about John.

Chapter Fifteen

Loyal to Abuser

The meeting finished at 2.30 p.m., with Jessie making an appointment to visit Beth on Monday after school. Jessie told me that I shouldn't say anything to Beth about their suspicions of abuse, and that she would explain to her on Monday why she couldn't telephone or see her father. Laura thanked me for attending the meeting and I left the room first, hurrying out of the building to my car. My thoughts were in turmoil and my stomach churned. I realized that I'd convinced myself Derek and Beth's behaviour towards each other was normal, when in fact it was indicative of abuse. I felt guilty. I thought I should have been more insistent with Jessie and stood my ground when I'd originally reported my concerns, but it was difficult to know what else I could have said or done. As a foster carer, my authority was very limited and I didn't feel I had the expertise or confidence to persist. I felt I'd let Beth down, but then again, Jessie hadn't acted on Marianne's or Miss Willow's concerns either.

Yet as I drove from the building I felt that something didn't sit right, as though a piece of the jigsaw had been fitted incorrectly. Obviously I was relieved that it was now out in the open and Beth would receive the help and protection she needed, but I was struggling to accept that Derek had been sexually abusing

Beth. True, I didn't know him; I'd never even met him, although I'd seen photographs of him and had spoken to him on the phone. He didn't look or sound like a paedophile, he looked and sounded normal, although of course paedophiles did appear normal, which was how they could prey on children. And while I knew that child sexual abuse was often perpetrated by a family member – not a stranger – Marianne, who knew Derek very well having been part of his and Beth's lives for a long time, had been convinced he wouldn't hurt Beth. Clearly, if Derek was sexually abusing his daughter then he was hurting her, and in a most dreadful and appalling way. Had it gone on without Marianne knowing? It was certainly possible.

I arrived in the playground still deep in thought but put aside my worries to greet Paula. I spotted her immediately, waiting with Vicky and Kay. Paula spotted me too. 'Mummy!' she cried. Leaving Kay's side she rushed over and I scooped her up and smothered her with kisses, grateful for the uncomplicated love that my family, like most others, enjoyed.

'She's been fine,' Kay said, as Paula and I arrived at her side.

'Thank you so much for looking after her,' I said.

I stood with Kay as first her son came out of school and then Adrian and Beth, arriving almost together. I thanked Kay again for helping me out and we said goodbye. Once we were outside the school gates, Beth said to me: 'You've been to that meeting. Can I telephone Daddy?'

I had hoped we'd be home before she asked so I could deal with it in private. 'We're going to have to be patient a little bit longer,' I said.

'You said that the last time!' Beth flared angrily. 'I'm fed up with being patient! I want to see my daddy and you can't stop me. I'll go on the bus if I have to!'

We were walking along the pavement outside the school and I saw Adrian glance over his shoulder, hoping none of his friends were close enough to hear Beth's outburst.

'Jessie is coming to see us on Monday,' I said to Beth. 'She's going to explain to you then what is happening. Monday isn't long to wait. Just tomorrow and the weekend.'

'That's too long!' Beth said, stamping her feet as she walked. 'I'm fed up with waiting! I want to see my daddy!'

She stamped all the way to the car, causing Adrian much embarrassment, and I quickly opened the rear door for the children to get in. Beth shot in first and then flattened herself against the door on the far side, right away from Adrian and Paula. Clearly she didn't want anything do to with us at present. Adrian and Paula climbed in, and I checked all their seatbelts. Beth glared at me but didn't say anything.

All three children were silent as I drove home. I asked them, as I usually did, if they'd had a good day. Adrian and Paula nodded, but Beth met my gaze in the rear-view mirror and glared at me. When we arrived home Beth threw off her coat and shoes and, dumping them in the hall, stomped upstairs to her bedroom. I heard her door slam. I thought I'd give her a little cooling-off time, but just as I was hanging my coat on the hall stand we heard a loud crash come from Beth's room. Leaving Adrian to look after Paula, I shot upstairs as another crash sounded from her room. I gave a quick knock on her bedroom door and went in. Beth was standing in the middle of the room with one of the framed photographs in her hand. Two others lay on the floor with their glass smashed.

'Put the photograph down,' I said, going further into her room. 'Breaking them won't help.'

'Yes, it will!' she shouted angrily.

I was more concerned she might cut herself on the glass than with the actual breakages. I went over and quickly but gently removed the photograph from her hand. 'That's better,' I said. 'Now calm down and we can have a talk.'

'No,' Beth said, scowling at me and stamping her foot. 'I don't want to talk to you.'

Outwardly calm, I returned the photograph to the shelf with the others and then sat on the edge of her bed and patted the area beside me for her to join me. 'Come on, love. I need to talk to you.'

Beth scowled.

'Please come and sit down.'

Few children can resist an adult they trust making the time to talk and listen to them, and a few seconds later, still scowling, Beth sat beside me on the bed. 'Good girl,' I said.

'It's about the hospital, isn't it?' she said, still angry and jutting out her chin. 'That's why I can't see Daddy.'

'What do you mean — about the hospital?' I asked, puzzled.

'I know Jessie is annoyed with me. She stopped me playing games at the hospital.' Cleary Beth had felt Jessie's disapproval and had realized something was wrong, without understanding what. It was probably guilt that had resulted in her claiming she couldn't remember the games they'd played when I'd asked her at the weekend.

'Jessie isn't annoyed with you,' I said. 'Certainly not. And she doesn't blame you for anything.'

'Are you sure?' Beth asked suspiciously.

'Positive. Let me try to explain. Sometimes children can act in a way that adults don't think is safe. It's not the fault of the child. They're just behaving in the same way they always do, but adults can spot danger that children can't. Jessie stopped you from playing kiss chase and sitting on other patients' laps because she felt it wasn't right.' I felt I'd phrased it as best I could, given I was very limited in what I could tell her.

Beth thought for a moment. 'But I play those games with my daddy,' she said naïvely. Which, of course, was the problem. Her father had taught her how to behave towards men, so she didn't know any different.

'Jessie will explain more when she sees you on Monday,' I said. 'But for now you need to understand that the decisions Jessie has had to make are to keep you safe while she makes some enquiries.'

'What are enquiries?' Beth asked.

'Asking questions of other people to find out the truth.'

'Will Jessie ask me questions?'

'She may,' I said.

'If she does, I'll tell her I love my daddy and I miss him and I want to see him soon.'

'You can tell Jessie whatever you like,' I said. 'She's your social worker and her job is to help you.'

Beth accepted this. I asked her if she wanted a hug, and she did. She was over her anger for the time being. After a minute or so I gently eased away. 'I'm going to clear up the broken photographs now and then make some dinner,' I said.

'Don't throw the photos away!' Beth cried, leaving my side and rushing to the photographs that lay on the floor.

'No, I won't,' I said, also going over. 'But don't touch them. I don't want you to cut yourself. I'll just get rid of the glass.'

Beth watched me closely as I carefully picked up the two broken photographs and then came with me as I carried them downstairs. Derek's and Beth's images looked up at me, but were distorted from the cracks in the glass. In the kitchen I carefully took the broken glass from each frame and wrapped it in newspaper before putting it in the bin.

'There! As good as new,' I said, handing the photographs in their frames to Beth. 'You can't even see the glass is missing unless you look very closely.'

'Thank you,' she said, finally managing a smile. 'I'll put them on the shelf in my bedroom. I promise I won't break any more.'

'Good girl.'

I watched Beth walk away carrying the photographs protectively in front of her. While I could appreciate the anger that had led her to smash the photographs, I really didn't understand why she treasured them so much and idolized her father if he'd been abusing her. Was it because he was the only person she had in the world and without him she'd be completely alone? It was an unsettling but very plausible reason.

The following day, Friday, the children and I had a nice surprise. Unknown to us, John had managed to leave work early and had arrived home while I'd been collecting Adrian and Beth from school. Adrian was the first to spot his car parked in the road outside our house. 'Dad's home!' he shouted. 'Yippee!'

As soon as I'd parked the car and opened the rear door, Adrian rushed up to the front door where he pressed continuously on the bell. The door was quickly opened from inside and all three children fell into John's outstretched arms. 'I've missed you,' John said as he hugged them and kissed their heads.

'We've missed you too, Dad,' Adrian said.

I watched as Beth hugged and kissed John with a passion and intensity that I guessed was similar to the way she embraced her father and, from what Jessie had said, other men too. It really wasn't appropriate for someone she barely knew. After a moment John straightened and we all went inside. I closed the front door.

'Hello, love,' he said, finally getting a chance to kiss me. 'How are you?'

'All the better for seeing you.' I smiled. Then I mouthed quietly, 'I need to have a word with you.'

John understood, and once the children were seated at the table in the kitchen having a drink and a snack to see them through to dinner, John motioned for me to go with him into the hall.

'What's the matter?' he asked quietly, when we were outside the room and couldn't be heard.

'I had a meeting yesterday with Beth's social workers, and it seems likely Beth's father has been abusing her.' John gasped in horror. 'The social services are investigating and, while they are, Beth's not allowed to see or telephone her father. But you need to be careful.'

'Why?' John frowned. 'What's it got to do with me?'

'Nothing directly, but Beth can be too familiar with men – because of the way her father has treated her. For example, when Beth wanted you to lie on her bed. And the way she's always touching you – rubbing your arm or your back or running her fingers through your hair. And the way she hugs and kisses you. She hasn't seen you that much, but she's all over you. I'm not saying you shouldn't hug her, but do it as you would a friend's child, not as you do Adrian and Paula.'

I could see John was struggling with this, just as I had. Having welcomed Beth into our home, he had treated her as a child of the family, his affection innocent and unguarded. But for Beth, any contact with John could have connotations – sexual connotations – based on the inappropriate relationship her father had with her. Now, foster carers have training that should help them recognize and deal with sexualized behaviour in children they foster, but then it was left to the carer to identify and cope with it as best they could.

'I don't like the sound of all this,' John said as I finished. 'I hope this doesn't affect Adrian and Paula.'

'I'll make sure it doesn't,' I said, although of course anything that affected Beth affected other family members too.

We heard the children leave the table and when they appeared in the hall we all went into the living room where we chatted about the past week: Beth and Adrian's school, Paula's visits with me to the park and to play with Vicky, and a little about John's work. Presently, I said I'd better go into the kitchen and start dinner.

'Does Beth want to help you?' John asked, now cautious at being left alone with her.

I looked at Beth and she shook her head. 'I want to stay here,' she said.

'All right.'

I nodded a reassurance to John, and as I left the room I propped open the door so that John could hear me in the kitchen and I could hear all of them. It seemed a sensible precaution to safeguard everyone.

Despite the new precautions we put in place, we had a pleasant evening, although John was tired and nodded off on the sofa a couple of times. When it was Beth's bedtime, John said goodnight to her downstairs but didn't go to her room to kiss her goodnight as he did with Adrian and Paula. Once all three children were in bed, I sat beside John on the sofa and began telling him more about the meeting I'd had with Jessie and her manager. As foster carers, there is always something to discuss about fostering and the issues we have to deal with. The telephone rang shortly after 9.30 p.m. and with a small sigh I reached out and picked up the handset, ready to tell any friend of mine that I'd call back another time. However, it was Marianne again. 'I hope this is a good time to call,' she said. 'I need to talk to you.'

John heard, yawned and said, 'I'm going to bed.'

I was disappointed, as I'd hoped we'd spend time together, although I appreciated he was tired.

'Yes?' I asked Marianne. John stood, threw me a kiss and left the room.

'Have Jessie and her manager seen you yet?' Marianne asked anxiously.

'Yes, yesterday.'

'I had to see them on Wednesday,' Marianne said. 'It was like an interview. I came out feeling I'd done something wrong. They didn't tell me anything, but I'm sure they think Derek is a paedophile. Did they say anything to you?'

'Not a lot,' I said carefully. 'I just answered their questions.'

'Questions about Beth and Derek?' Marianne asked.

'Yes, some were.'

'He's still not allowed to see Beth or speak to her on the telephone, is he?'

'Not at present, no.'

I heard Marianne sigh. 'Derek's beside himself with worry,' she said. 'I can see him having another nervous breakdown over this, and there's nothing I can do to reassure him. I feel so sorry for him.'

I chose my reply very carefully. 'Marianne, when you came to see me – to bring Beth's swimming costume – you told me how worried you were about Derek's relationship with Beth. You knew Miss Willow and I had concerns too and you wanted me to tell Beth's social worker.'

'Yes, but I never thought it would come to this,' she said, interrupting me. 'Derek's been forcibly separated from his daughter. He can't even speak to her. It's awful for him. Does Beth know what's happening?'

'She understands that the social services are investigating,' I said.

'What is there to investigate?' Marianne cried, her voice rising. 'I've told them everything!'

'I assume they're looking into the nature of the relationship Derek has with Beth.' I was purposely vague, as it wasn't for me to give Marianne details if Jessie and her manager hadn't done so.

'There's nothing to investigate!' Marianne said. 'Derek and Beth are very close, that's all.'

I was starting to feel a bit annoyed with the view Marianne was taking and her misplaced sympathy for Derek. 'Marianne, that wasn't what you told me when you came here. You said you thought their relationship wasn't healthy, and not like a father and daughter should be.'

'But I didn't see all this coming,' she said, 'or I wouldn't have said anything. Of course I wouldn't.' I was aware that some people who report child abuse run scared when action is taken and regret reporting their concerns, but there can be no half-measures. Children have to be protected.

'I think we'd better leave all this to the social services,' I said diplomatically.

'But I have to see Derek and face him! You don't!' Marianne cried, now very upset. 'What am I going to tell him?'

Marianne didn't *have to* see Derek; she chose to. It was her decision. 'I don't know,' I said. 'My concerns are with Beth and I am supporting her as much as I can.'

'I suppose that leaves me to support Derek,' Marianne said curtly. 'I must say I thought you'd be a bit more sensitive and understanding.'

'I'm sorry,' I said. There was silence on the other end of the telephone, so I added, 'I'm sorry I can't help you any more.'

'Don't worry. I won't telephone you again!' she snapped. And put down the phone.

I replaced the handset and stayed where I was on the sofa for a moment. I was genuinely sorry I'd upset Marianne. I'd never intentionally hurt anyone, but I really didn't see what else I could have said. I wasn't about to offer words of reassurance or commiseration for Derek. He was being investigated for child abuse. When I'd met Marianne, I'd formed the impression that she was a responsible and sensitive woman, who would have made a good stepmother for Beth, but her loyalty to Derek clearly undermined this. I hoped she'd keep her word and wouldn't telephone me again.

Pushing thoughts of Marianne from my mind, I let Toscha out for her last run and then went upstairs, hoping for a cuddle. But when I went into my bedroom I found John in bed and fast asleep. He was clearly exhausted from working away, as it was only 10.20 p.m. I thought an early night would do me good too, so I washed and changed and then quietly climbed into bed. John stirred but didn't wake. I lay on my back gazing into the darkness as John slept and I waited for sleep to come, but thoughts chased through my head. Marianne had believed Derek's relationship with Beth was unhealthy but now regretted saying anything, while I stood by my concerns, as I assumed Miss Willow did. I knew that sometimes the wives or partners of child abusers sided with them against the victim for fear of upsetting the status quo and being deserted, which seemed to be what Marianne was doing. It also occurred to me that, with Beth no longer in contact with her father, Marianne's pathway to Derek had been cleared. Was that why Marianne was being so loyal to Derek, because she was seizing the opportunity to spend the rest of her life with him? It was an uncomfortable thought.

Chapter Sixteen
Are You Happy Here?

After a lovely day at my parents' on Sunday, John left early on Monday morning for another week working away. He said goodbye to me in bed and then stole silently from the house so he didn't wake the children. I climbed out of bed and went to the window so I could wave him off. It was still dark outside and a frost had settled during the night. I hoped John would telephone to say he had arrived safely, but I knew it wasn't always possible with all his work commitments.

Like many parents, I find my children are reluctant to get up on a Monday morning, especially after a great weekend. This Monday was no exception. When I woke Paula she grumbled she was 'too tired to get dressed' and told me I should leave her in bed while I took Beth and Adrian to school, which she knew wasn't an option. Beth also groaned when I woke her. 'It's still night-time,' she said, screwing her eyes tightly closed. And when I woke Adrian he mumbled something about breakfast and then turned over and went back to sleep. I gently shook his shoulder and told him he'd have to get up to have breakfast.

I helped Paula dress and we went downstairs. Adrian and Beth came down later than they should have done for a school day, and I had to chivvy them along so we weren't late. After very quick washes and teeth brushing we were in the car and

arrived in the playground with a few minutes to spare. A friend
of Adrian's called him and he ran over to play, while Beth stayed
with Paula and me. I noticed Jenni and her mother standing not
so far from us. Jenni kept looking over longingly, as if she would
have liked to talk to Beth. I threw her a reassuring smile, but
her mother saw and turned her back on me, then turned Jenni
away. Fortunately, Beth didn't see. I really couldn't understand
why the woman was being so hostile to me when all I'd done
was uphold Derek's wishes and refuse to be drawn into a derogatory discussion about him. I hoped it wasn't rubbing off on
Jenni.

'Do you still play with Jenni?' I asked Beth.

'Sometimes,' she said.

'And she's nice to you? She hasn't said any more hurtful
things?'

'No. She's OK, but I play with my other friends more.'

'You could invite one of them to tea this week,' I suggested, as
I would to any child I fostered.

'I'm not allowed to,' Beth said. 'Daddy wouldn't like it.'

Clearly, not only was Beth not allowed to go to friends' houses,
she also couldn't invite friends home. Although I didn't agree
with Derek's views on this – children need to socialize – I
decided that, with everything else going on, now wasn't the time
to raise the subject with Jessie. Although I did wonder what
Beth thought about Adrian and Paula visiting friends and
having friends home, which, like many children, they did
regularly.

When Paula and I arrived home from taking Beth and Adrian
to school, Paula played with her dolls while I set about vacuuming the carpets. Today's cleaning was especially thorough as
Jessie was visiting after school. Paula began to help with her toy

vacuum cleaner, which my parents had given her as a Christmas present. I began vacuuming my bedroom, closely followed by Paula, and noticed John's wedding ring lying on his bedside cabinet. 'Oh dear,' I said, switching off my vacuum cleaner and picking up the ring. 'Daddy's forgotten his ring. He will be worried.'

'Why will he be worried?' Paula asked, also 'switching off' her vacuum cleaner.

'Because he'll think he's lost it,' I said. 'It's precious to him, just as my wedding ring is precious to me.'

Paula peered at John's ring and then at mine. 'Why are your rings precious?' she asked.

'Because we chose our rings together, and put them on each other's fingers when we got married and made our vows.' I saw her next question coming and pre-empted it. 'Vows are promises you make to the person you love when you get married,' I said. '"For better, for worse; for richer, for poorer; in sickness and in health; to love and to cherish; till death us do part." Then you take the rings and say: "With this ring I thee wed, with my body I thee worship and with all my worldly goods I thee endow ..."'

'Oh, I see,' Paula said, looking as though she wished she hadn't asked.

'I expect Daddy will telephone when he realizes his ring is missing,' I said.

'Can I speak to him?' Paula asked.

'Yes, if he has time.'

We continued our vacuuming and then, once finished, returned our cleaners to the broom cupboard, with Paula storing her cleaner next to mine. Ten minutes later the telephone rang, and sure enough it was John, worried that he'd lost his ring.

'It's on your bedside cabinet,' I said. 'You must have missed it when you left in the dark this morning.'

'Thank goodness,' he said, clearly relieved. 'I thought I'd left it at the hotel.'

'Paula would like to say a quick hello,' I said.

'Very quickly, then, as I'm due in a meeting soon.'

I held the telephone to Paula's ear and she said, 'Hello, Daddy. Mummy has found your ring, so you can still worship her with all your worldly goods.'

I dissolved into laughter. I could hear John laughing too. Paula grinned and said, 'Bye Daddy, see you soon.'

'What was all that about?' he asked me as I drew the telephone to my ear.

I was still laughing. 'Paula asked why our rings were precious, so I explained about our marriage vows.'

'Oh,' John said. 'Well, glad my ring is safe. Have a good week.'

'And you. See you Friday.'

'I hope so, although there's a slim chance I might have to work through the weekend.'

'Oh no, not again,' I said.

'Sorry. It can't be helped. I'll telephone you when I know for sure.'

We said goodbye. I replaced the receiver and hid my disappointment from Paula. If John couldn't make it home at the weekend, it would mean another two weeks before the children and I would see him again, which seemed a long time. There was no point in telling the children and upsetting them unnecessarily, so I'd wait until John knew for sure before I told them.

After lunch I took Paula to the park to meet up with a friend who had a son of a similar age to Paula and they played together. Although it was chilly, we stayed for over an hour and then I went to school to collect Adrian and Beth. When they came out

Adrian reminded me that he would be staying for football practice after school the following day, and Beth reminded me that
her social worker was coming that afternoon, neither of which
I'd forgotten. It occurred to me that since Beth hadn't been in
contact with her father she didn't talk about him as much, and
her references to being 'Daddy's little princess' and what she
would wear when she saw him or spoke to him on the telephone
had largely stopped. Now all she asked, as she did that afternoon, was when would Jessie let her see or telephone her daddy
again, which was sad.

Once home, I quickly made the children a drink and a snack
to see them through to dinner. As this was only Jessie's second
visit (the first being when she'd brought Beth to me), I wasn't
sure what format her visit would take or how long it would last.
Different social workers worked differently.

Jessie arrived as arranged at 4 p.m. and I showed her through
to the living room, where Beth was already sitting on the sofa,
waiting expectantly. I offered Jessie a drink, but she didn't want
one. 'I'd like to speak to you first,' she said to me. 'Then I'll have
a chat with Beth and look at her room.'

Beth looked disappointed.

'You could play with Adrian and Paula,' I suggested to her.
They were seated at the table in the kitchen with puzzles, paper
and crayons, which I'd set out to keep them amused during
Jessie's visit.

'When will you tell me about my daddy?' Beth asked Jessie.

'As soon as I've spoken to Cathy,' Jessie replied.

Beth accepted this and left the room to join Adrian and
Paula. I pushed the door to so we couldn't be overheard and sat
on the sofa, while Jessie took the armchair.

'I thought I'd get an update from you first,' Jessie said. 'How
has Beth been?'

'Not too bad,' I said. 'She's missing her father. I've reassured her as best I could.'

'Has Beth said any more about their relationship?' Jessie asked.

'Not really. Nothing new. Only what I've told you already.'

Jessie nodded. 'It's possible this may become a police investigation, in which case Beth will be interviewed and you may be asked questions too.'

'I'll obviously do what I can to help,' I said.

'I'm still looking into all of this,' Jessie said. 'I'm trying to arrange to see Derek's psychologist again. After that, my manager and I will be in a better position to make a decision on how to proceed. There is one thing I need to ask you.'

'Yes?'

'The make-up Beth was wearing when I took her to the hospital ... She told me her father bought it for her. Is that right?'

'Yes, as far as I know. It just appeared here. She said she'd taken it to school to show a friend and had left it in a drawer.'

'You didn't buy it for her, then?'

'No. Certainly not.'

'And there's nothing else you've heard Beth say about her father that might help us?'

I thought for a moment. 'No. I'm sure I've told you everything. Beth doesn't really talk about him so much now.'

'Is there anything from before, when she was in contact with him?' I felt the pressure to try to remember.

I shook my head. 'I'm sure I've told you all I know,' I said.

'And Beth's eating and sleeping well?'

'Yes. She's had a couple of nightmares. One when contact first stopped, but she normally sleeps well.'

Jessie nodded thoughtfully. 'I've spoken to Beth's teacher and she says that Beth is coping well in school.'

'Yes. Beth seems quite a resilient child. I suppose she's had to be, not having a mother and then having to cope with all of this.'

'Or maybe she's good at hiding her feelings, as a way of coping,' Jessie said. 'I'd like to have a look at the photographs now, please – the ones you took.'

I had them ready and passed the packet of prints to Jessie. She opened the packet and taking out the prints began looking through. There were about twenty in all, taken on our outings and at local parks. 'I've given Beth a copy of all the photographs,' I confirmed.

Jessie nodded.

She flipped to the end of the photographs and then returned them to their packet and passed it to me. 'Thank you,' she said. I'd no idea what she'd been looking for and she didn't tell me.

'I'll talk to Beth now, please,' she said. 'I'll call you when we've finished.' From which I concluded my presence wasn't required.

I went into the kitchen where the children were crayoning. Beth looked up at me in anticipation. 'Jessie would like to see you now,' I said.

I saw Beth into the living room and closed the door so they couldn't be overheard. I returned to the kitchen where I began the preparations for dinner, while Adrian and Paula continued playing at the table. Foster carers and their children have to get used to being excluded from meetings that take place in their home, uncomfortable though this may be.

Fifteen minutes later we heard the living-room door open and Jessie call out, 'You can come in now, Cathy.'

'Stay here, please,' I said to Adrian and Paula, for I assumed Jessie just wanted me.

In the living room Beth was sitting on the sofa beside Jessie and looking very glum. I smiled at her reassuringly.

'We've had a good chat,' Jessie said brightly. 'Beth now understands that my job is to protect her and act in her best interest, although it may not seem like it at the time. We've also talked about the different ways people touch us and we touch them. How some parts of our bodies are private and shouldn't be touched by others.'

'I can't see my daddy,' Beth blurted, looking at me.

'No, not yet,' Jessie said.

Having not heard their conversation, I'd no idea how much Beth now understood about why she couldn't see her father, but I hoped Jessie had explained sufficiently and had answered Beth's questions.

'We'll go up and see your room now,' Jessie said to Beth. Then to me: 'You can come too, if you like.'

I nodded. Beth stood and came over and slipped her hand into mine. We went upstairs to Beth's room, with Jessie following.

'What a lovely room!' Jessie exclaimed as we entered.

'Yes, Beth keeps it very tidy,' I said, throwing Beth another smile.

'Fantastic,' Jessie said. 'I'll be able to tell your daddy when I next speak to him what a good girl you're being.' Although I appreciated this comment was designed to give Beth comfort, it seemed a bit insensitive to me, given that she couldn't see him.

'Look at all your photographs,' Jessie said, going to the shelves. 'What a collection.' She began looking at each one closely, picking it up and then setting it down again. 'What happened to the glass in these two?' she asked, coming to the two Beth had smashed in anger.

'I broke them,' Beth said sadly.

'You didn't mention it,' Jessie said to me.

'Sorry, it slipped my mind.' It was difficult to know what was significant enough to tell Jessie and what wasn't.

'I was angry, that's why I broke them,' Beth admitted.

'Angry with your dad?' Jessie asked.

'Yes,' Beth said.

'But she was sorry after she'd broken them,' I added. 'And she's promised she won't do it again.'

'Why were you angry with your dad?' Jessie asked, still studying the photographs without glass.

'Because I couldn't see him,' Beth said.

'No other reason?' Jessie asked, looking at Beth.

'No,' Beth said.

Jessie looked at the remaining photographs while Beth and I stood together by the door, watching her. When she'd finished she turned to Beth. 'I think you keep a photograph under your pillow? Can I see it, please?'

Beth went to her bed, took the photograph out from under her pillow and passed it to Jessie. There was silence as Jessie studied the photograph, then she returned it to Beth who slipped it back under her pillow.

'You've got lots of photographs at home,' Jessie said, turning again to the shelves. 'Why did you choose these to bring?'

'I don't know. I guess because they're all of me and my daddy.'

'You look very grown up in them,' Jessie said. 'Why didn't you bring some of you when you were younger?'

I'd no idea of the significance of this question, and Beth just shrugged.

'Can I have a look in your wardrobe now?' Jessie said to Beth.

'Yes.' Beth opened her wardrobe door.

'You've got lots of clothes,' Jessie said, flicking through the hangers. 'Who chose them for you?'

'Daddy,' Beth said proudly.

'Did he used to choose all your clothes for you?'

'Yes.' Beth said.

'And all your underwear?'

'Yes,' Beth said.

Jessie closed the wardrobe door, opened the top drawer of the chest of drawers and began looking through Beth's underwear, moving some of the pants, petticoats and frilly vests that were on top to see those underneath. She did the same with the second and third drawers and then turned to Beth. 'You seem very comfortable here with Cathy. Are you happy?'

Beth gave a small nod.

'Excellent,' Jessie said and began towards the bedroom door. 'So you'll be fine here with Cathy for the time being.'

Beth stared at Jessie's back and I knew that she'd heard the finality in Jessie's words, as I had: Beth wouldn't be going home any time soon and would be staying with me indefinitely.

Chapter Seventeen

Special Present

'Jessie says I can't see my daddy,' Beth told me after Jessie had gone.

'And did she tell you why?' I asked.

'She said it was because she has to make sure I'm safe. But I don't understand. I am safe with my daddy.'

'I'm sure Jessie is doing what is best for you,' I said positively. Based on the little I'd been told, this was all I could say.

Beth had been living with me for a month now, although it seemed much longer with all that had happened. The week continued in the usual way with the school routine, homework and playing and television fitted in between. Beth began joining Paula for her bedtime story again, which was nice for both girls and distracted Beth from the fact that she no longer telephoned her father at seven o'clock – something she rarely mentioned now. I realized that Beth and Paula were bonding, like sisters. To begin with, Beth had played more with Adrian, who was closer to her age, but now she went out of her way to play with Paula and chose games and books that were suitable for Paula's age. Beth was very gentle in her manner with Paula and also very patient; she looked out for her and treated her as a younger sibling, which I found very touching. I thought this must come naturally to Beth, for as far as I knew she'd had no experience of younger children, having led a very insular life with her father, which was further proof of what a kind and sweet-natured child she really was.

The week went well until Thursday, when we arrived home from school to see the light on the answerphone flashing, signalling a message had been left. Without any thought that it might be bad news, and with the children listening as they took off their coats, I pressed play. John's voice came through, and all three children stood very still and silent. 'Hi everyone. Hope you are all OK. Sorry, folks, but I won't be able to make it home this weekend. Daddy's got to work. I'm sure you'll still have a fun weekend. Speak soon. Love you.' The digital voice said the message had been left at three-thirty. The machine reset.

Adrian's face fell. He dropped his coat in the hall and ran upstairs to his bedroom. Beth, able to identify with Adrian's disappointment, said, 'Shall I go and make Adrian better?'

'That's kind of you, love,' I said. 'But I'd prefer it if you could look after Paula while I go up.'

I helped Paula out of her coat, then Beth took her through to the living room while I began upstairs. It occurred to me that the only upsets in the house in recent weeks had been as a result of absent fathers – Beth's, and Adrian and Paula's. And although the reasons for their absences were different, the results were still the same: very unhappy children who needed comforting and reassuring.

Adrian's bedroom door was closed, so I knocked lightly before going in. He was sitting on the floor with his back resting against the side of the bed, gazing down at the model aeroplane he held in his lap.

'Can I join you?' I asked, as I entered his room.

He gave a small nod but didn't look up.

I went over and sat beside him, also using the bed as a back-rest. 'You made a good job of that plane,' I said. He'd spent weeks making it and had been looking forward to showing his father at the weekend.

'I'm going to give it to Grandpa,' he said. Which surprised me, as all the other models he'd made were displayed on a shelf in his room.

'That's nice of you. Grandpa will be thrilled, but are you sure you don't want to add it to your collection?'

'I'm sure. Can we see Grandpa and Nana on Sunday?'

'Yes, if they're free. We'll ask them to come for dinner. I'll telephone them later.'

'I love my Nana and Grandpa,' Adrian said, still concentrating on the plane.

'I know you do, and they love you, lots. But your dad loves you too. It's not his fault he has to work away.'

'Isn't it?' Adrian said, finally looking at me.

'No, love, it isn't. Your dad misses us as much as we miss him. I'm sure you know that really.'

'I don't want to talk about him right now,' Adrian said firmly, returning his attention to the plane.

I hesitated. 'All right, but promise me you'll talk to me when you feel you want to. I don't want you bottling it up.' He gave a small nod. 'Good boy. Now, I'm going down to start dinner, and then I'll telephone Grandpa and Nana. Will you come down soon?'

He gave another small nod.

I respected Adrian's wish to be alone and, kissing his cheek, I came out and closed the door behind me. Because Adrian was my son – whom I'd raised from birth – I knew him very well and felt confident in leaving him alone for a while, but with a foster child I'd only known for a short time I always erred on the side of caution and never left them alone if they were upset. Even so, ten minutes later I checked on Adrian. He was half-heartedly playing with some cars. I then went into my bedroom to telephone my parents. There was something I wanted to ask Dad, apart from inviting him and Mum to Sunday dinner.

Dad answered. 'Hello, love. What a nice surprise. Is everything all right?' I usually telephoned my parents in the evening, so this was out of character.

'Yes. We're fine, but I've just heard from John that he can't make it home this weekend. Adrian is very disappointed. I was wondering if you could have a chat with him. You know, man to man. And also, can you and Mum come to dinner on Sunday?'

'I'm sure we can,' Dad said. 'Let me talk to Adrian first and then I'll ask your mother about Sunday.'

'Thanks.' I blew him a kiss down the phone.

I put down the handset and went round the landing to Adrian's room where I gave a brief knock on his door and then stuck my head round. He was now propped up on his bed. 'Grandpa's on the telephone for you,' I said. 'He'd like a chat. Take the call in my bedroom.'

His face lit up and, scrambling off the bed, he went to my room as I returned downstairs to continue with the preparations for dinner. Half an hour later dinner was ready, but there was still no sign of Adrian. I went to the foot of the stairs to call him for dinner and then realized he was still talking on the phone. My bedroom door wasn't fully closed so I could hear the hum of his voice, although not what he was saying. I decided to leave him to finish talking to his Grandpa and I joined the girls in the living room.

Fifteen minutes later Adrian burst into the living room, grinning from ear to ear. Rushing over, he threw his arms around me and hugged me hard. 'I love you so much!' he declared.

'I love you too,' I said, hugging him. 'Has Grandpa gone now?'

'Yes. He said to tell you that they can come on Sunday and Nana will make an apple pie for pudding.'

'Wonderful,' I said.

We hugged for a few moments longer and then Adrian let go and announced: 'I'm starving, Mum. Is dinner ready?'

'It is,' I said.

'I'm hungry too,' Beth said.

'So am I,' Paula added, not wanting to be left out.

It was past their usual dinnertime and I led the way to the dining table. I didn't know what my father had said to Adrian – and I wouldn't ask him, as it was private, between the two of them – but whatever it was must have been exactly right, for Adrian had returned to his usual happy self. And of course now he had recovered, Beth and Paula were happier too, and we were all looking forward to seeing my parents on Sunday. Although we saw my parents regularly, their visits were always much anticipated and had a sense of occasion. I think grandparents are so important, and not just in times of crisis. Their knowledge, wisdom, patience, love and understanding gained from years of experience are invaluable, and their presence can provide stability for the whole family.

I didn't hear from Jessie again that week – I wasn't really expecting to. She'd said she'd telephone when she had any news, so I assumed she was still making enquiries. On Friday afternoon I took Paula to the mother and toddler group and then went straight from there to collect Adrian and Beth from school. All the children were very noisy as they came outside, excited by that start-of-the-weekend holiday feeling, and that evening, despite John not being home, was pleasant. On Saturday we went shopping to buy the food for Sunday dinner and also to stock up on some basics. Once in the supermarket, Adrian said he wanted to buy some wrapping paper to gift-wrap the aeroplane he was going to give to Grandpa. Then Beth said it wasn't fair to give Grandpa a present and not Nana. (All foster children very quickly call my parents Nana and Grandpa.) Paula agreed and she and Beth chose a box of chocolates and a sheet of wrapping paper. When we'd finished the shopping we went home, and after lunch the children sat at the table and carefully wrapped their presents: Adrian his plane and the girls sharing the task of wrapping the chocolates for Nana. Adrian then said he was going to make a card to go with his present and so the girls naturally wanted to make cards too. Adrian wrote inside his: *To the best grandpa in the world. Love you loads. Adrian xxx.* Beth wrote in her card: *I wish I had a nana like you. Love Beth x.* And I helped Paula write: *To Nana, lots of love. Paula.* She filled the rest of the page with kisses. We put the presents and cards safely away and the rest of the day passed in the happy expectation of my parents' visit.

The children were awake early the following morning and wanted to dress smartly for their grandparents' visit. Adrian chose a warm sweater and jeans, and I helped Paula choose a winter dress from her wardrobe. From Beth's wardrobe I took out the long-sleeved grey-and-pink check dress that I'd previously chosen for her to wear when she'd visited her father and she'd decided otherwise.

'It's perfect for Nana and Grandpa's visit,' I said.

Thankfully Beth didn't put up any argument, for her choice of suitable clothes was limited. I'd bought her some joggers and a matching top and I wanted to buy more, but I had reservations in case I upset her father again. I thought the next time I spoke to Jessie I would ask her if it would be all right to restock Beth's wardrobe with more suitable casual clothes.

We were all ready by eleven o'clock and when the doorbell rang we rushed down the hall to open the front door. With lots of excited 'His', 'Hellos' and 'Good to see yous', my parents came in and hugged each of us in turn. There was an air of conspiratorial silence between the children as they waited for the right moment to present their gifts. I made coffee and once we were all settled in the living room the children suddenly stood and left the room without saying a word.

'What are they up to?' my mother asked suspiciously, with a smile.

'You'll have to wait and see,' I said.

A minute later the children returned in a small procession bearing gifts: Adrian first, and then Beth and Paula, carrying theirs between them. Adrian went over to Grandpa and a little sheepishly set his present in his lap.

'Thank you, but it's not my birthday,' my father said, puzzled but delighted.

'Nor mine,' my mother said as Beth and Paula presented her with their present and cards.

Adrian looked slightly embarrassed and came over and sat next to me as Grandpa unwrapped his gift, while the girls stayed by Nana's side and watched her. I could tell from my father's expression when he saw the plane how very touched he was.

'What an amazing piece of workmanship,' he said to Adrian. 'Did you make it all yourself?'

Adrian grinned proudly. 'Yes.'

'It's fantastic,' Dad said. 'You've done a superb job, but I don't think you should be giving it to me. Don't you want to keep it with your other models?' Dad knew how proud Adrian was of his collection from having been invited to view it at each and every visit.

'I want you to have it,' Adrian declared.

'Thank you very much,' Dad said. 'I'll find a special place for it in the display cabinet in our sitting room. Then, when we have visitors, I'll show them what my clever grandson made for me. Thanks, lad, it's much appreciated.'

Adrian now went over and, perching on the arm of Grandpa's chair, threw his arms around his neck and gave him a big hug. Meanwhile, Beth and Paula were asking Nana if she would like to try one of her chocolates, meaning they'd like to try one.

'I think we could have just one before dinner, don't you?' Mum asked me.

'Yes. One won't spoil their appetites,' I agreed.

Carrying the box between them, Beth and Paula offered it to each of us and then Mum put the box to one side, 'out of temptation's way', she said. Mum and I chatted for a while as the girls played and Adrian talked to Grandpa. When I said I needed to check on dinner Mum came with me into the kitchen, but once there she looked at me seriously. 'Cathy, your father and I are worried about you. Looking after three children with John working away is an awful lot of work.'

'I'm fine, Mum,' I said. 'Beth's no trouble. And it's unusual for John not to be home at the weekend.' I took the oven gloves and opened the oven door to check on the roast.

'John has missed coming home twice this month,' Mum said.

'It couldn't be helped, and we've managed. I don't suppose it will happen again for a long time.' I basted the chicken and potatoes and then closed the oven door.

Mum was still looking at me as though she had something to say.

'What's the matter?' I asked. 'I always know when there's something bothering you.'

'Please don't take this the wrong way,' Mum said awkwardly, 'but is everything all right between you and John?'

'Yes, of course it is!' I said, surprised she could think any differently. 'Whatever makes you ask?'

She shrugged. 'I guess it's just me being silly, but John doesn't seem to be home as much as he used to be. I know you say it's because of his new job, but I remember your father was once offered a post that involved working away, and he refused it on the grounds that he wanted to spend more time with his family, not less. I suppose things are different now; jobs are scarce and there isn't the same choice.'

'John is very career oriented,' I said, trying to reassure Mum. 'Promotion is important to him and I respect him for that. Please don't worry. Everything is fine between John and me.'

And as far as I knew, it was.

Chapter Eighteen

Sudden Turn of Events

February continued to rattle along at great speed as a cold northeasterly wind blew in small flurries of snow – bitterly cold but not enough to make snowmen and enjoy it. I didn't hear from Jessie during February, although I did telephone her half-way through the month after Beth asked me to, to find out how her father was. A colleague of Jessie's answered her telephone and told me Jessie was on annual leave for two weeks. I left a message asking Jessie to telephone me when she returned to work.

With no contact between Beth and her father, her bond with him appeared to be slowly weakening. She talked about him less and less. When she did mention him, it was usually something like: 'I don't think I have a daddy any more,' or, 'My daddy has gone away and is never coming back.' While I felt very sorry for her and obviously comforted her as best I could, I thought that perhaps it was for the best if Beth accepted that her father would be permanently missing from her life, for it seemed highly unlikely she'd ever live with him again or, possibly, even see him again.

The last week in February was half-term, so the children had a week's holiday from school. The weather stayed bitterly cold and I provided activities to do at home. We also visited some indoor attractions: a small local museum, a ball pond and an activity centre. John only missed coming home one weekend in February but to our delight took the Monday of half-term off work, and we all went to the cinema in the afternoon, which was great. That evening I raised the subject of our annual summer holiday with him, as I felt we needed to book it before long. Since we'd had children, we hadn't gone abroad but had rented an apartment on the English coast. John said he wasn't sure what his work commitments would be for summer, but that he'd look into it and we'd book something as soon as he knew.

'I'm not sure if Beth will be coming with us,' I said to John. 'Although my guess is she will be.'

'You need to ask that social worker what her plans are for Beth,' John said, slightly disgruntled. 'It's difficult to plan ahead, not knowing. I assume Beth's not staying with us forever.'

I gave a small laugh. 'It would never surprise me!' I said. 'But you're right. I'll ask Jessie when she phones.'

As it turned out, when Jessie did telephone – on the first Thursday in March – I didn't ask her about the long-term plans for Beth, or if she could come with us on holiday. I was too shocked by what she was telling me.

'Derek was discharged from hospital on Tuesday,' she said. 'He's home now and I want to set up telephone contact for Friday. I'll need you to monitor it.'

'Discharged?' I repeated in disbelief. 'Is he better, then?' I'd been expecting to hear he was in police custody charged with child abuse.

'He's well enough to go home,' Jessie said guardedly. 'And he'd like to speak to Beth. I assume Beth would like to speak to her father?'

'Well, yes. I expect she would,' I said, completely nonplussed and thrown by what Jessie was saying.

'Good. You can telephone him any time after five o'clock on Friday. But you must monitor the call. Do you have a telephone that can be put on speaker?'

'Yes, the answerphone in the hall can be.'

'Use it, please, and stop the call if Beth becomes upset or Derek says anything inappropriate.'

The obvious question was: what sort of things? But my thoughts were all over the place and all the questions I should have been asking flew from my head.

'If this call goes well,' Jessie continued, 'we can start regular telephone contact, but that's in the future. And I need you to come to a meeting – Tuesday, one o'clock. The same room as before. It's likely to be a long one, so allow most of the afternoon. You can tell me how the telephone call went then, so it might be a good idea to take some notes.'

'Yes,' I agreed as I scribbled the date and time on the notepad I kept beside the phone. 'How long should the telephone call last? They used to be on the telephone for ages before.'

'I should think fifteen minutes is sufficient for the first call,' Jessie said. 'Do you have Derek's home telephone number?'

'No. Just the hospital.'

'Pen handy?'

'Yes, go ahead.' I wrote down the telephone number and then repeated it back to Jessie to check I had it down correctly.

'I'll tell Derek to expect Beth's call on Friday evening,' Jessie said. 'It's possible Marianne may answer the telephone, so you make the call.'

'Marianne is with Derek?' I asked, even more amazed.

'Yes. She's moved in for the time being. Why? Is there a problem?'

'No,' I said, my thoughts somersaulting. 'Should I speak to Derek or do I just pass the telephone to Beth as I did before?'

There was a pause and then Jessie said: 'You can speak to him, but tread carefully. I'm in a meeting soon. Is there anything else?'

'No, I don't think so,' I said, not understanding what was going on.

'I'll see you Tuesday, then,' Jessie said. 'I'm out of the office tomorrow and Monday, so if there's a problem, call my colleague.'

'All right,' I said.

We said goodbye and I hung up. My heart was racing and my stomach churned as I struggled to make sense of what I'd been told. All contact between Derek and his daughter had been stopped over a month ago, and now – with no explanation – we were to telephone and I was to monitor the call. Had he been cleared of child abuse? It didn't seem likely, given the evidence against him. And Marianne had moved in, so it seemed I'd been right in suspecting her motives. But then again, who would want to live with a child molester? It simply didn't make sense, and I assumed some explanation would be given at the meeting the following week.

Beth no longer asked me every afternoon when she came out of school if there was any news about her daddy, so I waited until we were home and Adrian and Paula were occupied before I told her she could telephone her father. She'd gone up to her bedroom to fetch a toy, so I went up after her.

'Beth,' I said, going straight in as the door was open. 'Jessie phoned today.'

She immediately turned and looked at me.

'She said you could telephone your father tomorrow evening. He's left hospital and is home now.'

Beth's mouth dropped open and her eyes rounded in astonishment. 'Does that mean I'll be going home soon?' she asked.

Although Jessie hadn't mentioned Beth going home, I'd formed the impression that she wouldn't be. 'Not as far as I know,' I said gently. 'But Jessie said if the telephone call goes well then you'll be able to telephone him again another evening. I'm seeing Jessie on Tuesday, so I should know more then.'

Beth crossed the room and, slipping her arms around my waist, laid her head against my chest for a cuddle. I held her close. I could appreciate how confusing this must be for her. She didn't say anything for some moments, then she raised her head to look at me. 'Is my daddy better, then?' she asked.

'He's well enough to go home,' I said, using Jessie's phrase.

'He needs me,' Beth said, dropping her arms and immediately looking worried. 'Daddy can't be alone. He needs me to look after him, like I used to.'

I made the snap decision not to tell Beth that Marianne was at home with her father, as I knew it would upset her, so I said, 'I'm sure Jessie would have thought of that and arranged for a carer if necessary.'

'As long as it's not Marianne,' Beth said, her old hostility returning. 'My daddy hates her and so do I.'

Clearly Derek didn't hate Marianne – far from it – but I wasn't about to tell Beth that.

'I hope someone nice is looking after my daddy,' Beth said.

'I'm sure they will be. So please don't worry.'

Beth picked up the toy she'd come for and then came with me downstairs. She joined Adrian and Paula in the living room while I began the preparations for dinner. As we ate, and throughout the rest of the evening, Beth was quiet. She told Adrian and Paula once that she was allowed to telephone her father the following day, but only once. There was no excitement, as there had been previously when she'd been in regular contact with her father and had talked non-stop about her daddy, being his little princess and all the things she and her superhero father did together. I guessed she was feeling apprehensive, as I was, but there was little I could say to reassure her.

Later, as I tucked her into bed, she asked, 'What time am I phoning my daddy tomorrow?'

'About five o'clock,' I said. Jessie had left the timing of the telephone call to me, and five o'clock was good, as Adrian and Paula were usually occupied watching television at that time. 'Jessie said the call should last about fifteen minutes,' I added, so Beth knew.

I hugged and kissed Beth goodnight, and then she slid the photograph from beneath her pillow and kissed the image of her father goodnight. 'I knew you hadn't forgotten me,' she said smiling. 'Night, Daddy, I love you. Night, Cathy.'

'Night, love.'

The following afternoon, when we returned home from school, Beth said she was going to her room to change. I didn't think much of it, because Beth always changed out of her school uniform and into one of her dresses when we got home. But twenty minutes later, when she hadn't appeared, I became concerned she might be upset as the time of the telephone call approached, so I went upstairs. Her bedroom door was shut. 'Are you all right?' I called through the door.

'Yes! I'm fine!' her cheerful voice came back. 'I'll be down soon.'

Reassured there was nothing wrong, I returned downstairs. Ten minutes later Beth appeared. It was immediately obvious why it had taken her so long to change. She had dressed for her father in a little black skirt, a frilly see-through cream lace blouse, fishnet tights, high heels, thick make-up and bright-red nail varnish, again looking like a child prostitute. Adrian laughed when he saw her, while Paula stared aghast. We hadn't seen Beth dressed like this or wearing make-up since she'd stopped seeing her father.

'Are you seeing your daddy?' Paula asked, as she had done previously.

'No. I'm phoning him. He likes me to look nice.'

Neither the children nor I made the obvious comment that her father wouldn't be able to see her down the phone, or that in fact she didn't look nice. Why she felt she had to dress like this for her father I didn't understand, but it worried me. All my previous concerns about Derek's relationship with Beth resurfaced. I was dreading having to speak to him on the telephone – albeit briefly – and was almost hoping that Marianne would answer. Jessie had told me to make notes about the telephone contact, so away from Beth I now took a sheet of paper and made a note of what Beth was wearing to telephone her father. I guessed Jessie would see the significance in it; she was trained to spot these things.

Just before five o'clock, when Adrian and Paula were watching children's television and the dinner was in the oven, I told Beth we'd telephone her father and she came with me down the hall. 'We'll use this phone,' I said, pointing to the one on the hall table, 'because it can be put on speaker, which means you won't have to hold the handset.' I wanted to make the idea of using the telephone on speaker attractive to Beth so that she wouldn't be worried that I was listening to what she and her father said. 'You can sit in the chair by the telephone and I'll show you how it works.'

Beth sat by the hall table and watched as I pressed the speaker button on the telephone. Immediately we heard the dialling tone. 'I'll dial, and get your father on the line first,' I explained. 'Then I'll press the speaker button and you'll talk to him as normal. He'll be able to hear you, and you'll hear him through that mic there. Jessie wants me to stay with you during the call,' I added.

Beth nodded, although she seemed a little nervous and kept clasping and unclasping her hands, which was hardly surprising as this was the first contact with her father in over a month. I was nervous too.

I pushed the button to end the speaker function and then picked up the handset and keyed in Derek's telephone number. Beth was watching me carefully. I listened to Derek's telephone ringing for what seemed a long time but was probably no more than six or eight rings. My pulse quickened. Then a male answered, 'Hello?' But the voice was so quiet it was nearly inaudible and I wasn't completely sure it was Derek.

'Is that Derek?' I asked.

'Yes.'

'It's Cathy Glass, Beth's carer.'

'Oh, yes,' he said, a little louder. 'Is she there?'

'Yes, I'll put her on.'

I pressed the speaker button and replaced the handset. All was quite. Beth was looking at me, uncertain. 'Just speak as normal,' I said. 'Your dad can hear you.' And of course he could hear me too.

'Hello, Daddy,' Beth said cautiously.

'Hello, my princess. How are you?'

'I'm all right,' Beth said. 'How are you?'

'I'm home now. I'm going to be OK.' His voice faltered and then recovered. 'Your daddy is doing all right.'

'I'm worried about you,' Beth said, now less self-conscious. 'I want to come home and look after you. Why can't I, Daddy? Why can't I come home and be with you?' Her bottom lip trembled.

'Don't worry about me, princess,' Derek said. 'I'm being well looked after.'

'Who's looking after you?' Beth asked.

There was a pause before Derek replied. 'A nice lady Jessie knows.' Which was a clever half-truth, and I wondered how many more clever half-truths Derek had told over the years.

'Tell me about school,' Derek said, changing the subject. 'Are you still doing well in all your work?'

'Yes,' Beth said. She began telling her father about the book the class was reading.

I sat on the bottom step of the staircase so I could use my lap as a rest and began making notes on what they were saying, although there wasn't really anything of significance. Their conversation went from school to food, and Derek asked Beth if she was eating well.

'Yes,' Beth said. 'I like Cathy's meals.'

I smiled, but I noticed there was silence on the other end of the telephone, and then Derek said a muted, 'Good. What do you do in the evenings?'

Beth began telling her father how she changed when she got home, then played or watched television until dinner was ready, and then she did her homework and played some more. She broke off once and said, 'I don't have to hold this phone. Cathy's pressed a button and we can both hear you.'

'I know,' Derek said, so I assumed that Jessie had told him I would be listening and monitoring the call.

Derek asked Beth if she was sleeping well and she said, 'Yes. But I miss you, Daddy. Cathy gave me Mr Sleep Bear and I've got your photo, but it's not the same.'

'I know, princess. I miss you too.'

Beth then began describing what she was wearing, but unlike before, when Derek had enthusiastically joined in, wanting to know all the details, including which petticoat and underwear she had on – he now remained very quiet. Even when Beth said, 'I put on my own make-up, but it's not as good as when you do it,' there was no response. So Beth asked, 'Can you hear me, Daddy?'

'Yes, I can hear you,' Derek said. I wondered if his reticence in discussing what Beth was wearing was because he knew I was listening.

Ten minutes passed and then we suddenly heard a bang come from Derek's end.

'What's that?' Beth asked.

'The front door,' Derek said. 'Marianne's just come in.'

I knew straight away he'd said it without thinking, for he immediately added, 'She's just popped in with some shopping.'

Beth flared. 'Tell her to go!' she demanded. 'She shouldn't be there when I'm not. Tell her to go, now. I don't want her there. Or I'll never speak to you again.'

I looked up from my notes. Beth's face was set in anger and her eyes blazed. She was trying to bully her father. While I didn't have any sympathy for him, I don't like to see a child disrespecting an adult or another child, so I said lightly, 'Beth, please don't be rude.'

'I'll talk to him how I want!' Beth snapped at me. 'He'll do as I say, or else!' Beth never normally spoke to me like that, and later I would sanction her, but for now I waited to see what Derek would say.

After a moment his voice came through weak and ineffectual: 'Please don't be horrible to me, princess. You know how much I love you.'

'You can't love me if you let her in,' Beth thundered. 'Has she still got a key?'

Derek was silent and I had the feeling he'd covered the mouthpiece so he could talk without being heard. When he came back on the line his voice was unsteady. 'You've upset your daddy,' he said shakily.

'You deserve it. For choosing her over me!'

'It's not like that,' Derek moaned. 'You know your daddy loves you more than anyone else in the world.'

'You can't if she's there.'

Jessie had given me the responsibility for ending the call if necessary, and with only a minute to go before the fifteen minutes was up, I saw no point in continuing the conversation – for either of their sakes.

'Beth, I think you should say goodbye to your father,' I said. 'We'll be having dinner soon.'

For a moment I thought she was going to say something else rude to me, but she didn't. Now staring at the telephone, she said quietly, 'I have to go now, Daddy.'

'Yes, I heard,' Derek said. 'Go and have your dinner, princess. And try not to be angry with me. I love you. I'm sorry.'

Beth's face lost some of its anger, but she wasn't willing to let go of the subject yet. 'Will you tell her to go, then?' she asked.

'Yes. I'll tell her,' he said.

'Promise?'

'Yes, I promise.'

I wasn't sure if this was a promise Derek could keep, but he shouldn't have allowed himself to be placed in that position. He was an adult, and despite all he'd been accused of and was being investigated for, as an adult he had a right to choose whom he saw. Beth had far too much power over him and it wasn't good for her.

They said a subdued goodbye, then I cut the call and looked at Beth seriously. She knew she'd done wrong.

'You've lost ten minutes of your television time for being rude to me,' I said. 'You can either go to your bedroom or come and help me lay the table.'

'Help you,' Beth said without hesitation, for she loved helping me.

Although it wasn't really a punishment, I'd made the point. Beth was only a child and as such needed to learn boundaries and respect, for her own good.

It wasn't long before Beth bitterly regretted the way she'd spoken to her father. 'Can I telephone Daddy again, so I can say I'm sorry?' she asked me, nearly in tears.

'I don't think we can, love. Jessie said one call for about fifteen minutes.'

'Oh dear. Can you tell Jessie to tell my daddy I'm sorry and I love him?'

'I will,' I said. 'But don't upset yourself. I'm sure he knows that already.'

Chapter Nineteen

Dr Jones

That Friday evening we sat down to dinner without John. I was expecting him to arrive home any minute, although I never knew exactly what time he would appear – it depended on how far away he'd been working, the traffic and road conditions, but it was usually around dinnertime, sometimes earlier. We finished eating shortly after 6.30 p.m. and there was still no sign of John. He wasn't so late that I was worried, but as the evening passed and he didn't arrive my concerns for him grew, although I hid it from the children.

When it was time for Paula to go to bed, she asked, 'Isn't Daddy coming home this weekend?'

'Yes, he is, love. He's just late. He must have got delayed.'

I took her up for her bath thinking John would very likely arrive by the time she'd finished and was in bed, so he'd be able to give her a goodnight kiss. But as I read her a bedtime story and then tucked her in and said goodnight, there was still no sign of John. 'You'll see Daddy first thing in the morning,' I reassured her.

My worries for John's safety grew during the evening. Now, if someone is late you phone or text their mobile, but back then they weren't in common use and not many people owned one. I told Beth that John was running late, and then reassured Adrian that his father was fine but that he had been delayed, which was all I could say, not knowing the reason for the delay. Adrian stayed up later than usual in the hope of seeing his father before bedtime. To our great relief, John telephoned at 9.30 p.m. from a petrol station but said the bad weather was causing havoc on the roads and he wouldn't be home for another hour and a half at least. He said a quick hello to Adrian and told him he would see him in the morning. Reassured that his father was all right, Adrian went to bed.

With all three children asleep, I sat in the living room with Toscha on my lap and watched the ten o'clock news. It was the usual assortment of doom and gloom, followed by the weather, which was a lot brighter. The forecaster said that the sleet showers had died out, leaving a clear night, and that all the main roads were running smoothly. I thought, therefore, that John would be home sooner than he'd expected – at any moment.

A little after eleven o'clock I was still waiting for John and was worried again. The telephone suddenly rang, making me jump. I picked up the handset and was surprised to hear John's voice: 'Cathy? Are you still up? I was expecting the answerphone.'

'Yes. Is everything all right? How far away are you now?'

'Too far,' he said with a heartfelt sigh. 'I've decided to call it quits for tonight. I've booked into a motel. I'll do the rest of the journey home in the morning.'

'Oh. How much further have you left to go, then? I thought you were quite close.'

'No, and I'm knackered. I'm not going to risk driving further while I'm so tired. I'll get my head down and see you first thing in the morning. And if the bad weather sets in again, I'll leave on Sunday afternoon.'

'Yes, of course. Take care and see you in the morning.'

* * *

I was obviously disappointed that John hadn't made it home that evening, but he'd made the sensible decision to book into a motel and not risk driving while tired. I settled Toscha in her bed for the night and then went to my own.

The following morning I explained to the children what had happened and reassured them John was on his way. When he walked in at ten o'clock, just as we'd finished breakfast, the children rushed to greet him. 'I wanted you to come home yesterday,' Adrian said, hugging his father.

'But you wouldn't want your dad having an accident, would you?' John said.

Of course Adrian wouldn't; he was just disappointed he wouldn't have so long with his father this weekend.

I made John a cooked breakfast, as he'd left the motel with just a coffee, and as he ate we all chatted and caught up on the week's news. As the weather forecast had predicted, the sleet had died out and Saturday was fine. In the afternoon we wrapped up warm and went for a walk in a local wood. John said that, after sitting in meetings all week and the long drive home, it felt good to 'stretch his legs and have some fresh air'. We played hide and seek with the children, hiding behind the trees, and generally had fun, and then on the way home we bought a Chinese takeaway for dinner.

On Sunday morning we rose to another fine day. Although the air temperature was still chilly – it was only the beginning of March – the clear skies and birdsong suggested spring wasn't far away. Adrian's thoughts turned to his birthday, which was at the end of March. He said he'd like to take some friends bowling for his birthday treat, which John and I agreed to. I told Adrian I'd book the bowling in plenty of time. Paula, hearing talk of birthday treats, wanted to know how long it was until her birthday. It was a week after Adrian's, but at her age she had little concept of time, so I showed her the number of sleeps on the calendar — twenty-five in all. 'That's a long time!' she exclaimed. 'Can't you make my birthday sooner?' which made us all smile.

'Will I be able to see my daddy on my birthday?' Beth asked.

Beth's birthday wasn't until October. 'I don't know,' I replied honestly. 'I should know more when I see Jessie on Tuesday.'

I'd assumed that as the weather had improved John wouldn't need to leave on Sunday afternoon but could wait until early Monday morning to drive to work. However, at five o'clock on Sunday, to my disappointment and surprise, he said he needed to make a move soon. 'I don't want to risk leaving it any later,' he said. 'You can't trust the weather at this time of year.'

This was true. The weather in the UK is changeable at any time of the year, but especially in spring and autumn when the temperature can rise or fall by ten degrees or more from one day to the next, bringing frost and ice when previously it had been fine. I worried about John driving, so I was quick to agree with him that it was 'better to be safe than sorry', as he said. I fetched his clean shirts, which I'd ironed that morning, and he repacked his suitcase. I remained positive as we all stood in the hall and he kissed us goodbye. Adrian, in particular, was very subdued as we waved John off. Once his car was out of sight, I closed the door and turned to see three glum faces.

'Let's microwave some popcorn and watch a film,' I said. Which helped a little.

I hadn't yet arranged a babysitter to look after Paula on Tuesday while I was at the meeting, and possibly also to collect Adrian and Beth from school if I wasn't back in time. Jessie had said that the meeting would be a long one and I should allow most of the afternoon. The obvious person to ask was Kay, but I was a bit reluctant to ask her for another favour, having not had a chance to reciprocate the last one, even though she was a good friend and I knew she wouldn't mind. Later that evening, when the children were playing, I telephoned her.

'That's a coincidence!' she exclaimed, hearing my voice. 'I was going to telephone you later. I need to ask you a favour.'

'Good.' I laughed. 'That makes me feel much better. I need to ask you another favour too. You go first.'

Kay said she had a long dental appointment, three hours, booked for Wednesday morning and asked if I could look after her daughter, Vicky.

'Yes, of course,' I said. 'I'd be happy to.'

'I'm afraid the appointment is rather early – nine-thirty,' Kay said. 'Can I leave Vicky with you in the playground? I'll need half an hour to get to the dentist.'

'No problem. And don't rush back. I'll give Vicky lunch, and she can stay and play for the afternoon if you like. It will give you time to recover. Then I could meet you in the playground with her at the end of school.'

'That would be perfect,' Kay said. 'Thank you. I'm going to have a very sore mouth for a while. But it will be worth it in the end.'

I knew Kay had been saving up for some time to have some cosmetic work done to straighten her front teeth. And, of course, having been able to help her out, I felt less guilty asking her for help on Tuesday. She was happy to oblige.

Monday saw the start of the school week and clear skies, so I said we'd walk to school, and we left home a little earlier. During Monday I thought a lot about the meeting the following day, imagining all sorts of hypothetical discussions and outcomes. Jessie had said very little about the meeting when she'd telephoned, but I assumed I'd be brought up to date on what was happening to Derek, and the social services' long-term plans for Beth. It crossed my mind that if Beth couldn't live with her father again, which I assumed would be the case, as she had no other relatives who could look after her then perhaps she could continue staying with us. Obviously John, Adrian and Paula would need to agree, but it seemed silly to me to move her to another foster carer when she was already settled with us. I thought I'd raise this at the meeting if it seemed appropriate.

On Monday evening I explained the arrangements for the following day to the children. Paula was delighted at the thought of spending another afternoon playing with Vicky, Adrian didn't mind being met by Kay if necessary and Beth told me many times to tell Jessie that she loved her daddy and she was very sorry she'd been rude to him on the phone.

'Make sure Jessie knows I won't be rude if I'm allowed to telephone him again,' she said.

'I will,' I reassured her. 'Please don't worry.'

I felt so sorry for her.

The following morning I was up and dressed early, even though the meeting wasn't until one o'clock. I put the notes I'd made about the telephone contact into my handbag so I wouldn't forget them later. We had breakfast and then I took Adrian and Beth to school in the car and returned home with Paula. The morning whizzed by, which was just as well, because Paula was so excited at going to Vicky's that she asked me repeatedly if it was time to go yet. Finally, at 12.20 p.m., I was able to say yes.

Having taken Paula to Kay's, I continued to the council offices. Jessie had told me that the meeting was in the same room as the last meeting, so I signed the visitors' book at reception and continued up the stairs to the first floor, then along the corridor to Room 3. The door was closed and I could hear the low hum of voices coming from the other side. I was a couple of minutes early, so I assumed a previous meeting hadn't finished yet. I stood in the corridor to the side of the door and waited. A few minutes later there was still no sign of the meeting ending – I could hear talking, although not the actual words. When it went past one o'clock, I became concerned that perhaps I had the wrong room or the venue had been changed at the last minute. I was about to return downstairs and check the room number at reception when I heard a female voice come from inside the room. I was sure it was Jessie. I knocked on the door and the woman called out: 'Come in!'

I opened the door. It was Jessie. She was seated at the table with three others. She and her manager, Laura, were facing me, and two men had their backs to me.

'Come on in and take a seat,' Jessie said, seeing me hesitate.

'Sorry I'm late. I've been waiting outside,' I said, flustered. I sat in the empty seat beside Jessie.

'You're not late,' Laura said. 'We asked Dr Jones and Derek to meet with us early.'

I looked across the table at the two men: Dr Jones, whom I'd never met before, and Derek, whom I recognized from the photographs. Feeling confused and self-conscious, I threw them a weak smile.

'Pleased to meet you,' Dr Jones said in a rich, mellow voice. Tall, with fair hair and blue eyes, and in his early forties, he leaned across the table to shake my hand.

'And you,' I said.

Derek glanced at me with a small nod, clearly feeling as uncomfortable as I did. He was wearing a suit with an open-neck shirt, and although he looked older than he did in the photographs he was easily recognizable: receding grey hair, blue-grey eyes and regular features. He had his hands on the table and he twiddled his fingers nervously.

'Thank you for coming,' Jessie said to me. 'Dr Jones is the psychologist working with Derek.' I nodded. Then to Dr Jones she said, 'Cathy is Beth's foster carer.' He smiled.

'Laura will minute the meeting,' Jessie said to me. 'Although we're keeping it very informal.'

Laura and Dr Jones had notepads open on the table in front of them and Laura jotted something on hers. I was still struggling with the shock of suddenly meeting Derek, and I wondered why he and his psychologist were here. I could feel my heart racing and my cheeks flush.

'We have Derek's permission to share certain things with you,' Jessie said, turning slightly towards me. 'But you appreciate what you hear in this room stays in this room?'

'I understand,' I said. Most meetings I attended at the social services were confidential and of course I respected that confidentiality.

'I'll give Cathy a bit of background information before we continue,' Jessie said. Dr Jones and Laura nodded. 'As you know,' Jessie said, again turning to me, 'Derek was discharged from hospital last week. He is now home and making good progress. Marianne, his long-time friend, has moved in with him to support him until he is completely back on his feet.' Derek nodded but concentrated on the table. 'We've just been hearing from Derek that he accidentally mentioned Marianne to Beth during their telephone call last Friday,' Jessie continued, 'and Beth became very agitated and angry. That is one of the issues we shall be exploring, but I think it would be useful if you could tell us how Beth has been generally, and how that telephone call went. I asked you to monitor it?'

'Yes. I did,' I said. I reached down into my handbag and took out my notes. 'Shall I read what I've written?'

'Do you think you could save that for a bit later?' Dr Jones put in. 'To begin with, I'd like to hear your impression of Beth – as her foster carer. How she's settled into your family's life – or not – and how she comes across as a person. I believe there are five in your family, including Beth?'

'Yes. I have two children of my own, and a husband, John.'

Dr Jones made a note. 'And the ages and sexes of your children?' he asked.

'Adrian is six, soon to be seven,' I said, 'and Paula is nearly three.'

'And your husband is supportive of fostering?' he asked, glancing up from writing.

'Oh yes, very much so. Although he's having to work away quite a bit at present, so he's only home at the weekends.'

Dr Jones nodded as he wrote. 'Now, perhaps you could describe Beth and how she relates to you and your family.'

He had his pen poised, ready to write, while I felt Laura and Jessie looking at me. Derek was still concentrating on the table. I wasn't sure what exactly Dr Jones wanted from me, but I began anyway. 'Beth is generally very friendly and polite,' I said. 'We all like her. She comes across as being quite mature for her age. She's well organized and self-sufficient, but she can worry about household matters to an extent I wouldn't normally expect from a child of seven. Occasionally she becomes angry, but that's understandable. She soon recovers and says she's sorry. She's become quite attached to my two children and plays with them nicely. She's doing well at school and is eating and sleeping well. Considering all that has happened, I think Beth is coping remarkably well. She misses her father and was very sorry she was rude to him on the phone. She asked me a number of times to make sure Jessie told her daddy that she was sorry and she loved him.'

Derek looked up at me, pain in his eyes. 'Tell Beth it doesn't matter. Of course it doesn't. I love her too.'

There was silence as Dr Jones and Laura wrote. Dr Jones finished last and then looked at me. 'Thank you, Cathy. That was very helpful, but what about the problems you've encountered and the concerns you've expressed to Jessie?'

Conscious that Derek was present, I'd been careful to avoid saying anything too negative, and although Dr Jones had now asked a direct question I still wasn't sure how much I should say. He saw my hesitation and said: 'You're aware of our concerns about incest?'

I heard the word incest and went cold.

Chapter Twenty

He's Mine!

'I'm aware of some of the concerns,' I said, concentrating on Dr Jones and not daring to look at Derek. 'But I'm not aware of the details or the findings of the social services enquiries.'

Dr Jones looked at Jessie and Laura as he said: 'If we are all going to work together then Cathy needs to be fully in the picture.'

Laura whispered something in Jessie's ear and then Jessie asked Derek: 'Are you happy for Cathy to be made aware of our findings?'

Derek nodded but didn't look up.

'Go ahead, then,' Jessie said to Dr Jones.

Dr Jones laid down his pen, setting it precisely in the centre of his notepad, and then looked at me. 'Beth came to stay with you when her father was admitted to hospital. I am attached to that hospital, and I was assigned Derek's case. Derek wasn't coping and was displaying classic symptoms of what is generally known as a nervous breakdown. He was treated with medication and therapy. At the start Derek made good progress and I was expecting him to be discharged within a fortnight. However, one evening after Jessie had visited him and raised various concerns, he suffered a setback and had to be sedated. I wasn't on duty that evening, but I was made aware of what had happened. Subsequently, Beth made her first visit to see her father in hospital, accompanied by Jessie. I was on duty that afternoon and Jessie asked me to observe some of their contact, as she was very worried by what she was witnessing. As a result of Jessie's and my observations, combined with the previous concerns that you, Marianne and Beth's teacher had raised, we called a professionals meeting, where it was decided that in order to safeguard Beth all contact with her father should be suspended pending a full investigation.'

Dr Jones took a breath and I looked at Derek, who was now sitting hunched forward over the table, head in hands, as if weighed down by the pressure of what he was hearing. I returned my gaze to Dr Jones as he asked, 'Cathy, I don't suppose you know what the term "emotional incest" means? Most lay people don't.'

'I know what incest means,' I said, 'but I'm not sure about emotional incest.'

'I'll explain,' Dr Jones said. 'There are very good reasons in societies why fathers and daughters, and mothers and sons, are not allowed to have sexual relationships.' I felt myself tense at his directness. 'Any children born of those liaisons would weaken the genetic pool, and their relationships would undermine the moral and social structure of the family on which developed societies rely. In order for children to thrive, they need to grow up in an atmosphere where they feel loved and protected by their parents and not in competition with them. Sometimes – and it is more common than people think – the boundaries in the parent–child roles become foggy or even break down altogether, and the parent forms a relationship with the child that is inappropriate. It can happen for a number of reasons, including an absent or dead parent, mental illness in one of the parents or a vulnerable, needy or immature parent who is unable to provide the correct boundaries and support for their child. Emotional incest is seen in two-parent families as well as single-parent families. Nearly half of all cases of emotional incest go on to become sexual incest, where the child is either coerced into having sexual intercourse or is raped.'

Dr Jones paused and there was deafening quiet. No one moved, and I could feel my heart drumming on the inside of my chest. Then he continued, looking at me as he spoke. 'Emotional incest can be very difficult to spot, even by clinicians, and you and Beth's teacher did well to report your concerns. What often happens in these cases is that an adult close to the child will instinctively feel something is wrong but won't be able to identify what it is. Or they dismiss their suspicions as ludicrous, and ignore the evidence of their eyes. Marianne, Derek's long-term friend, knew something was wrong but couldn't identify it. She came to you with her concerns and you did right in passing them on to Jessie. Your actions probably saved Beth and changed the course of her destiny.'

I gave a small, appreciative nod. Yet while I felt vindicated in having reported my concerns, I didn't feel any less anxious for Beth. Indeed, now I knew more, I felt worse.

'There's a lot of work to be done if Derek and his daughter are to stand any chance of having a proper father-and-daughter relationship,' Dr Jones said, addressing us all. 'They will have to completely change the way they relate to each other, and to do that they will have to alter their perceptions of each other. I'm hoping some of this will be achieved through therapy. Derek will continue therapy with two sessions a week. Cathy, it may be helpful if, at some point, you could join us for a session so you will be in a better position to help Beth.' I nodded. 'I shall also be inviting Marianne and Beth to join us at some stage, but that is for the future.' He paused and then added, 'Beth must be a very confused little girl.'

'Yes, she is,' I said without hesitation. 'But until now I didn't understand why.'

'Emotional incest is very confusing,' Dr Jones said. 'The child has little idea how to behave as a child in the relationship with the parent. They often have an elevated status and are made "special" – Daddy's little princess – but that comes at a price. If emotional incest is left, it can have a devastating effect on the child for the rest of their life. Children who are victims are often incapable of forming meaningful relationships with the opposite sex in adult life, hankering after their fathers – or, in the case of boys, their mothers. Inevitably they become isolated and depressed and turn to drink and drugs as a way of coping. They often develop suicidal tendencies. Early intervention is crucial if the child is to be saved.' Dr Jones stopped and then added, 'It's a big subject, but I hope this helps you understand?'

'Yes, thank you,' I said sombrely. Jessie and Laura nodded, while Derek kept his head down.

'Good. Now, perhaps you could tell us about the telephone contact last Friday,' Dr Jones said. 'Then we'll end for today. I'm sure Derek must be exhausted and I know Jessie and Laura want to talk to you after we've gone.'

I'd almost forgotten the existence of the sheet of paper lying on the table in front of me. I now looked down and unfolded it. Using these notes as a reminder, I gave details of the phone contact, including Beth's dress and make-up and that I'd eventually brought the telephone call to an end when Derek had mentioned Marianne and Beth had become angry. 'There was only a minute or so left,' I explained. 'I couldn't see that anything positive would come from prolonging the call.'

'No, indeed,' Dr Jones agreed as Laura made notes. 'A sensible decision. I'm not going to analyse that call in depth now, but it does raise two important issues, ones which I will be covering in therapy. Briefly, Beth wore make-up and dressed up to make herself look older because of the adult role she has had to assume in her relationship with her father. She's not his child but his partner and believes she has to make herself look sexually attractive to keep her father's love. She is in the role her mother vacated when she left the marriage when Beth was a small child. Secondly, and this leads from the first point, Beth's anger and hostility towards Marianne is because Beth sees herself as her father's partner. Marianne therefore automatically becomes a rival – a threat – someone Beth needs to see off. Beth did this remarkably well when Derek tried to have a relationship with Marianne last year. But we need to be very clear that incest – of any type – is never, ever the fault of the child, even though the child may appear to be flirtatious with the parent. The child is simply responding in the way they have been taught and are trying to please the parent. They may also respond to other males in the same way. Now, I think that's enough for today. I shall be exploring these and other issues in therapy.'

'Thank you, Dr Jones,' Laura said.

Dr Jones nodded, closed his notepad and returned it, with his pen, to his briefcase. He then touched Derek lightly on the shoulder. 'I'll see you out,' he said gently.

Derek, who'd hardly said a word, now slowly raised his head from his hands and straightened. His brow was knotted in pain, but for what reason – guilt, or regret that he'd been found out – it was impossible to say. Dr Jones stood and, coming round to where I sat, shook my hand. 'Lovely to meet you,' he said charmingly. 'I hope to see you again soon.'

'Thank you,' I said.

He said goodbye to Laura and Jessie and then left the room with Derek. Once the door had swung shut, Jessie leaned back in her chair and let out a heartfelt sigh. 'That was a bit of a marathon!' she said. I could appreciate what she meant. I'd only joined them for the last hour, but I felt exhausted.

Laura was sitting very quietly too, then she turned to me and asked, 'Well? What did you think of Dr Jones?'

'He's clearly very knowledgeable, and what he said made a lot of sense,' I said.

'He's an expert in his field,' Laura said. 'We're lucky to get him. But Derek is going to have to be receptive to what he's being told and willing to make some very big changes if he is to stand any chance of having Beth returned to his care.'

'And is there a chance?' I now asked.

'It will depend,' Laura said. 'Derek will be assessed as part of the therapy. We will be working closely with Dr Jones. His report will be crucial to any decision we make on where Beth will eventually live. Thank you for agreeing to participate in the therapy.'

'I'm pleased to be able to help,' I said. Although I'd no idea what I was letting myself in for.

'I need to be going soon,' Jessie said. 'Do you have any more questions, Cathy?'

There was one that had been burning in my thoughts, but I was almost too afraid to ask it for fear of hearing the answer. 'Do you know if Beth has been sexually abused?' I said.

'We don't at this point,' Jessie said. 'And it would be wrong of us to speculate. We'll wait for the outcome of Dr Jones's report and the assessment.'

'In the meantime,' Laura said, 'Beth won't be seeing her father, but she can telephone him once a week. I suggest you make it on a Friday so she has the weekend to recover if she's upset. Monitor the call, please, and make notes. Stop the call if you hear anything that is not appropriate or if Beth becomes upset.'

I nodded. 'And what shall I tell Beth when I get home?' I now asked. 'She's anxious about her future and she is already asking if she will be seeing her father on her birthday, although it's not until October.'

'We'll have made a decision by then,' Laura said.

'I'll see Beth and explain,' Jessie said. 'But I can't visit until next week. Can you reassure her until I have a chance to speak to her?'

'Yes.' I was getting good at reassuring Beth with very little information. 'Shall I tell her I met her father at this meeting?'

'I don't see why not,' Jessie said, glancing at Laura.

'No, go ahead,' Laura agreed. 'It can't do any harm.'

But I don't think either of them appreciated the effect this would have on Beth.

I arrived in the playground a few minutes before the end of school. My thoughts were still swimming from all Dr Jones had said at the meeting. There was a great deal to think about and come to terms with, and I knew Beth was going to need a lot of support in the months to come. I hadn't mentioned at the meeting that I'd like to be considered as Beth's permanent carer if she couldn't return home, as there hadn't been an appropriate opportunity, but it was still in my mind.

Paula saw me and rushed over. I picked her up and hugged her hard, acutely aware of the horrors that some children had to live through. I set her down and we went over to Kay. 'Thank you so much,' I said.

'No problem, she's been fine, haven't you, love?' Kay said.

Paula nodded vigorously.

I confirmed with Kay that I'd see her in the playground the following morning when I'd be looking after Vicky for the day. The girls were excited at the thought of spending another day playing together. Adrian came out of school before Beth, bursting to tell me his good news. 'Mum! I've been chosen to swim for the school at the county sports!' he cried proudly.

'That's fantastic. Well done,' I said, giving him a kiss on the cheek, which he immediately wiped off. 'That's two years in a row you've been chosen. Fantastic.'

I was still talking about his achievement when Beth came out. 'Did you see Jessie?' she asked, nudging my arm.

'I did,' I said, turning away from Adrian to speak to her. 'I'll explain in the car.'

'Did you tell Jessie what I told you to say?' Beth persisted.

'Yes, and I'll tell you all about it in a minute, when we are in the car.' I thought that Beth might react or be upset when I told her that I'd met her father, so I wanted to be away from the playground, to give us some privacy and also to avoid Adrian being embarrassed in front of his friends by another outburst.

I turned and began towards the school gates. 'Tell me now,' Beth said, tugging on my arm. 'I want to know now.'

'I'll tell you when we are in the car,' I said again, this time more firmly.

Beth finally realized that I meant what I said and I wouldn't be bulldozed into doing what she wanted. Once we were all in the car with the doors closed, Beth asked me again. 'Did you tell Jessie I was sorry and I want to phone my daddy again?'

'Yes, I did,' I said, turning in my seat to face her. 'I was also able to tell your father. He was at the meeting too. So I explained you were sorry for the way you spoke to him.'

Beth's eyes widened in astonishment. 'What? You saw my daddy?'

'Yes, love. He said it didn't matter that you were angry with him and he forgives you. He said to tell you he loves you.'

I thought Beth might dissolve into tears and I was ready to comfort her, but instead her anger flared.

'Why couldn't I go to the meeting?' she demanded, kicking the back of the seat in front.

Adrian and Paula shifted away from her.

'Don't kick the seat, Beth. The meeting was for adults only.'

'That's not fair!' Beth shouted. 'You shouldn't be able to see my daddy when I can't. He's mine! You can't have him!' Which seemed a highly significant comment in the light of what Dr Jones had said about Beth viewing other women as threats. 'What else did my daddy say?' Beth now demanded.

'Nothing. That was all.'

'I don't believe you!' Beth fumed. 'You're lying, just like Marianne used to!' And again, I saw the significance in this comment, which previously I might not have done.

'Jessie and her manager were also at the meeting,' I said. 'Now calm down. I'm going to drive home and then I'll explain more.'

'You'd better,' Beth said fiercely, folding her arms across her chest.

'Don't be rude, please,' I said. 'You don't want to lose television time.'

I threw Adrian and Paula a reassuring smile and then turned to face the front to drive home.

Once home, I settled Adrian and Paula in the living room and took Beth into the front room where, drawing out two chairs, I sat in front of her and took her hand in mine. All her anger had now gone and she looked at me with sadness in her eyes. I told her that Jessie would be visiting us the following week to explain more, and that she would be able to telephone her father on Friday.

'Does that mean I'm never going home?' she asked, her eyes filling.

'We don't know yet, love,' I said honestly. 'Your daddy will be seeing a doctor regularly and Jessie will explain when she sees you.'

'I don't think I will be going home,' Beth said, a tear escaping and running down her cheek. 'Daddy loves Marianne now. He doesn't love me any more.'

'Your daddy does love you,' I said, 'but he has to make a lot of changes. I know it's difficult to understand.' I hoped it would become clearer when Jessie explained, but I had my doubts. A child of seven doesn't have the vocabulary or understanding to grasp the implications of what Jessie would try to explain to her.

'Cathy?' Beth said, wiping her hand across her eyes. 'If I can't go home and live with my daddy, can I stay here with you? I've nowhere else to go.'

My heart went out to her. She'd clearly been thinking about her long-term future, as I had, but I couldn't give her false hope by saying a definite yes. It would be the social services' decision where Beth lived.

'I hope so,' I said, and gave her a big hug.

Chapter Twenty-One
The Telephone Call

The following morning I met Kay in the playground as arranged. Vicky and her brother Oliver stayed with me while Kay went to her dental appointment. When the klaxon sounded, Oliver, Adrian and Beth lined up in their classes ready to go into school, while Vicky came home with Paula and me. The two girls played nicely together all day and ate lunch seated at the small play table, using the little dolls' plates, cutlery and china, which they found great fun. When we met Kay again in the playground at the end of school, her mouth was swollen and she said she'd had a lot of local anaesthetic, which had only just worn off. I winced at the thought of all those injections.

'Tell me it will be worth it in the end,' Kay said, feeling a little sorry for herself.

'It will be worth it,' I said.

On Thursday Adrian stayed behind at the end of school for swimming practice in preparation for the competition. Those participating would be practising every week from now until the event. I collected Beth at the usual time and then returned an hour later to collect Adrian. He was pleased, as they'd been allotted their races and he'd been chosen to swim in the mixed-stroke relay as well as the 50 metres freestyle. He handed me a

215

printed letter, which gave the date, time and venue for the competition with a tear-off slip to request the number of tickets the family wanted. 'It's on a Saturday,' Adrian said. 'So Dad will be able to come.'

'Excellent. We'll tell him tomorrow when he's home, so he can put it in his diary in plenty of time.'

On Friday, when I collected Beth from school at the end of the day, she didn't say anything about telephoning her father that evening. Neither did she mention it when we got home. She just went quietly up to her bedroom to change, and then appeared downstairs half an hour later all dressed up and wearing make-up and high heels. She tottered into the kitchen for a glass of water, very subdued, and I wondered if she was worrying about speaking to her father. 'Is everything all right?' I asked as I handed her the glass.

She nodded and took a sip of water.

'We'll telephone your dad in about half an hour, when I've got dinner in the oven,' I said.

'I'm going to try not to be angry with him,' she said sombrely. 'But it makes me so mad when I know Marianne is there.'

'Why?' I asked.

'Because Marianne is with my daddy and I'm not,' Beth said, her face set. 'She's trying to take him from me.'

'I'm sure she's not,' I said. 'I think she's trying to help your dad. Like she wanted to help you before.' Since hearing what Dr Jones had said, the thoughts I'd entertained about Marianne working to her own agenda and against Beth had largely gone. I now believed she was supporting Derek and that any threat Beth perceived in Marianne was because of the distorted relationship she had with her father.

'But Marianne loves him,' Beth said, as if it was a crime. 'And she'll make him love her. I know she will.'

'Beth, if your daddy loves Marianne it is because he wants to,' I said. 'And it doesn't mean he loves you any less. A parent's love for their child is very different from their love for a partner.' Or should be, I thought. 'And the parent shows their love and affection in different ways too.' I was tempted to add something about the way Beth dressed to speak to her father, but I felt I'd said enough for one day and thought I should leave further explanation to Jessie, and to Dr Jones's therapy.

Once dinner was in the oven, I called Beth from the living room to telephone her father in the hall. As with the previous call, she sat on the chair beside the hall table and watched as I dialled Derek's telephone number. He answered almost immediately with a quiet 'Hello'.

'It's Cathy,' I said. 'Beth's here to speak to you.'

'Thank you,' he said.

I pressed the speaker button and replaced the handset. 'Hello, Daddy,' Beth said quietly.

I perched on the bottom step of the stairs with a notepad and pen, ready to take notes. Derek asked Beth how she was, and she said she was all right, and then he asked her about school. A minute into the call, as Beth was telling her father what she'd had for dinner, a key sounded in the lock and the front door opened. 'What was that?' Derek asked edgily.

'John, Cathy's husband,' Beth said, and continued talking to her father.

I stood and went over to John and kissed his cheek. 'She's talking to her father,' I whispered. 'I have to stay and monitor the call. Adrian and Paula are in the living room.'

John nodded, put down his suitcase and then went into the living room, where he quietly closed the door. But even through the closed door I could hear the children's excited whoops of joy at seeing their father. I smiled. John was home early and we had the whole weekend ahead of us.

Beth's conversation with her father was uneventful and seemed quite 'normal' to me. I noticed Derek didn't ask Beth what she was wearing, and the flirtatious undertones of their previous conversations that I'd found so uncomfortable had gone. His voice sounded quite flat as he asked Beth about school, what she was having for her meals and the games she liked playing with Adrian and Paula. I didn't know what was responsible for the sudden change in Derek, but Beth answered his questions sensibly, and then asked evenly, 'Daddy, is Marianne there?'

There was a long pause before Derek said, 'Yes. She is.'

I'm pretty certain he was expecting Beth to explode – I know I was – but instead she said in a small voice, and rather sadly, 'You know I don't like her being there.'

'I know,' Derek said, and changed the subject.

To my surprise, Beth kept her word that she wouldn't get angry and didn't react. Possibly what I'd said to her about Marianne wanting to help her father might have helped a little, I don't know. But the result was a pleasant telephone conversation, more like the ones a father and daughter should have. Jessie hadn't told me how long the call should last, but Derek seemed to assume (or had been told) that it should be of the same duration as the last one, for as fifteen minutes approached he began winding up their conversation. 'Have a nice weekend and be a good girl,' he said. 'Don't forget to telephone me next Friday.'

'Can't I phone you sooner?' Beth bemoaned. 'Friday's a long time away.'

'We have to do as we're told,' Derek said. 'Jessie and Dr Jones said you can telephone once a week for now.'

'Is Dr Jones your doctor?' Beth asked.

'Yes,' Derek said.

They said goodbye to each other and I added a polite goodbye to Derek before I cut the call.

'Well done,' I said to Beth. 'You did very well.'

She shrugged a little sulkily. 'Daddy didn't ask me what I was wearing. I chose it specially.'

'But he enjoyed talking to you and that's more important.'

'I shan't wear my best dress again if he doesn't care,' Beth said moodily, and then she went off to find Adrian, Paula and John in the living room.

I put my notes safely away in a drawer and then joined them. John was sitting on the sofa with Adrian and Paula either side of him, listening to the children's news. Beth began doing a puzzle and I could see he was looking oddly at what she was wearing. I'd explain later. 'Everyone OK?' I asked cheerily.

There was a chorus of 'Yes'.

I smiled and went into the kitchen to complete the preparations for dinner and then called everyone to the table. John was first in and said he was looking forward to some homemade food after eating in hotels and restaurants all week. He was in very good spirits and did most of the talking during dinner. Among other things, he said he'd had an appraisal at work and the feedback from his manager had been very positive. 'It makes all the hard work and nights away worthwhile,' he said. And I agreed.

Adrian made sure his father had the dates of his bowling party, which I'd now arranged, and the county swimming event. 'I wouldn't miss them for the world,' John said to Adrian, ruffling his hair.

'And my birthday party,' Paula added. 'It's only a week after Adrian's.'

'Yes, I'll make a note of that in my diary too,' John said.

Beth kept quiet about her birthday, and there wasn't anything positive I could say, for we didn't know where she would be in October. It's at moments like this that I'm reminded of just how insecure all the uncertainty must make a child in care feel – not knowing where you will be living from one month to the next, and not having any say in the moves.

That evening, when the children were in bed, John and I chatted and he told me more about the appraisal he'd had at work, and I told him about the meeting I'd attended with Dr Jones. John was surprised I'd met Derek, and more surprised by what I'd learned.

'You always thought there was something odd about their relationship,' he said, referring to Derek and Beth. 'I thought they were just close and loved each other.'

'They do love each other,' I said, 'but Derek shows his love and affection in a way that isn't appropriate. He treats Beth like a partner, rather than a daughter, which is why Beth saw Mari-anne as a rival and not a possible stepmother.' I continued by explaining why Beth dressed as she did for her father, and reminded John to practise safer caring, for his sake and Beth's. 'Beth doesn't know how to relate to a father figure,' I said. 'So you will need to set the boundaries as you have been doing.' John, like most adult males, knew instinctively how to relate appropriately to children because of the examples he'd been set as a child. Our chat had turned into a heavy conversation for a Friday evening, but afterwards I felt considerably relieved at being able to share the burden of it all with John.

We had a lazy morning on Saturday and in the afternoon we went to a wildlife reserve at an old flooded quarry about half an hour's drive away. The weather was reasonable, and we stood in the hide as quietly as the children were able to, watching the birds, ducks and geese land and take off on the water. Between us we knew the names of some of the birds and fowl, but not all. On the way home we stopped off at a café and ordered an all-day breakfast each. The meal was huge and even Beth, who had a good appetite, struggled to finish. John and Adrian ate half of Paula's and some of mine. However, we all found room for an ice cream with chocolate topping for dessert. The only disappointment in the day was that when we returned home John received a telephone call from a work colleague who had something urgent to discuss that couldn't wait until Monday. John said he'd have to meet the man and arranged a rendezvous with him at a pub equidistant between their two homes, about an hour's drive from us. John left at half past seven, having reassured the children he'd be home later that night, although after they were asleep.

I felt him slip into bed beside me just before midnight. 'Is everything all right?' I mumbled, half asleep.

'Yes, all sorted,' he said happily.

We had another lazy morning on Sunday, and then in the afternoon we went to a local park with some bread to feed the ducks. John didn't have to leave for work again until eight o'clock on Monday morning, so we had the whole of Sunday together, and he was able to see the children off to school on Monday.

Jessie telephoned on Monday afternoon and said she would visit Beth after school on Wednesday. She asked how Beth had been since our meeting and how the telephone call to her father had gone. I told her that the telephone call had gone well, although Beth had dressed up for it, and had then got a bit moody when her father hadn't asked what she was wearing.

'It sounds as though Derek is taking on board what Dr Jones is saying,' Jessie said positively.

'It left Beth a bit confused,' I said.

'It will, because her father is changing the way he relates to her. I'll try to explain it to her when I see her, but she'll be starting play therapy next week, which should help. Have you got a pen handy?'

'Yes.' I reached for the pen and notepad.

'I've arranged for Beth to see Dr Weybridge, who is a child psychologist. I'm afraid it will mean Beth missing some school, but it can't be helped. There's a long waiting list for appointments out of school time. It will be Tuesday and Thursday afternoons, starting next week. The times have yet to be confirmed. Dr Weybridge will be working closely with Dr Jones, and the plan is for Beth to see Dr Weybridge twice a week, and then, in a month or so, they'll join Dr Jones and Derek in family therapy.'

I made a note of all this. 'Do you want me to tell Beth's teacher she'll be missing school?' I asked.

'I've already spoken to Miss Willow. I've told her I've asked for the appointments to be as late as possible in the afternoon, so minimizing the time Beth has off school. I'll see you and Beth on Wednesday, then.'

'Yes, thank you.'

I was pleased that things seemed to be moving forward, for I felt sure therapy would help Beth in a way I could not.

That evening, to my astonishment and slight embarrassment, Marianne telephoned. It was 9.30 p.m. and the children were in bed, asleep.

'I've just popped back to my flat to collect some more of my things,' Marianne said. 'So I thought I'd give you a quick ring.'

'Oh, I see,' I said hesitantly. 'How are you?' The last time Marianne had telephoned me – when Derek had been in hospital and all contact with Beth had been stopped – she'd become quite angry and had hung up.

The Telephone Call

'Derek doesn't know I'm phoning you,' she said, 'so please don't tell him. I don't want him to think I'm checking up on him, but I was wondering if you could tell me how the telephone call went on Friday? It seemed all right from our end, but how was Beth?'

While it was thoughtful of Marianne to be concerned about Beth, it wasn't my place to give her feedback – Jessie or Dr Jones would tell her what she needed to know – but at the same time I didn't want to appear rude, so I said, 'I think it went quite well.'

'Is that what you told Jessie?' Marianne now asked, an edge of anxiety creeping into her voice.

'I gave her an honest account of the call, yes.'

'And Jessie was pleased?'

I could understand why Marianne was anxious – the telephone calls would form part of Derek's assessment – but it wasn't for me to go into detail or second guess Jessie's opinion of the call or anything else.

'It's all right, you can tell me,' Marianne added. 'Jessie has told me all about the assessment. I shall be included in it and the therapy at some point.'

'I gave Jessie an honest account,' I said again. 'It's probably best if you ask her.'

Marianne went quiet for a moment and then said, 'I blame myself, you know. I knew there was something wrong and I should have intervened. But it was difficult; the two of them against me, and I felt very hurt. I didn't know what to do for the best.'

'I don't think you can blame yourself,' I said.

'That's what Jessie said. She also said this type of thing can be very difficult to spot, which is one of the reasons so many cases go unreported.' I noticed Marianne hadn't been able to use the word incest. 'Does Beth hate me?'

'She's very confused,' I said diplomatically.

'So am I,' Marianne said. 'I broke down at work last week and ended up confiding in my manager. It won't go any further, but I knew she'd had similar problems in her family. Her niece dated an older man who had a child from a former relationship. The way he and his daughter behaved towards each other was worse than Derek and Beth. Her niece couldn't understand what was going on and eventually ended their relationship. She was very upset, but you wonder about the child left there.'

'Absolutely,' I said. 'She couldn't walk away.'

'But Derek didn't do anything, you know.'

Marianne heard my silence.

'Derek didn't sexually abuse Beth,' she said. 'I know the way he behaved towards her was wrong, but it never went that far. And he certainly didn't rape her. I've told Jessie that.'

'She's the best person to tell,' I said, wondering how Marianne could be so sure. She hadn't been certain at one time: *Some of their kissing and cuddling could be described as sexual*, she'd said when she'd brought Beth's swimming costume.

'Don't you believe me?' Marianne asked, her voice rising slightly.

'I don't know what happened between Beth and her father,' I said. 'I think we should leave it to Dr Jones and Jessie to make their assessment.'

There was a pause and then Marianne's voice broke as she said, 'I'm sorry to have bothered you.' And she hung up.

I was sorry I hadn't been able to offer her the reassurance she sought, but I didn't know what else I could have said. No one knew the outcome of the assessment and, as Laura had said, it would be wrong to speculate.

I went to bed that night with thoughts of Beth, Marianne, Derek and Marianne's manager's niece chasing through my head. I was finally drifting off to sleep when I was startled by the phone ringing. I reached out and picked up the handset on the beside cabinet. 'Hello?'

A woman's voice asked, 'Is John there?'

'No, he's at work,' I said blearily.

'Of course he is, how silly of me. Sorry to have troubled you.' She hung up.

I thought nothing more of this call until some months later, when I was forced to think a lot about telephone calls to John, and his nights away.

Chapter Twenty-Two

Icing On the Cake

The following night an incident occurred that made me realize I'd become a little too complacent with Beth. When a foster child first arrives and I don't know them, I am hyper-vigilant, not only to make sure all their needs are met, but also that they and my family are safe. As time passes and I get to know them and they feel more settled, depending on their level of needs I start to relax. The longer the child is with me the more relaxed I become, until eventually they are just one of the family, and I know and trust them implicitly. That is, unless something happens to put me on alert again.

Having had a restless night on Monday, I was tired the following day and planned to have a reasonably early night. I might have mentioned this to the children – a throw-away comment – and possibly Beth heard me, for she spied the opportunity she'd been waiting for. I was in bed shortly after ten o'clock and went to sleep very quickly. Fortunately, regardless of how tired I am, I'm a light sleeper – from years of listening out for children – and tend to wake at the slightest noise. It was just before eleven o'clock when my eyes opened. To begin with I thought that one of the children had called out, or possibly I'd heard cats fighting or a fox barking in the garden, which happened quite a lot where we lived. I lay in the small light coming through the parted curtains from the streetlamp outside and listened. All was quiet for a few seconds, but then I heard a strange tapping sound, which seemed to be coming from downstairs.

With John working away, I can feel quite vulnerable at times, especially with unidentified noises in the night. I don't consider myself a nervous person, but one of the reasons I keep a telephone by the bed is so that I can call for help if necessary. But, the intermittent tapping I was hearing didn't seem like a burglar – they certainly weren't being very quiet about breaking in if they were. I listened a moment longer and then gingerly eased back the duvet. With my heart starting to race, I got out of bed and padded quietly across my bedroom in my nightdress. Once on the landing, I knew the noise was definitely coming from downstairs and I continued slowly round the landing until I could see the hall below. The night-lights in the hall and on the landing were on and I could see Beth in her pyjamas standing beside the telephone table in the hall below. She had her back to me, but I could see that in one hand she held the telephone handset and she was tapping the numbers on the keypad with the other.

Not wanting to wake Adrian and Paula, I went part-way down the stairs before I spoke. 'Beth, what are you doing?'

She jumped and, spinning round, dropped the handset. 'Nothing!' she said guiltily.

I continued downstairs into the hall where I picked up the handset, which was sounding the dialling tone, and replaced it in its cradle. 'Who were you phoning?'

'No one,' Beth said, clutching a piece of paper to her chest.

'Beth, love, I'm not silly. You were trying to phone someone. You won't get into trouble, but I'd like to know who it was and why.'

'A friend,' Beth said.

'It's rather late to be phoning a friend,' I said. 'Won't they be in bed?'

Beth looked at me, then, perhaps realizing she'd been caught out and would at some point have to confess, she pushed the crumpled piece of paper towards me. I opened it out. In Beth's childish handwriting was a row of numbers, which I recognized as Derek's telephone number with the area code.

'So you were trying to telephone your father,' I said.

'Yes, but he didn't answer. I tried lots of times, but the answerphone is on, like here. So I didn't speak to him.'

Just as well, I thought, for I could imagine the bad impression that would have given: a child chatting to her possible abuser as the foster carer slept.

'Why were you trying to phone your father in the middle of the night?' I asked.

Beth shrugged.

Aware Adrian's and Paula's bedroom doors were ajar and our voices might carry up and wake them, I said, 'Come in the front room, Beth, and talk to me.' I opened the door to the front room, switched on the light and then closed the door behind us.

Beth stood in the centre of the room and looked at me a little defiantly. 'I wanted to speak to my daddy,' she said.

'But we phone your daddy on a Friday, as Jessie told us to. And at the time that was agreed, not in the middle of the night.'

'But I want to speak to him more often,' she said.

'I understand that. And the correct thing to do is to tell Jessie how you feel when you see her tomorrow. I can't make the decision for you to phone your father, as you know. Neither can we take it upon ourselves to phone him whenever we like.'

'I don't like you listening when I talk to him!' Beth now blurted out.

'I can understand that too,' I said. 'But I have to do as Jessie tells me, just as you do.'

'Does my daddy have to do what Jessie says?' Beth now asked.

'Yes, he does.'

'Why?'

'Because he's working with Jessie for his own good,' I said. 'Jessie will explain more when she sees you tomorrow, but you can't decide to telephone your father when you want to. I thought you were asleep. Were you awake all this time, waiting for me to go to bed?'

She nodded.

'Well, you need to promise me you won't do it again, Beth. You could have tripped and fallen downstairs in the half-light.' Which, of course, was another worry.

'I promise,' Beth said a little sulkily.

'Good. How did you get your father's number?' I asked, glancing at the paper I held.

'When we phoned I watched which numbers you pressed and then I wrote them down. Not all at once, I couldn't remember them all, but a few each time.'

Full marks to Beth for ingenuity, I thought, and another minus point to me for letting her see the numbers as I'd keyed them in.

'Thank you for being honest,' I said. 'Now off to bed and no more wandering around in the night.'

Beth nodded and we went upstairs and I saw her into bed. However, for a few weeks following this incident, to be on the safe side, I began unplugging the telephone in the hall before I went to bed, and then plugging it in again the next morning. The doors to the rooms downstairs where there were other phones were closed at night, and of course I'd hear Beth if she came into my bedroom to use that telephone.

The following day a letter arrived from Dr Weybridge's secretary, confirming Beth's appointments for therapy on Tuesdays and Thursdays at 2 p.m., commencing the following week. It said each session would last an hour and would be held in the Butterfly Wing, which was a unit attached to the children's ward of our local hospital – the same hospital Derek had been in. Enclosed was an information leaflet giving instructions on how to get to the hospital and a map showing where the unit was situated and where to park. It also said there was a waiting area for parents and their children not attending the session, from which I concluded that Beth would be seeing Dr Weybridge alone, and that I would be able to wait with Paula in the designated waiting area, although I'd phone to check. The timing of the appointments was also good, as Beth wouldn't miss too much school, and I should have time at the end of the session to meet Adrian from school, so I wouldn't have to ask Kay for another favour.

That afternoon Jessie visited us as arranged at four o'clock. She wanted to speak to Beth alone first, so I made her a cup of coffee and then left the two of them in the living room with the door closed, while I began making dinner and Adrian and Paula amused themselves. It was three-quarters of an hour later when Beth emerged from the living room and came to find me.

'Jessie says you can go in now,' Beth said. 'She's finished with me.' She seemed happy and with a little hop and a skip went off to play with Adrian and Paula.

I went into the living room where Jessie was sitting on the sofa with some papers, and a notepad and pen on her lap.

'Beth appears to be taking it all very well,' she said as I sat down. 'Although she can become very anxious about her father.'

'Yes, I reassure her as best I can.'

'I've told her that her father is being well looked after,' Jessie said, updating me. 'She asked if Marianne was still at home and

I've told her the truth – that she's staying with her father so she can help him. Beth needs to know. Marianne's not going to disappear. But their relationship is something that'll be addressed in therapy. Beth also told me she wants to telephone her father more often, but I've said it will stay at once a week for now. I understand she tried to phone him when you weren't looking.'

'It was worse than that,' I said, and I confessed all.

Fortunately Jessie saw the funny side to it. 'Little madam!' She laughed. 'She can be very strong-willed when she wants to be.'

'Yes, although she does accept what I say once I've explained the reasons for a decision.'

Jessie then asked me about the telephone contact on Friday and I gave her a résumé as she made some notes. I showed her the letter I'd received from Dr Weybridge confirming Beth's appointments and Jessie noted the times.

'It's been decided that, as of next week, Marianne will join one of Derek's therapy sessions,' Jessie said. 'She'll be taking time off work to attend. You have to admire the woman's commitment, whatever the outcome of all this.'

I nodded, and I knew I should mention Marianne's telephone call to me, so I gave Jessie a brief outline.

'Marianne's very anxious,' Jessie said. 'I'll speak to her and give her some feedback.' She made another note and then looked at me. 'But generally, Beth is happy here with you?'

'Yes, I think so,' I said.

'Good. That's what I thought. There's something I need to ask you.'

'Yes?' I said, puzzled, wondering what was to come.

'When the assessment is complete – in a couple of months – if it's decided that Beth can't go home to live with her father, would she be able to stay here with you and your family?'

I smiled. 'I'd thought about asking you the same question,' I said. 'Obviously I'll have to discuss it with my husband and children, but I have a feeling they'd be happy if Beth stayed, and I certainly would.'

'Excellent,' Jessie said. 'I am pleased. No one wants to move a child unless it is absolutely essential, and Beth is so settled here. It would be a long-term foster placement, as Derek would never give permission for Beth to be adopted.'

'I understand,' I said.

Jessie left shortly after, calling goodbye to the children as she went. We ate and then after dinner we sat in the living room where I read another chapter from Roald Dahl's book *Matilda*, which all three children were enjoying. The telephone rang. I reached out and answered it and was initially delighted to hear John's voice: 'Hi, how are you?'

'We're all fine, thanks, love,' I said. 'How are you?'

'Not so bad, but unfortunately I won't be able to make it home this weekend. Sorry. It's unavoidable.'

'Oh dear. Not even for a day?' I asked, disappointed.

'Not possible, I'm afraid. But I'll definitely be home the following weekend for Adrian's birthday party.'

'And the weekend after that for Paula's birthday party?' I reminded him.

'Yes, of course. I haven't forgotten. It's in my diary, so is Adrian's swimming competition. It's just this weekend that's causing a problem.'

'Oh well, I suppose it can't be helped,' I said, aware the children were listening and I needed to stay positive. 'And the weeks go quickly.'

'They do indeed,' John said. 'Can I speak to the children now?'

'Yes, of course.'

Icing on the Cake

I passed the phone to Adrian, who talked to his father about his party and then he passed the phone to Paula, who talked about her party. She passed the phone to Beth, who said she was looking forward to both parties, which was so sweet of her. When she'd said a few words she passed the phone back to Adrian, who chatted and then let Paula have another turn. And so it went on with the phone being passed around the children three times, amid lots of laughing, before it was returned to me to say goodbye. Although John had told the children he wouldn't be coming home at the weekend, all the talk about the birthday parties and the laughter had minimized their disappointment, so they weren't unhappy. Once we'd said goodbye, I continued with the story of Matilda and her magic powers of being able to make objects move by thought alone.

'I wish I could do that,' Beth said.

'Me too,' Adrian, Paula and I agreed.

Torrential rain and gale-force winds set in on Friday morning and were forecast for most of the weekend, making driving conditions hazardous, so in a way I was relieved John wasn't driving home. On Friday evening Beth got dressed up again to telephone her father, but the conversation was a good one – with nothing untoward – just as it had been the previous Friday. When Beth told her father what she was wearing he said, 'Oh,' and changed the subject. I noticed that Beth didn't tell him she'd tried to phone him on Tuesday night, but she did tell him that Jessie had visited. Then she asked him if he was still 'cooperating'.

'Who told you that?' Derek asked.

'Jessie,' Beth said. 'She said you were cooperating with the social services. Is that a good thing, Daddy?'

'Yes, it is,' he said. 'It means I'm listening to what I'm being told and I'm trying to change.'

The relentless rain and wind over the weekend meant that the children and I were confined mainly indoors. Even Toscha only went out to do her business and then quickly returned. By Sunday morning the children had virtually exhausted all the games in the house and were becoming a bit niggly with each other. I organized some cake making and then we made some fresh play dough, which the children modelled for an hour or so. After lunch the rain finally eased and we all put on our coats and boots and went for a little walk to a local 'open space'. The air was fresh and the exercise was just what we all needed. When we returned home the children were in better spirits and watched a movie, while I made dinner. After dinner I read some more of *Matilda* and then it was time for the bath and bedtime routine. The following weeks were going to be busy – with Beth's therapy starting, Adrian's extra swimming practice, Paula's mother and toddler group and then the birthday parties and the swimming gala. There was a lot in the diary.

On Tuesday morning, when I took Adrian and Beth to school, I went into reception and asked the school secretary if she'd let Miss Willow know that I'd be collecting Beth at 1.30 p.m. Jessie had already told Miss Willow that Beth would be starting therapy but hadn't given her the times. The secretary said she'd pass on the message, and then said that I should wait in reception when I collected Beth that afternoon. When Jessie had visited us the previous Wednesday, she'd told Beth about the play therapy, so Beth had an understanding of what to expect. However, what Jessie hadn't told her was which hospital we would be attending, and I hadn't thought to mention it either.

That afternoon, when I drove into the hospital car park, Beth cried out anxiously, 'I'm not going in there!'

'Why? Whatever is the matter?' I asked.

'They took my daddy away!' Beth said.

'Really?' Paula asked, turning to Beth in sympathy. 'I hope they don't take my daddy away.'

I parked, cut the engine and turned in my seat to face the girls. They both looked at me anxiously. 'It's a hospital,' I said. 'They make people better. They don't take daddies away.' Although I could see why Beth might think that. 'Beth, your daddy stayed here for a while and you visited him. Then the doctors made him well enough to go home. You know that.'

'You won't leave me here to sleep, will you?' she asked.

'No, of course not. People come to hospital for appointments; they don't all stay. They see the doctor and then go home again. That's what you'll be doing. You're not sleeping here.'

Paula looked at Beth. 'Is that all right, then?' she asked her.

'I guess so,' Beth said. 'So you haven't brought my pyjamas?' she asked me.

'No, love. You'll see the doctor for one hour and then we'll all go home again.'

Which showed how easily a child could misinterpret a situation that seems clear to an adult. The only time Beth had been to the hospital was when she'd visited her father who, as an inpatient, had slept there and, in Beth's eyes, had effectively been 'taken away' from her.

Using the map that had been enclosed with the appointment letter, we easily found the Butterfly Wing. It was a small new outbuilding attached to the far end of the children's ward by a short corridor. I gave Beth's name to the receptionist and she pointed us to the waiting room where there were comfortable chairs, toys and books. The whole unit appeared very welcoming and child friendly, with the walls painted pastel shades of blue and lilac, and decorated with brightly coloured friezes and pictures of cuddly animals. A woman was sitting in the waiting room reading a magazine. She glanced up and smiled as we entered and I said hello. There were no children present. I sat in one of the chairs while Beth and Paula went to the large toy box at one end of the room. Squatting on the floor, they began taking out the toys and playing with them. At little before two o'clock I heard a door along the corridor open and close, and then footsteps, before a woman whom I took to be a doctor appeared with a child of a similar age to Beth.

'Goodbye, Clare,' the doctor said to the child, and she ran over to the other woman.

'Thank you, Doctor,' the woman said. 'See you next week.' She began helping the child into her coat.

'Dr Weybridge,' the doctor said, coming over and introducing herself to us.

'Hello, I'm Cathy Glass and this is Beth,' I said. 'And this is my daughter, Paula.'

Dr Weybridge said hello to both girls, and they smiled back shyly. I guessed Dr Weybridge was in her mid-forties; she was of average height and wasn't wearing a white coat, but a woollen skirt and jumper. She had rather unkempt hair, suggesting she'd more important matters on her mind than styling her hair. I'd noticed on the appointment letter she was very well qualified, with lots of letters after her name.

'Does Beth understand why she is here?' Dr Weybridge asked me.

'Yes. Her social worker and I have both explained.'

'Good. Say goodbye to Cathy,' Dr Weybridge said to Beth. 'You'll see her here again in an hour.'

'Bye,' Beth said without hesitation.

'Bye, love, see you soon,' I replied.

Paula gave a little wave, and Beth went with Dr Weybridge along the corridor, and I heard a door open and close. Paula returned to playing with the toys and I picked up a magazine, then a little later I read to her from some of the books that were in the toy box. The time passed quickly and towards the end of the hour another woman came into the waiting room with a young boy. We smiled at each other and the boy joined Paula on the floor by the toy box.

Just before three o'clock I heard the door along the corridor open and close, footsteps and then Dr Weybridge and Beth appeared. Beth ran over to me with a big smile.

'OK, love?' I asked.

Beth nodded.

'See you on Thursday, then,' Dr Weybridge said to Beth and me. She then went over to the other woman, whose child went in next.

I had wondered if I would receive some feedback at the end of the session, but that didn't happen, so we put on our coats and left.

'Was everything all right?' I asked Beth as we crossed the car park.

'Yes. I had fun,' she said with a little hop.

'Good.'

I wouldn't question Beth about what had happened in her therapy session, as that was private and between her and Dr Weybridge. Dr Weybridge would write a report as part of the assessment and hopefully I'd be told what I needed to know. Paula, however, a young child, didn't have the same reservations as I did. 'What did you do with that doctor lady?' she asked, as we got into the car.

'Drawing and colouring, and we played some games,' Beth said easily.

'That sounds nice,' Paula said. 'Can I come in with you next time?'

'No,' Beth said. 'It's only for kids with problems. You haven't got problems.' Which Paula accepted. I thought Beth's reply was rather sweet, although I wondered where the idea had come from. I hadn't told her she had problems. Maybe it was something she'd deduced.

I drove to school to collect Adrian and then we all went home. Later that evening, when Beth was getting ready for bed, she said to me, 'I like Dr Weybridge.'

'That's good,' I said. But again I didn't press her for details. If Beth wanted to tell me about her therapy that was fine, but it wasn't for me to ask.

On Thursday Beth had no reservations about going to the hospital for therapy again. Indeed, that morning she told us that she would rather go and play and draw with Dr Weybridge than do her lessons in school. Paula and I collected Beth from reception at 1.30 p.m. and drove to the hospital. The routine was the same as before: I registered our arrival at reception and then we sat in the waiting room until Dr Weybridge had finished the previous session, and when she came out Beth went in. As before, there was no feedback at the end of the session, but in the car Beth said she'd enjoyed herself. She also said she'd been playing, and talking to Dr Weybridge about lots of things. Because Adrian had swimming practice after school that afternoon, I had time to return home briefly and give the girls a drink before we collected him. Adrian came out in high spirits, having won a practice race, and also because he and his friends had been talking about his birthday party on Sunday. Apparently there'd been some lighthearted banter in the changing rooms about who was best at bowling and who would win, with everyone claiming they would.

On Friday afternoon Adrian's excitement reached new heights when we returned home from school to find John was already home. He said he'd left work after lunch so he could spend as much time as possible with 'the birthday boy'. Adrian was overjoyed, as we all were, and the atmosphere in the house that Friday evening was so merry that it seemed Adrian's party had already begun.

On Saturday I left Adrian at home with his father while I went into town to collect his birthday cake. Paula and Beth came with me but knew they had to keep the secret of Adrian's cake, which I'd ordered specially and was in the shape of a football; football was another of Adrian's favourite sports. He stayed up late on Saturday playing chess with his father, which was lovely to watch. John had begun teaching Adrian chess a couple of years before, but when he'd started working away he hadn't had much time to play with him.

Sunday was Adrian's actual birthday as well as the day of his party, so we began the day by watching him open his presents. His little face lit up as he peeled off the gift-wrapping from each one and thanked us. We arranged Adrian's cards on the mantelpiece in the living room, and then Adrian, John and the girls played with one of Adrian's new boxed games in the living room, while I made a light lunch. After that we all got changed – Beth into a new dress I'd bought her – and then I smuggled the cake in its box into the boot of the car, and John drove us to the leisure centre. We arrived fifteen minutes before the party was due to start, checked in at reception and then I sneaked the cake into the party room. Adrian's friends began arriving and they'd all brought presents for him, which was kind. He thanked them and put them aside to open later as there was so much going on. He had invited ten friends, but it seemed more like ten hundred with their noisy excitement. My parents arrived and having said happy birthday to Adrian they stood with John and me, as the party organizers – two staff from the leisure centre – took over.

The birthday-party package included two games of bowling, a party tea and some more games. We all bowled, including the adults. Beth teamed up with Paula and helped her, as even the lightweight balls were heavy. Fred, a boy from Adrian's class, won the bowling and we all cheered and clapped. Then the organizers led the way into the party room, gaily decorated with balloons and streamers, where the tea was already laid out on the table. I took lots of photographs, and when it was time for the cake I told Adrian to cover his eyes. 'No peeping,' I said.

I took the cake from the cupboard where I'd hidden it, added the seven candles and then placed it on the table in front of him. 'Wow!' he said, impressed. 'Thanks, Mum.'

I smiled, pleased that he liked his cake. John gave Adrian the box of matches and supervised him as he lit the candles. Of course, Adrian was embarrassed when we all sang 'Happy Birthday', but that's all part of having a birthday, and he loved every moment. He blew out all the candles with one breath and we gave three cheers – more embarrassment for Adrian. The party organizers then arranged some games for the children, while Mum and I cut the cake. At the end, when his friends' parents arrived to collect their children, we thanked them for the presents and Adrian handed each of his friends a party bag, containing a slice of cake, some sweets, novelties and a small gift. My parents retuned home with us for a cup of tea and to watch Adrian open the presents and cards from his friends, and also the present from them, which was a new cycling helmet. They left around eight o'clock and after we'd waved them off at the

Icing on the Cake

door Adrian thanked his father and me and said he'd had a fantastic birthday and loved his cake. But I knew the real 'icing on the cake' was that he'd been able to spend so much time with his dad over the weekend, and that John didn't have to leave for work until Monday morning.

Chapter Twenty-Three
She Must Hate Me

Paula's birthday party was on Sunday a week later and fell at the start of the Easter holidays. It was a different type of party to Adrian's but suitable for her age and she enjoyed it very much. We held it at home, and my family, Kay and her family and another two of Paula's friends and their parents were guests. I organized party games and made a buffet tea and her birthday cake. It was in the shape of the number three and covered in pink icing with a piped decoration. It looked impressive, although it had been simple to make using a shaped cake tin.

Paula's actual birthday was on the Monday, so she opened the presents from her friends at the party, and I put away those from the family until the next day. Because we'd broken up from school, Paula was able to open her presents the following morning without rushing, although unfortunately John had to leave for work at 6 a.m. so wasn't able to watch. As usual I took lots of photographs, which I would show him the following weekend. The mother and toddler group Paula and I attended had broken up for two weeks in line with the school's Easter holidays, but Beth's therapy continued, as did the Friday telephone calls to her father. Out of the school routine we all relaxed and the children either played at home or I organized trips to the local parks and open spaces, where we met up with friends and their children. John had the national holidays off work – Good Friday and Easter Monday – and we arranged a couple of day trips, to the zoo and to a forest with an outdoor activity centre. Having the Friday and Monday off work also meant that John had two four-day working weeks, which made his absence from home seem much shorter.

It was on the Friday after Easter, the third week in April, and just before the schools went back for the summer term that something interesting happened. It was five o'clock, time for Beth's telephone contact, so I called her to the telephone in the hall. We'd got into the habit of telephoning her father at five; the time suited me and seemed to suit Derek too. Beth came straight to the telephone as she always did and sat on the chair beside it as I pressed the speaker button and then keyed in Derek's number. I could have let Beth make the call herself, but I wanted to reinforce to her that I was in charge of the telephone, in case she was entertaining any more thoughts about creeping downstairs at night to phone her father, or anyone else for that matter.

We listened to the telephone ringing and then her father answered, 'Hello.'

As usual, I said, 'Good evening, Derek. Beth is here.' I moved away from the hall table and sat on the bottom step of the stairs with my notepad and pen ready. It was only then, as I looked over at Beth, that I realized she hadn't got all dressed up (tarted up) to speak to her father. She was in the same clothes she'd been wearing all day – a winter dress I'd bought her. And she wasn't wearing the ridiculous high heels, fishnet tights, make-up or nail varnish.

I wasn't sure what this meant, if anything, but I made a note and then listened as unobtrusively as I could to what they were saying. I didn't like having to listen to and record their conversation; it seemed intrusive, but I appreciated that sometimes it's essential for the welfare of the child. Foster carers are often asked to supervise telephone contact. Beth was telling her father what she'd been doing during the Easter holidays, including Paula's birthday party, which had taken place after their last telephone call.

Derek was quiet as Beth finished, and then he said, 'You have a lot of parties at Cathy's.'

'Not really,' Beth said. 'It's because Adrian's and Paula's birthdays are close together.' Which was sensible. Then she said, 'Daddy, can I have a party when it's my birthday?'

I waited for Derek's reply, as did Beth. Given that Beth had never been allowed to play with children outside of school and certainly not have them home to tea, I thought a party was highly unlikely, even if it was decided that Beth could return home, which was a big 'if'.

'We'll have to wait and see what happens,' Derek said eventually. 'Nothing's settled yet.'

'But if I can come home, can I have a birthday party?' Beth persisted. 'And invite lots of my friends from school?'

Another silence, then Derek said, 'I don't know.'

'Why don't you know, Daddy?' Beth asked. I could hear the insistence creeping into her voice and I knew she was challenging him.

'Because October is a long way off,' Derek said. 'We don't know what's going to happen before then.' Which was all he could say, really, with the decision on Beth's future unmade.

But Beth was ready with her reply. 'If I'm still at Cathy's, she'll give me a big party. I'll invite all my friends and we'll have a great time.'

Her face was set. The comment was designed to hurt her father. It went quiet on the other end of the phone and I almost felt sorry for Derek.

'Beth, that's not a nice thing to say,' I gently cautioned her. 'Your father's told you he isn't able to make a decision yet about your birthday.' It wouldn't do Beth any good to grow up believing she could blackmail or manipulate adults into doing what she wanted.

'What Cathy says is right,' Derek replied quietly.

But Beth hadn't finished with him yet. 'I'm not wearing one of your pretty dresses,' she said defiantly. 'And I'm not wearing any make-up or nail varnish or my black tights or heels.'

I glanced over again. I was writing and listening at the same time. There was another pause before Derek said, 'That's all right, princess.' Which, given his previous enthusiasm for Beth's dresses, surprised Beth as much as it did me.

'But you like me to wear those things,' Beth said, clearly wrong-footed by her father's reaction, or lack of it. 'I'm not wearing them ever again. I might even throw them away.'

There was another pause before Derek said, 'Is there a reason, princess?'

'Yes! Because I'm not your princess any more. I'm a normal girl and normal girls don't wear make-up or black tights. My friends don't.'

'I see,' Derek said.

'My friend's mothers wouldn't let them wear that stuff,' Beth continued, her anger now rising. 'And if I had a mother, she wouldn't let me. Cathy doesn't let me wear your dresses or make-up. I wear things that are suitable for children. Cathy knows how I should dress.' While all this was true, I'd no idea where it had come from or what had provoked Beth's attack on her father, which was clearly designed to hurt him.

I waited, as did Beth, for her father's reply. 'I know you're angry with me,' he said, 'and I can understand why. You're right. You are only a little girl and I haven't been treating you like one. I'm trying to learn how to treat you like a child, but it's not easy and it's taking me time.'

The significance of her father's words weren't lost on Beth. 'Is that so I can come home?' she asked. My heart went out to her.

'Yes,' Derek said.

They were both silent again, then I heard Derek take a deep breath before he said shakily, 'I'd better go now, pet. Be good and remember to phone again next Friday, please.' They'd only been talking a short while.

Beth didn't reply. 'Say goodbye to your father,' I prompted her.

'Bye, Daddy,' she said in a small voice.

'Bye, love,' Derek said. 'Bye, Cathy.'

'Goodbye, Derek,' I said, going closer to the phone. 'We'll telephone again at the same time next week,' I confirmed.

'Thank you.'

As I went to push the speaker button to cut the call, Beth called out, 'I am your princess really, Daddy!'

Derek didn't reply. He'd hung up.

Beth looked at me anxiously. She hadn't got the replies from her father she'd been expecting. 'Why can't I be my daddy's little princess any more?' she asked, confused.

'I think it's because your daddy is having to learn new ways to behave and talk to you,' I said. 'Perhaps this is something you could ask Dr Weybridge when you see her next. I'm sure she can explain it better than I can.'

'Yes. I'll do that,' Beth said quickly, now eager to put the telephone call and all the issues it raised behind her.

She went off to play with Adrian and Paula. I appreciated just how confusing all this must be for Beth. I was struggling with having to put aside my negative feelings towards Derek and remain neutral during the assessment period.

I finished my notes and put them safely away in a drawer.

We ate at six and as John wasn't home I plated up his dinner and put it in the oven to keep warm. He arrived home just as we'd finished eating and, having said hello and hugged all the children, he ate his dinner on a tray in the living room. I thought he seemed a bit quieter than usual, but when I asked him if everything was all right, he said he was just tired and he'd have an early night.

The weather dramatically turned warm over the weekend, as it can in England. The temperature rose ten degrees centigrade to the mid-twenties, and the sun shone in a clear blue sky. John said he could do with relaxing over the weekend after a very busy week, so we spent most of it in the garden. I did some gardening, while John sat on a lounger and read the newspaper. The children didn't mind that John didn't feel up to playing lots of games – it was enough that he was there, as it was for me. By Sunday evening, when it was time for John to leave, he said he felt much better and that the rest had done him good.

Jessie telephoned on Monday and began by asking if the kids and I had had a good Easter, and then she asked how Beth's therapy was going.

'It seems to be going well,' I said. 'Although Beth doesn't say much and I certainly don't press her.'

'But she's happy to go? And isn't upset after?' Jessie asked.

'No. She's fine. She said she'd rather go than stay at school.'

Jessie laughed. 'And the phone contact? How is that going?'

'Very well. Just a minute and I'll fetch my notes,' I said.

I collected my notes and at the same time checked on Paula, who was crayoning at the table. Leaving the door open so I could hear her if she needed me, I returned to the living room where I'd taken the call. I sat on the sofa and, using my notes, gave Jessie a résumé of the phone contact since the last time we'd spoken, finishing with the most recent.

'That's very interesting,' Jessie said. 'It seems the therapy is having an effect on both of them. Can you photocopy your notes, please, and put a set in the post to me.'

'Yes, of course,' I said.

'Thanks. Derek's therapist, Dr Jones, would like you to attend this Friday's session at ten o'clock. It's at the hospital you take Beth to, only in a different wing: the Chancery Suite.' I wrote the name of the suite on my notepad.

'Will Derek be there too?' I asked.

'Yes. It's his therapy you're joining.'

'Oh, I see,' I said, feeling a bit dim, but I'd never done anything like this before. 'Thank you.'

That afternoon I took Paula to the mother and toddler group and then later – in the playground at the end of school – I asked Kay if she could look after Paula on Friday morning. She said she would be happy to and that she'd got a number of dental appointments coming up when she would be asking for my help. Kay didn't ask where I was going and assumed it was a meeting in connection with fostering, which it was in a way. The week was busy and time flew. But I'd be lying if I said I wasn't apprehensive about the therapy session I had to attend on Friday. Not knowing what to expect, I imagined all sorts of weird and wonderful scenarios, including Dr Jones discovering my innermost thoughts, feelings and phobias simply by looking at me. Also, I had reservations about just how much I could contribute to the session or how my contribution could possibly help Derek. I'd only met him once and then he'd hardly said a word, and any communication between us on the telephone was confined to hello and goodbye.

On Thursday evening my anxiety reached a new level, but for a different reason. John telephoned late in the evening, after the children had gone to bed, to say he would be travelling home on Saturday morning, not Friday evening. Normally this wouldn't have caused me a lot of angst as it had happened before, but this Saturday was the county swimming competition that Adrian had been practising so hard for. Although the competition didn't start until half past one, the competitors had to be there by 12.45 p.m. I was immediately worried that John wouldn't make it home in time.

'You know we have to leave the house at twelve-fifteen,' I said.

'Yes, I know. I'll be there in plenty of time.' Which I had to accept.

But I remained concerned, and the following morning when I told Adrian, despite reassuring him that his father would leave his hotel very early on Saturday morning, he was anxious too.

'Supposing there's a lot of traffic, or an accident on the motorway?' Adrian said, remembering that these had delayed John on previous journeys home. 'What then?'

'Please don't worry. If necessary, we'll meet your dad at the swimming pool. We won't be late, I promise, and he won't miss it.'

I felt it was a pity that Adrian was now having to worry about his father arriving on time when he should have been concentrating on, and looking forward to, the competition.

Kay had suggested that I leave Paula with her in the playground on Friday morning, rather than return home for what would only be fifteen minutes and then drop her off at her house later. As a result, I arrived at the hospital early and had time to pick up a coffee from the vending machine in the foyer. I stood outside to drink it before returning to the building. The main hospital building was old and very different from the newer extension in which the Butterfly Wing was situated. Many of the wards were named after historic places or figures – Trafalgar Ward, Henry VIII Ward, Waterloo Ward, Shakespeare Ward. They were clearly signposted and I found the Chancery Suite without a problem. I went through the double swing doors and into a small reception area where a lady sat behind a desk.

'Cathy Glass,' I said. 'I'm here to see Dr Jones at ten o'clock.'

'Take a seat over there, please,' she said, pointing to an open-plan waiting area. 'Dr Jones will be with you shortly.'

I thanked her and went over and sat down in one of the steel-framed chairs. I was alone in the waiting area and with five minutes until the appointment time I wondered if Derek would arrive and sit in the waiting area, which might be embarrassing. I'd no idea what we would find to talk about. The waiting area was stark and poorly decorated compared to the Butterfly Wing. Derek didn't appear, but at exactly ten o'clock Dr Jones did, suddenly, from around the corner.

'Good morning, Cathy,' he said. 'Thank you so much for coming.' He shook my hand. 'We're in here,' he said, heading off in the direction from which he'd come.

I followed him around the corner and into a small room. Derek was already there, seated in one of three chairs arranged in a small circle in the middle of the room. He stood as I entered and offered his hand for shaking. He appeared nervous and I felt his hand tremble in mine.

'Thank you for joining us,' Dr Jones said as we sat down.

'Yes, thank you,' Derek echoed. I threw him a small smile. He was dressed smartly in navy trousers and an open-neck shirt. His forehead glistened slightly, but the room was very warm.

Dr Jones retrieved his notepad and pen from under his chair and placed them on his lap. 'As you may know,' he said, looking at me, 'Derek has been seeing me for some weeks now, and Marianne, Derek's partner, has being joining us for some sessions. It is intended that Derek and I will meet up with Dr Weybridge and Beth at some point. When you and I met before, when Jessie and Laura were present, I explained the framework in which I would be working with Derek – that of emotional incest. Derek and I have been addressing a number of issues in connection with this and we've now reached the stage where we feel some input from you would be useful.'

I nodded, although I still had little idea how I could be useful.

Dr Jones continued. 'Recently, Derek and I have been looking at the changes he needs to make in the way he relates to Beth, and the expectations he has of her. I think a good place to start now would be with the way Derek has been dressing Beth, as he tells me this came up in their telephone conversation last Friday.'

'Yes, I'm sorry,' I said, glancing at Derek. 'It was wrong of Beth to speak to you like that.'

'She was angry with me,' Derek said, justifying Beth's comments.

'That telephone call raises some interesting points,' Dr Jones said. 'But I'd like to stay with the issue of how Derek dresses Beth for now. Cathy, could you give us your views, please?'

I shifted in my chair. 'Beth arrived with a lot of clothes,' I began. 'Far more than she would ever need. But most of them were not practical or appropriate for a girl of her age. I've bought her some new outfits and she knows she wears those when we go out. She now keeps most of the clothes Derek bought her for dressing up in at home.' I'd no idea if I was on the right track, and I paused and looked at Dr Jones.

'When you say "not appropriate", what exactly do you mean?' Dr Jones asked, making a note.

'They're not what a girl of seven should be wearing. They're what I would call sexy, tarty. And the make-up doesn't help either. I don't let her wear make-up.'

'And Beth has accepted your boundaries?' Dr Jones asked.

'Yes,' I said.

There was a small silence and then Dr Jones said: 'Derek has struggled to put boundaries in place. As a result, there has been a lot of confusion in his role and relationship with his daughter. I explained some of this before in our previous meeting.'

I nodded.

'Marianne told me what I was doing wrong a long while ago,' Derek now said, rubbing his fingers nervously across his forehead. 'But I didn't listen. I thought Marianne was jealous because Beth and I were very close, and also because she didn't have a child of her own. Marianne told me Beth's clothes and make-up weren't right, and that I shouldn't keep giving in to her, or cuddling and kissing her the way I did, or having her in my bed. But I needed Beth so much. I didn't want her leaving me like her mother did. I can see now I was wrong, but I never meant to hurt her.'

Derek stopped and Dr Jones gave him a few moments to recover. I wasn't sure what I should be feeling about Derek's confession. Then Dr Jones looked at me and said, 'I believe you had to set boundaries in the way Beth acted towards your husband?'

'Yes, that's right,' I said. 'Beth was over-familiar with him. At the start it was difficult for me to work out exactly what was making me feel so uncomfortable, and my husband, John, didn't think anything was wrong. But I had the feeling that the way Beth behaved towards John – touching him and stroking him and almost flirting with him – wasn't right.'

'And you were able to put new boundaries in place, which Beth accepted?'

'Yes. She did. I felt I needed to do something to keep everyone safe. For example, John stopped going into Beth's bedroom to say goodnight, but did so downstairs.'

Derek was now clearly itching to say something and Dr Jones turned to him. 'Yes, Derek? Go ahead.'

'I'm pleased Cathy is looking after Beth so well,' Derek blurted, agitated. 'But it makes me feel so inadequate.'

'I'm sorry,' I said. 'That certainly wasn't my intention.'

'Of course it wasn't,' Dr Jones said, then to Derek: 'Would you like to expand on your comment?'

Derek looked at me and I met his gaze, uncomfortable though it was. I felt as though I was in a group therapy session as I'd seen in plays on the television.

'Please don't think I'm blaming you, Cathy,' he began, 'but when Beth tells me about all the fun things she does with you and your family, I feel awful, completely inadequate.'

'What sort of things?' Dr Jones asked Derek.

'The lovely meals Cathy makes, the games she organizes and the family outings she takes all the children on. I feel like I've done nothing for Beth, and she's my daughter. You have a lovely family,' he said, now addressing me, 'with a son and daughter and grandparents. I can't offer Beth anything like that. It's just her and me. I love her, but I've failed her miserably. She must hate me.' I could see tears glistening in his eyes.

Chapter Twenty-Four
A New Friend

The room was silent for a moment as Dr Jones wrote.

'Beth doesn't hate you,' I said gently to Derek.

'She has every right to,' Derek said, struggling to regain his composure.

I didn't reply.

Dr Jones gave Derek a few moments to recover and then looked at me. 'It's been a very valuable experience for Beth, living with you, for a number of reasons. She's been able to see what it's like living in another family – a two-parent family. It's set her thinking about her own family and she's made some comparisons. I understand Beth mentioned her mother during the telephone conversation on Friday?'

'Yes, she did,' I said. 'But it wasn't in a positive way. What she said was designed to hurt her father and make him feel bad about the way he's allowed her to dress.'

'It's significant, though,' Dr Jones said, glancing at Derek. 'Beth has never been allowed to mention her mother at home. Staying with you has allowed her to do that – by telephone.'

I didn't fully appreciate the significance of Dr Jones's comment, but Derek appeared to. 'I know I've got to start talking to Beth about her mother,' he said. 'And show her some photographs.'

'Has Beth ever seen a photograph of her mother?' I asked.

Derek shook his head. 'No. Never.'

'Has Beth ever talked to you about her mother?' Dr Jones now asked me.

I thought for a moment. 'Not as far as I can remember. I don't think she's ever mentioned her.'

Dr Jones nodded and made a note. 'Children need to grow up with a realistic image of their parents,' he said, addressing us both. 'If an absent parent is demonized by the parent left behind, or their existence ignored, the child can create all sorts of fanciful notions about the missing parent. If they believe they are bad, it is only a small step for the child to believe they are bad too, or that they were responsible for the parent leaving. It's a huge burden for the child to carry, and very unhealthy.'

'I know I need to talk to Beth about why her mother left,' Derek said, revisiting something he'd previously discussed with Dr Jones. 'I will, if I'm given the chance.'

Dr Jones gave a small nod. 'Beth's negative view of her mother also had an impact on her relationship with Marianne,' he said, again looking at me. 'It was one of the reasons Beth couldn't form an attachment to Marianne; that, and viewing her as a rival. Living with you has shown Beth what a mother can be – a role she refused to let Marianne have.' Again, I felt this was something Derek and Dr Jones had covered in a previous therapy session, for Derek nodded knowledgeably.

'Beth has led quite an isolated life,' I now felt confident enough to say. 'By her age, children often have close friends who they see outside of school. They spend time in their friends' homes, play outside or have their friends over. Beth would love to do this.'

Dr Jones looked to Derek for his response.

'I know, and it's something I need to address,' he said.

'Derek,' I said tentatively. 'How would you feel if I invited a friend of Beth's to my house to play and maybe stay for some tea?'

I saw him tense. 'Would Beth be invited back to that child's house?' he asked, as though this was a worry for him.

'Possibly, although of course she doesn't have to go.'

Dr Jones again looked to Derek for his reply.

Derek rubbed his hand over his forehead. 'I know I've been over-protective, but I wanted to keep Beth safe. I also now realize I wanted to keep her just for me.' He paused, then sat upright in his chair. 'Yes,' he said decisively. 'Please invite a friend for Beth, and if she's invited back she can go. As long as it's not Jenni,' he added. 'Her mother hates me.'

'It won't be her,' I said with a small smile.

Dr Jones looked at me questioningly. 'Jenni's mother can be rather outspoken and prejudiced about some things,' I said. 'Including a father bringing up his daughter alone.' I decided there was no point in mentioning all the other issues Jenni's mother had with Derek, like his mental health, as it wouldn't have been helpful. 'I don't think Beth is particularly friendly with Jenni any more,' I added, for Derek's benefit.

'That's a relief,' he said. At that moment I felt the atmosphere in the room lift slightly, as though Derek was at last beginning to trust me and view me as an ally, rather than a threat to his parenting.

The session continued with Dr Jones returning to the importance of setting boundaries for children, and also establishing routines. He asked me for my opinion and to give some practical examples of how this could be achieved, which I assumed was for Derek's benefit. At eleven o'clock Dr Jones drew the session to a close and thanked me very much for my input. 'We may ask you to join us again,' he said.

A New Friend

'Yes, of course.'

I said goodbye to Derek, and Dr Jones showed me to the door. I left the hospital with my thoughts racing over all the issues we'd talked about. Some of my impressions of Derek had been confirmed during the therapy session; he was needy, isolated and desperate to hold on to Beth. But he'd also come across as wanting to protect her. However, in so doing he'd fulfilled his own needs at the expense of hers. Derek had appeared sincere in his commitment to change, but whether that made him any less guilty or increased his chances of having Beth returned to him I'd no idea. What complicated and troubled lives some people lead, I thought as I drove home, and sometimes through no fault of their own. Again I was very grateful for the uncomplicated and rewarding life I had, with two loving parents, a devoted husband and two adorable children.

Kay offered me a cup of coffee when I arrived to collect Paula, which I readily accepted. I stayed for about half an hour and then I returned home and made Paula and myself some lunch. In the afternoon we went to the mother and toddler group, and from there we went straight to school to collect Adrian and Beth. Both children came out looking forward to the weekend, and also the county swimming competition the following day. Many of the other parents had bought tickets so that they and their children could see the event and support the school team.

'I hope our school wins at least one trophy,' Adrian said.

'They will with you swimming,' Beth said, which was kind of her.

Beth's telephone contact that evening was the best so far. Perhaps because Derek had met me and aired some of the issues that had been bothering him, or had simply been reassured by meeting me, I didn't know. He sounded far more relaxed and, I thought, more self-assured when he talked to Beth. Even when Beth asked him if Marianne was still there, he replied confidently that she was, and that she was helping him, so there was no need for Beth to worry.

'But I should be there looking after you,' Beth said, her face setting.

'No, you shouldn't,' Derek said. 'You should be playing. That's what children do. Has Cathy asked that friend back to tea yet?'

I hadn't – with all that had been going through my thoughts since I'd left the hospital it had slipped to the back of my mind. 'I haven't yet, Derek,' I said, loud enough for him to hear over the speakerphone. 'But I will soon.'

Beth looked at me incredulously, and then disbelief set in. 'Can I really have a friend to tea?' she asked her father.

'Yes. If Cathy says it's all right,' Derek said.

Beth looked at me again and I nodded.

'Thanks, Dad!' she cried.

'You're welcome, precious,' Derek said, and I could hear the emotion in his voice.

Beth wound up their conversation pretty quickly after that, as she was eager to start making the arrangements to invite a friend home, nearly forgetting to say goodbye to her father, she was so excited. And who could blame her? It wasn't just that Beth's father had finally agreed to her inviting a friend home to tea – exciting for children anyway – but that in so doing Derek had taken a big step towards normalizing Beth's childhood, and Beth knew that.

'I'll be just like all my friends!' she declared. She threw her arms around me and gave me the biggest hug ever.

'So all you have to do now is to decide which friend to ask,' I said.

A New Friend

Did I say 'all you have to do'? This turned out to be rather a lengthy business, and Beth deliberated most of the evening, deciding on one friend and then a few minutes later changing her mind and deciding on someone else. I think she named most of her class at some point – girls and boys – even suggesting Jenni, although she changed her mind. Finally, at bedtime, Beth announced, 'Cathy, I know who I'm going to ask to tea, and I won't change my mind this time.'

'Yes?' I asked, a little wearily.

'April. I'd like April to come to tea.'

'Oh. That's fine,' I said, slightly surprised. Beth had mentioned April in the past, but they didn't seem especially close friends. April was a sweet child whose parents were from Japan. I understood they'd settled here after arriving on a work contract. I didn't know the family – I was on nodding terms with April's mother, but I'd never actually spoken to her. 'Is there any particular reason for choosing April?' I asked as Beth climbed into bed.

'April's nice,' she said. 'She's always nice to everyone. But no one invites her to play or to their birthday parties. I think it's because she's different. She eats different food.'

'No worries,' I said. 'I'll see April's mother at school on Monday and we'll arrange a date. I'll also ask her what April likes to eat. It's not a problem.'

Beth was so excited that night that she needed Mr Sleep Bear to get her off to sleep. 'Thanks, Cathy,' she said as I finally kissed her goodnight and came out of her room. 'Thanks for making my dreams come true.'

My eyes immediately filled. This was just a child coming to play and have some tea – something my own children had done since they were toddlers – but it meant so much to Beth. 'You're very welcome,' I said. 'Sweet dreams.' And I drew her door to.

When I went into Adrian's room I found him sitting up in bed and looking worried. 'What's the matter?' I asked, perching on his bed.

'Suppose I'm rubbish at swimming tomorrow?' he said, fretfully. 'Suppose I come last and let the school down?'

'I'm sure you won't come last,' I said. 'But someone has to. And if it is you, you'll have done your best. Remember, it's the fun of being involved in the competition that counts, not the winning.'

He gave a small nod, but didn't look any less worried. 'Suppose Dad doesn't arrive on time?' he now asked.

I could see that Adrian – over-tired – was starting to worry about everything.

'He will,' I said. 'Now stop worrying and go off to sleep. Everything will be all right in the morning.'

He finally snuggled down, and I read to him until he dropped off to sleep.

The following morning we were all up and dressed earlier than usual for a Saturday – in plenty of time for what had become known as Adrian's Big Day. I cooked breakfast and then suggested to the children that they went into the garden to play as it was warm and sunny, but that they should try not to get messy as we would be going out in a couple of hours. I got the bikes, tricycles, bats and balls out of the shed, but I left the sand pit covered. They played in the garden while I cleared up the breakfast things, but Adrian kept popping in to see if his father had arrived yet.

'I'll tell you when he's here,' I said. 'I'm sure he won't be long.'

However, I must admit I was relieved when at 11.15 – an hour before we needed to leave – I heard the front door open and John call, 'I'm home! Where is everyone?'

I went into the hall and hugged him. 'The children are in the garden,' I said. 'Coffee?'

'Yes, please.'

As I filled the kettle John went into the garden. I glanced out of the kitchen window and saw Adrian spot him first. 'You're here! Daddy's here!' he shouted. He ran up the garden path and into his arms.

'Of course I'm here,' John said. 'You surely didn't think your dad would let you down?'

'No, of course not!' Adrian said, and neither had I.

I made John coffee and then the egg on toast he wanted. At 12.15 we all piled into his car and headed for the county swimming baths where the competition was to be held. The car park was already filling with parents from schools all over the county bringing their children to compete. I took Adrian into reception, where his swimming teacher signed him in and other members of the team were waiting. I wished them luck and then returned outside, as spectators weren't allowed in for another half an hour. The county baths were surrounded by shrubs and occasionally mown grass. John and I sat on the lawn and chatted while the girls ran around picking daisies and dandelions, and looking for four-leafed clovers. John talked about his work and I told him about my week, including the therapy session I'd attended with Derek and Dr Jones. None of what we said was earth-shattering news, just the stuff that makes up our daily lives and that partners like to share with each other.

Presently the doors to the baths opened and, brushing off the grass, we joined the queue filing in. Inside the baths the air was hot and humid. We sat, third row back, in the tiered seating around the pool. The noise level grew as the seats filled and spectators chatted excitedly until it was time for the competition to start. The organizer blew his whistle and asked for quiet. The girls sat forward in their seats, looking for Adrian, and I explained he would be waiting with his team somewhere out of sight until it was time for his races. The organizer introduced the Major, who was guest of honour, and passed the microphone to him. He welcomed us and thanked us all for coming and then declared the competition should begin. The younger children's races were first – three- and four-year-olds. They were so cute as they walked in and appeared very tiny as they swam their widths in the shallow end. Adrian's first heat was the 50-metre freestyle, and that came after about twenty minutes. We cheered when he and his competitors walked in, as did the rest of the audience. The swimmers took up their positions along the edge of the pool, and the organizer called for silence. He blew his whistle and the swimmers dived into the water and swam for all they were worth. We shouted encouragement and cheered at the tops of our voices. They completed one length, turned and swam back again to finish the race. Adrian came a respectable third and we all clapped and cheered again as he climbed out of the water and then disappeared into the waiting area. I didn't know if Adrian had seen us; there were so many people in the audience, we must have appeared a sea of faces from the pool.

Adrian swam again in the mixed-stroke relay and his team came second, which was a fantastic achievement for the school. Other heats followed, finishing with the older children – fourteen- to sixteen-year-olds – in a 200-metre freestyle. At the end of the competition the Major gave a congratulatory speech and then presented the trophies, medals and ribbons. Our school won a trophy and six medals, one of which went to Adrian for coming third. Each child participating was given a royal-blue ribbon to commemorate the day, so no child left empty-handed.

We met up with Adrian outside. 'Well done,' I said, giving him a big kiss. For once he didn't rub it off.

'Well done, son,' John said, clearly proud and ruffling his hair.

Adrian beamed as he showed us his medal and ribbon. Then he said he was starving hungry and rubbed his growling stomach. 'Burger and chips, please, Mum,' he said.

On the way home we stopped off at a fast-food restaurant, and that night Adrian didn't have any problem going to sleep – he was exhausted and also very happy with his achievement. John had to leave again on Sunday evening, but I was pleased he'd made it home in good time for Adrian's swimming competition and consoled myself that he wouldn't be working away forever. 'No more than a year,' John said.

On Monday morning – from when I woke Beth, to leaving the house for school – she reminded me every five minutes that I needed to ask April's mother if April could come to tea. I could see that Adrian and Paula didn't know what to make of Beth's continual fussing, so I took them aside, and out of earshot of Beth, I explained that she was very excited because she'd never had a friend home before.

'What, never?' Adrian asked, amazed.

'No, never,' I said.

'Why?' Paula asked.

'Because her daddy was a bit over-protective,' I said. 'He's getting better now.'

'Why was he over-a-detective?' Paula asked, mispronouncing the word.

'Over-protective!' Adrian shouted in her ear.

'Don't shout,' Paula said, rubbing her ear. 'Why was he over-protective?'

'Because he thought he was doing the right thing,' I said.

'But he wasn't,' Adrian added.

'Exactly.'

As we entered the playground, Adrian ran off to join his friends while Beth scanned the children looking for April. 'There she is!' she cried, grabbing my arm and then hauling me across the playground to where April was standing quietly with her mother.

'Hello,' I said, smiling at April's mother. 'I'm Cathy. Beth was wondering if April would like to come and play after school one day, and maybe stay for some tea?'

April's mother looked a bit startled at suddenly being descended on, while Beth and April were jumping up and down and shouting, 'Yes! Yes!'

'I'm Beth's foster carer,' I said, feeling I should explain. 'My son Adrian goes to this school and this is my daughter, Paula.'

'Yes, I've seen you in the playground. I'm Frances,' she said, a little more relaxed. 'Hello, Paula, how are you?'

'I'm fine,' Paula said shyly, and buried her head in my skirt.

'I'm sure April would like to come,' Frances said. Turning to April she asked, 'Would you like to go to Cathy's house to play with Beth?'

'Yes, please,' April said politely. Both girls began bouncing up and down again, clapping their hands in excitement.

'Wednesday would suit us,' I said to Frances. 'Is that any good for you?'

'Yes, April's free on Wednesday. Her piano lessons are on Tuesday and Thursday.'

'I could collect April at the end of school and then bring her home to you after tea, at about six o'clock?'

'Yes, that would be all right. Thank you.'

A New Friend

I found a piece of paper and a pen in my handbag, wrote down my contact details and passed the paper to Frances. Then I wrote down her address and telephone number on another piece of paper and tucked it into my purse.

'What does April like to eat?' I now asked, hoping it was something I could master.

'Oh, she's a good eater,' Frances said. 'She enjoys most things.'

'What's her favourite?' I asked.

'Fish fingers and chips,' Frances said, with a laugh.

'Fish fingers and chips it is, then,' I said, relieved.

'Yippee!' the girls cried.

The klaxon sounded and before Frances left she thanked me for inviting April, adding, 'And perhaps Beth would like to come to tea at our house the following week?'

'Thank you. I know she will,' I said.

Chapter Twenty-Five
The Decision

The word excitement did not do justice to the fervour that built up in our house as Wednesday approached. Beth might have been hosting a royal garden party at Buckingham Palace for the planning and anticipation that went into April coming to tea. She thoroughly tidied her already neat bedroom, then the living room, the toy cupboard and then her bedroom again. After that she began fussing about the meal, which couldn't have been simpler.

'Cathy, have you got enough fish fingers for us all?' she asked for a second time.

'Yes,' I said, again.

'Are you sure?'

I showed her the large packet of fish fingers in the freezer.

'Are the chips the thin, crispy ones we like?' she asked.

'Yes,' I said, and I opened the freezer door again and showed her the bag of chips.

'Can we have baked beans with the fish fingers, not peas like you usually do with fish?'

I hadn't realized I'd been so set in my ways. 'Yes, of course you can have baked beans,' I said. I opened the cupboard door to show Beth that we had plenty of cans of baked beans.

Then, a short while later, Beth asked, 'Cathy, you know you said you're going to make a trifle for dessert ...'

'Yes.'

'Well, what if April doesn't like trifle?'

'Then she can have something else,' I said. 'Please don't worry, Beth. I've had children to tea before. I promise you, everything will be fine.'

But this was such a big occasion for Beth, she wanted everything to be perfect. And it was.

April was a very polite and kind child and she loved the meal, including the trifle. She and Beth played nicely together, sometimes downstairs with Paula and sometimes in Beth's bedroom, as girls of their age do. Adrian joined us for dinner but otherwise kept out of their way, feeling that a 'house full of girls' was a bit much. But, of course, the two hours after school were nowhere near long enough, and when it was time for April to go Beth asked me if she could stay longer. I reminded her that April's mother was expecting her soon after six o'clock, but added to April she could come again another day if she wished, which helped. I took April home in the car and Frances thanked me, and then repeated her offer for Beth to go to tea at their home the following week, so we made a definite arrangement.

After this Beth and April became good friends and, interestingly, when the news got out at school that they were friends and had been to each other's homes for tea, barriers were broken down and other children in the class wanted to be friends with April too. In reaching out the hand of friendship, Beth had unwittingly removed the wariness that had made others cautious of a different culture.

Beth's therapy arrangements continued unchanged for the next two weeks, and then one Monday afternoon in the middle of

May Jessie telephoned to say that the next two therapy sessions would be group therapy. Dr Jones with Derek and Marianne would join Dr Weybridge and Beth in the Butterfly Wing. Jessie said she wanted to be present so she could include her observations in her final report, and would collect Beth from school and return her home after the session. I assumed, therefore, that we were getting close to the time when a decision would be made on where Beth would live permanently. This new arrangement was to start the following day, and as Jessie wouldn't have a chance to visit beforehand and tell Beth, she asked me to.

That evening after dinner I explained to Beth what was happening. She was delighted that she would be seeing her father again after so long, but then added rather grumpily, 'Why does she have to be there?'

'Who? Jessie?' I asked.

'No. Marianne.'

'Because Jessie and the doctors think it will be helpful,' I said.

'It's not helpful,' Beth grumbled.

Clearly Beth didn't know if it would be helpful or not. It was just the mention of Marianne that provoked the negative reaction, as it always had.

'I'm sure Jessie and the doctors know what they are doing,' I said. 'So try to keep an open mind.'

On Tuesday morning, when I took Beth and Adrian to school, I went in and told the receptionist that Beth's social worker would be collecting Beth that afternoon, and also on Thursday. She thanked me, made a note and said she would tell Miss Willow. Paula and I returned home and then, with the afternoon suddenly free (we didn't have to take Beth to therapy) and with the weather good, I took Paula to the park. From there we went to collect Adrian from school, and then the three of us went home. It felt strange not having Beth with us, as though we weren't a complete family, and I kept looking round thinking one of the children was missing.

When Jessie brought Beth home that afternoon, about half an hour after we arrived home, she said she couldn't come in but that the session had 'gone well'. However, for the rest of the afternoon Beth was very quiet, and although she joined Adrian and Paula in the living room where they were watching television, she didn't say much. Usually Beth had a lot to say after school and Adrian sometimes told her to shush while they were watching television. She was quiet during dinner too, although she ate well. After the meal, when Paula and Adrian had left the table, I asked Beth if everything was all right.

'Yes,' she said. But that was all.

She had homework to do, which she needed some help with, but as I sat beside her she seemed preoccupied and kept making silly mistakes. I asked her if there was anything bothering her that she might like to talk about.

'No,' she said.

I assumed she was thinking about the therapy session. Seeing her father again after such a long time, and also Marianne, must have given her a lot to think about. But as a foster carer (and parent) I have to respect the fact that sometimes a child doesn't want to talk and share their thoughts and feelings, and they shouldn't be pressed to do so. Beth wasn't unhappy or sitting alone in her bedroom, she was just quiet and preoccupied, so I said, 'You know you can talk to me whenever you want.'

'Yes,' Beth said. So I left it at that.

By the following morning Beth had recovered and was her usual chirpy self. She was a resilient child, as many who've led difficult lives are, and tended to bounce back. Over breakfast she and Adrian talked about how long it was until the next school holiday. Wednesday continued, uneventful, and on Thursday morning I reminded Beth that Jessie would be collecting her from school again that afternoon and taking her to therapy as she had done on Tuesday.

'Daddy and Marianne will be there,' she said reflectively and went quiet.

I knew there was a lot going on for Beth, not all of which she wanted to share, so I asked, 'Is everything OK?'

'Yes,' she said, but again that was all.

When Jessie brought Beth home later that afternoon she didn't come in but said this was the last of the therapy sessions and that she'd telephone me the following day to explain what was happening. Again, Beth was very quiet after her return, but then, as I was washing up the dinner plates, she came to find me.

'Cathy, do you like Marianne?' she asked.

I stopped what I was doing to look at her, aware I needed to choose my words carefully. 'I've only met her once,' I said honestly, 'but she seems a nice person to me.'

'Do you think my daddy needs her?' Beth asked, watching carefully for my reaction.

I guessed Beth's questions had been sparked by something that had been said in therapy, but, not knowing what, again I was careful in my reply. 'I think Marianne has been helping your daddy a lot,' I said. 'And he's happy to have her help.'

Beth nodded and then asked, 'Do you think Marianne likes me as much as she likes my daddy?'

'Yes. I think she does,' I said.

Satisfied, Beth went off to play, and I was relieved. While I'm always happy to answer a child's questions if I can, without knowing what was behind Beth's questions I was concerned I might inadvertently say something that wasn't helpful or ran counter to the therapy. From Beth's questions, it seemed to me she was re-evaluating her view of Marianne.

As it turned out, I wasn't wrong.

Jessie telephoned the following morning and began by asking how Beth had been after the two group therapy sessions. I told her she'd been quiet at home on both occasions, and then I told her about the questions she'd asked about Marianne.

'Mmm,' Jessie said thoughtfully. 'Some of the work covered in the sessions has been to help Beth and Marianne form a relationship. Dr Weybridge, Dr Jones and myself are in the process of writing our final reports. The assessment has been lengthy, because it was important we got it right this time. But we are now of the opinion that Beth can be successfully rehabilitated home to live with her father and Marianne.'

'Oh, I see,' I said.

'Yes, so it's reassuring that Beth is starting to adjust her perception of Marianne, which is essential if this is to work. While Derek has made huge progress, it is unlikely we would be making the decision to return Beth home without Marianne being there.'

'I see,' I said again. 'Does Beth know she's going home? She hasn't mentioned it here.'

'No. I haven't told her yet. Once we've had the planning meeting I'll see her and explain what's going to happen. I'm allowing a month for Beth to be rehabilitated home, but I shall be monitoring the situation carefully. I'll extend the time if necessary. We'll go at Beth's pace. It's important she feels comfortable. Derek has asked Marianne to marry him, but don't say anything to Beth. Her father will tell her when the time is right. But first things first. I know it's short notice, but can you come to a planning meeting tomorrow morning, here at the council offices?'

'As long as I can get a sitter for my daughter,' I said. 'What time?'

'Ten o'clock. I don't know which room yet, so when you arrive, ask at reception. Derek and Marianne will be attending, possibly my manager, and me of course. And bring your diary.'

'I will,' I said.

'See you tomorrow at ten,' Jessie said.

As soon as Jessie had hung up, I telephoned Kay. Full of apologies for the short notice, I explained I'd been called to an urgent meeting the following morning.

'No problem,' she said, before I'd even finished. 'But you'd better warn Paula that we shall be going shopping. My cupboards are bare.'

'She won't mind if Vicky is there,' I said.

'Tell her we'll have a drink and a sticky bun at the café when we've finished. That should help.'

'Thank you so much,' I said gratefully. 'I owe you big time.'

'No you don't,' Kay said. 'You've helped me out plenty of times.'

Nevertheless, I bought Kay a box of her favourite chocolates, which I gave her the following morning when we met in the playground.

'You shouldn't have,' she said. 'But I'm glad you did.'

Sometimes it's difficult for foster carers to accept the decisions made by the social services, usually because we don't have access to all the information that they do. I'd be lying if I said I had no reservations about the decision that had been made for Beth to return to live with her father, but then I guessed Jessie did too, for her comments about Marianne were very telling: *While Derek has made huge progress, it is unlikely we would be making the decision to return Beth home without Marianne being there.* So

The Decision

Marianne was critical to Beth going home, which was why she'd been in the group therapy with Beth. I wouldn't be shown the reports that Jessie and the doctors had written, so it was unlikely I'd ever know the extent of Derek's inappropriate physical contact with Beth, although clearly it hadn't been the worst-case scenario, for there'd been no police prosecution and Beth was returning home. She wouldn't have been, even with Marianne there, if the emotional incest had led to sexual incest. I had to accept that Jessie, Dr Jones and Dr Weybridge, having seen and discussed all the evidence, and having worked with Derek and Marianne, were satisfied that Beth was in no danger and it was in her best interest to return home to live with her father and Marianne.

I dressed smartly for the meeting, choosing a navy skirt and jacket, and as I entered the meeting room I was pleased I had. Marianne and Derek, the only ones present so far, were looking very smart too: Marianne in a skirt and jacket and Derek in a suit and tie. They were seated at a small rectangular table in the centre of the room and both looked up and smiled as I entered.

'Jessie has been called away,' Marianne said. 'She said to tell you she shouldn't be long.'

'Thank you,' I said.

I sat in one of the two empty chairs on the opposite side of the table to Marianne and Derek. It was a different room to the one I'd been in for the previous meetings; this room was much larger, and being seated at the small table in the centre of the large room gave the feeling of being exiled on a small island. I slipped off my jacket and hung it on the back of my chair and then took my diary from my bag and set it on the table in front of me. There was an uncomfortable silence.

'How is Beth doing?' Marianne asked after a moment.

I looked up. 'She seems to be doing very well,' I said, addressing them both.

'It was nice of you to invite her friend to tea,' Marianne said. 'Jessie told us how much she enjoyed it.'

'Yes, they had a great time, and also when Beth went to April's for tea.'

'Thank you for arranging that,' Derek said, a little stiffly.

There was another awkward silence and then Marianne suddenly said, 'I owe you an apology.'

'Oh?' I met her gaze.

'The last time we spoke on the telephone I was rather rude to you and hung up without saying goodbye.'

'Don't worry,' I said, with a reassuring smile. 'It was a fraught time for us all. I'm pleased everything is sorted out now. I expect you're both very excited and looking forward to Beth's homecoming.'

'I'm also very nervous,' Marianne admitted, her expression serious. 'I so want to be a good stepmother, but I've still got bad memories of the last time I tried. The therapy has helped. I can see what went wrong before, so I won't make the same mistakes. But my only experience of children is my niece and nephew, and I only see them a couple of times a year. I've signed up for some parenting classes that Jessie recommended, but I'd also appreciate any help and advice you can give me.'

'I'd be pleased to help in any way I can,' I said. 'Beth's a good kid, but she will need some boundaries, as all children do.'

'Yes, Dr Jones is very keen on boundaries and routine,' Marianne said, glancing at Derek. Derek nodded but didn't say anything. I was forming the impression that Marianne would be leading the parenting of Beth.

The door opened and Jessie came in, cradling a large folder and a desk diary. 'Sorry I'm late,' she said, slightly out of breath.

'We had an emergency. My manager is dealing with it now.' She sat in the chair next to me and with a little sigh set her folder and diary on the table in front of her. 'So, how are we all?' she asked brightly, looking across the table at Marianne and Derek.

'Nervous,' Marianne admitted. Derek nodded in agreement.

'And how's Beth?' Jessie asked, turning to me.

'All right. Not saying very much, but doing a lot of thinking,' I said with a smile.

'There's a lot to think about,' Jessie agreed. Marianne and Derek nodded. I thought, of the two, Derek appeared the more nervous.

'OK. Now, to the reason we're here today,' Jessie said. 'To plan Beth's move home. Have you brought your diaries with you?'

I opened mine as Marianne took hers from her handbag and positioned it on the table between her and Derek, together with a pen.

'Because this is a planned move,' Jessie began, addressing us all, 'and not an emergency, we have the time to do it properly, in stages, and it's important we do. As you all know, I'm allowing a month to complete Beth's move home, but this can be extended if necessary. I'll be monitoring progress as we go and asking you all for regular feedback. Before we draw up the timetable for the move, does anyone have any questions?'

I shook my head.

'I'm sure I should be asking lots of questions,' Marianne said, with a small, nervous laugh, 'but I can't think of a single thing.'

'Stop me if you think of anything,' Jessie said. 'We all need to feel comfortable with the pace of this.' Marianne nodded. 'So,' Jessie continued looking at her diary, 'I need to start Beth's rehab home by visiting her, when I'll explain the reason for our decision, and outline the timetable of the move to her. Although she'll obviously need reminders as we go.' Jessie glanced at me.

'Yes, of course,' I said.

'I'd like to visit Beth on Monday after school,' Jessie said to me, then, glancing across the table to Marianne and Derek: 'This visit doesn't affect you two.'

'Monday is fine with me,' I said, making a note in my diary.

'Four o'clock,' Jessie said. 'I'm allowing a couple of hours. It's important Beth understands what is happening. Now, to Tuesday,' Jessie continued, looking around the table. 'Marianne and Derek will visit Beth at Cathy's house. I'm scheduling their visit in the early evening to avoid Marianne having to take more time off work. So what time can the two of you get to Cathy's on Tuesday?' Jessie now asked Marianne and Derek.

Marianne turned to Derek. 'If you catch the bus to my office and we go to Cathy's from there it will be quicker than me coming home first.'

'Yes, I can do that,' Derek said.

'Good,' Jessie said. 'So what time would you arrive at Cathy's?'

'We can be there for five-thirty,' Marianne said decisively.

We all noted this.

'This first visit will be for an hour,' Jessie continued. 'And it's important Beth sees the three of you getting along and working together. Keep it casual and relaxed. I suggest that over a cup of tea you chat and play some games with Beth.'

'Beth may want to show you her bedroom,' I said to Marianne and Derek. 'She's proud of it, as many girls of her age are.' I'd been involved in rehabilitating a child home before, so I had expectations of what was involved.

'That's fine if she does,' Jessie said. 'And you can go in the garden with her if it's a nice day, but you're not taking her out on that day,' Jessie said, now addressing Derek and Marianne. 'Beth can be very insistent and she won't necessarily appreciate the reasons why these visits are structured. The timetable gives everyone involved time to adjust to all the changes, so it's important to keep to it. Understood?'

'Yes,' Marianne said. Derek nodded.

'I'll telephone you all on Wednesday to see how the visit went,' Jessie said. 'Then on Wednesday evening Marianne and Derek will telephone Beth.' I made a note of this in my diary, as did Marianne. 'Let's set it for six o'clock. The phone call should last about fifteen minutes, and both Marianne and Derek will talk to Beth.'

Marianne and I noted this in our diaries. Then something suddenly occurred to me. 'It's Friday today,' I said, glancing at Jessie. 'Beth would normally telephone her father this evening. Will she still do that?'

'Good point,' Jessie said. 'I'd forgotten.' She looked at me thoughtfully. 'What do you think?'

'If Beth doesn't telephone her father as usual this evening she'll want to know why, so I'll need to give her some explanation.'

Jessie nodded. 'Let her phone as normal, then, but please no one mention the move home until I've seen her on Monday and had a chance to explain everything.'

'So only Derek will be talking to Beth tonight?' Marianne queried.

'Yes, unless Beth asks to speak to you, which is possible. She knows you're living with her father and is more accepting of you now.'

Marianne and Derek both nodded and I saw Marianne smile, clearly pleased by Jessie's comment and the progress Beth had been making in their relationship.

'As usual, Cathy will make the telephone call tonight,' Jessie said to Marianne and Derek. 'But once we've started the move home you'll make the calls. It will send Beth the message that you want to phone her – you're taking the initiative.'

Derek was watching Marianne writing. He was now supporting his head on one hand and looked rather worried. Jessie must have seen this for she said: 'I know it's a lot to take in, and it all seems a bit daunting, but once we get started it will all fall into place.'

'Thank you,' Marianne said.

'Now, to Thursday,' Jessie continued, pen in hand. 'Marianne and Derek will visit Beth at Cathy's house. This time it will be for two hours and you will take Beth out for some of that time. I'll leave it up to you how much time you spend away from Cathy's, but the whole visit is for two hours. You can include a drink and something to eat while you're out. I expect Beth will be hungry.'

Marianne and I were making notes in our diaries again.

'Then on Friday', Jessie continued, 'I'll phone you all, and see how the visit has gone. Marianne and Derek will phone Beth on that Friday evening, and they will both speak to her as they did on Wednesday, which brings us to the weekend.'

Chapter Twenty-Six

The Visit

The planning of Beth's move home continued. It was a gradual introduction, for although Beth was returning home she hadn't lived there for over five months – a long period in a child's life – and Marianne had made some changes to the flat, refurbishing and redecorating, which Beth needed to get used to. The meeting lasted an hour and a half, but I left the room feeling positive. Marianne had clearly gained confidence in her role as stepmother, although she still had some doubts in her ability – only natural given her past experience of trying to look after Beth. Derek seemed to follow Marianne's lead in any matter relating to Beth; whether this was because he felt more comfortable with Marianne in charge or it had been decided in therapy, I didn't know. I thought that Derek and Beth were very lucky to have Marianne. Many women wouldn't have stood by their partner and his child to the extent Marianne had. She clearly had their best interests at heart and I hoped that, in time, Beth would grow to appreciate and love her just as Derek obviously did. At the end of the meeting Derek had thanked Marianne for all she was doing, and as they'd left he'd held her hand. I thought that their relationship was clearly back on track, and all that remained was to fit Beth in so they could be a proper family at last.

I collected Paula from Kay's, we had some lunch and then that afternoon I took Paula to the mother and toddler group. From there we went straight to school to collect Adrian and Beth. That evening we telephoned Beth's father and they talked about school and the weekend, among other things. Beth didn't ask to speak to Marianne, but she did ask after her: 'What's Marianne doing?' she said, without her usual grumpiness or anger.

'Relaxing after work,' Derek replied.

'OK,' Beth said easily, and continued talking about something else.

Clearly a lot of work had taken place in therapy to change Beth's perception of Marianne, and once we began the programme to move Beth home, what had been learned would be put fully into action and to the test.

It was nearly nine o'clock before John arrived home that Friday evening; he said there'd been an accident on the motorway. Paula was already in bed asleep and Beth and Adrian were on their way up to bed. John said goodnight to them both, kissed Adrian and said he would see them in the morning. John and I didn't have much time to talk, as he was very tired and said he needed an early night, but as he drank the cup of tea I'd made I did have the chance to tell him that Beth would be able to go home, and he was pleased for her. John had to leave again on Sunday afternoon, but we'd made the most of the weekend, and he promised that the following week he'd book time off work for our summer holidays.

Monday morning for Beth was an ordinary morning, just like any other Monday, but that was because she didn't know what I knew: that later Jessie would be telling her she could go home. I was so excited for Beth, for although we would miss her dreadfully, as a foster carer nothing is more rewarding than seeing a

The Visit

child successfully rehabilitated home. The anticipation I felt on waking grew as the day went on, so that by the time I collected Beth and Adrian from school I could barely contain myself.

'Jessie is coming to see you at four o'clock,' I reminded Beth.

'Yes, I know,' Beth said, without much enthusiasm.

'I expect she'll want to talk to you alone,' I said.

'She usually does,' Beth said flatly.

'It'll be nice to see your social worker,' I said.

'Will it?' Beth said, now looking at me a little oddly.

Once home, I made us a drink and a snack to see us through to dinner and then, when the doorbell rang, I rushed down the hall to answer it, butterflies churning my stomach. Beth, unfazed, was in the living room petting Toscha. Adrian and Paula were upstairs. I opened the door and saw that Jessie was smiling too, clearly delighted that she was able to bring Beth the news she wanted to hear.

'Big day,' Jessie said, stepping in.

'Absolutely. Would you like a coffee?'

'Yes, please.'

Jessie went into the living room while I made coffee. She left the living-room door open and I could hear her making light conversation with Beth and putting her at ease. I took the coffee through, set it on the occasional table within Jessie's reach and then came out, closing the door behind me.

I knew that Beth, like many children in care, had been keeping a tight lid on her emotions in order to cope, and that once Jessie told her the good news all her built-up emotion would be released. I wasn't wrong. Suddenly I heard Beth let out a loud, excited scream, and the door to the living room burst open.

'Cathy!' she cried at the top of her voice, running into the kitchen. 'Jessie says I can go home!' She threw herself into my arms.

'Oh, love, that is good news,' I said, holding her close. 'How wonderful.'

'Jessie says I can live with Daddy and Marianne!' Beth repeated, as though she was unable to believe it.

'That's fantastic,' I said, and my eyes filled. Beth had her head buried in my chest and both arms tightly around me. I knew it wouldn't be long before I no longer felt her hug. 'I'm so pleased for you, love,' I said, my voice faltering. 'But we're going to miss you loads.'

'I'm going to miss you too,' she said and burst into tears. Which set me off.

Jessie appeared in the kitchen. 'Oh dear. What have I done?' she said, with a smile.

'It's all right,' I said. 'We're happy, really, aren't we, Beth?'
Beth nodded and sniffed.

I could see Jessie wanted to continue talking to Beth, so I gently eased her away, then I took a tissue from the box and wiped her eyes. I took another tissue and wiped my own.

'You'll still be able to see Cathy if you want to,' Jessie said to Beth.

Beth nodded and blew her nose.

'And while you're at the same school, we'll see you in the morning and afternoon in the playground,' I added.

'There!' Jessie said positively. 'Now, let's go into the living room and I'll show you the timetable for your move home.'

Beth blew her nose again and followed Jessie out of the kitchen. I heard the living-room door close. Adrian and Paula appeared, having heard Beth's cries of delight from upstairs.

'Is Beth really going home?' Adrian asked, his face serious, while Paula looked at me, hoping she'd misheard.

'Yes, she will be in a few weeks,' I said.

'Oh dear,' Paula said, close to tears.

Fostering involves the whole family, so the carer's children miss the foster child as much as the carer. Having to say goodbye to a child you've all grown close to is the downside of fostering, and you never really get used to it. The best we can do is to reassure ourselves and our families that the child will be happy, which is what I did with Adrian and Paula. And in Beth's case I was able to remind them that we would still be seeing her in the playground.

'That's cool,' Adrian said, partly reassured.

'Is Beth very happy to go home?' Paula asked.

'Yes, love. She is.'

'So am I, then,' Paula said. 'But I'll still miss her.'

'I know, love, we all will.'

Jessie was with Beth for an hour, and by the time she left Beth had a reasonable understanding of the timescale of her move home. Jessie gave Beth and me a printed copy of the timetable of the move, and on Beth's copy Jessie had drawn a picture of a little house and written *Home* beneath the date she would actually move. Beth wanted to put her copy on her bedroom wall so she could tick off the days as they went, and also count the days to *Home*. We mounted the chart on her bedroom wall with Blu-tack, then she called Adrian and Paula in and showed them, proudly explaining what each day meant until *Home*. Paula was so impressed she wanted a timetable in her bedroom.

'You're home already, silly,' Adrian said.

'You can help me tick off mine,' Beth said kindly.

That night Beth took a long while to go to sleep – hardly surprising with everything that must have been going through her mind. She asked me to run through the timetable again with her, which I did. Then she wanted confirmation that I would be staying with her during her first visit home. I said I would and pointed it out on her timetable: *Cathy and Beth to visit Beth's home. One hour.* Beth then wanted reassurance that she would still see us in the playground after she'd moved. I understood she was feeling a bit insecure and that this would ease once the programme got under way and she slowly transferred the trust she'd put in me to her father and Marianne. I talked to her, hugged her and eventually Mr Sleep Bear got her off to sleep. I too was feeling anxious, although I didn't let Beth know. Rehabilitating a child home can and does go wrong sometimes, resulting in the child returning into foster care. It doesn't happen often, fortunately, but when it does it's traumatic for the child and they can suffer feelings of rejection and worthlessness into adulthood. While I didn't think that would happen here, you can never be completely sure.

The following morning Beth was very excited again. Over breakfast she told Adrian and Paula more than once that they would be meeting her daddy and Marianne tonight – their first visit. Then she described them in detail, even the 'little lines' Marianne had when she smiled, which I didn't think she'd be too pleased about if she knew. Paula had actually met Marianne once before – when she'd brought Beth's swimming costume – but it was a long time ago and she didn't mention it. The way Beth now talked about her daddy was very different to the gushings of 'Daddy's little princess' when she'd first arrived. Now her talk of her father was normal for a girl of her age. The contrast between this and her previous comments was so great that she could have been talking about a different person, which in a way she was for all the changes Derek had made and was still making. Adrian and Paula must have felt comfortable with Beth's talk, for they were happy to sit and listen until it was time to get ready for school.

The Visit

That afternoon, when I collected Beth from school, Miss Willow came into the playground to see me. For a moment I thought there might have been a problem in school, as that's often the reason a teacher seeks out a parent or carer at the end of the day – the child had fallen, or was upset, or hadn't done their homework. But Miss Willow was smiling as she approached me.

'Beth's been telling me all about her visitors tonight,' she said. 'I'm so pleased.'

'Yes, so are we,' I said. 'Jessie told you about the decision?' For it occurred to me that perhaps the school hadn't been updated, as they should have been.

'Yes, she did,' Miss Willow confirmed. 'Jessie has been very good at keeping us informed.' Then, addressing Beth, she said: 'You have a lovely evening. I'll look forward to hearing all about it tomorrow, and to seeing your dad and Marianne again when they bring you to school in the future.' It was a lovely thing to say, and Beth beamed.

'Thank you for all your help,' I said to Miss Willow.

'You're welcome. I'm just pleased everything seems to be working out all right.'

Derek and Marianne arrived at exactly 5.30 p.m. as timetabled. Hearing the doorbell, Beth flew down the hall and then waited for me to open the door, as I liked all the children to do. 'Hello. Come in,' I said to them both.

Beth was so very excited and she hugged them both hard as they came in. Then, grabbing her father's hand, she led him down the hall and into the living room, where she introduced him to Adrian and Paula. Marianne and I followed and I threw her a reassuring smile, for she looked even more nervous than Derek did.

'And this is Marianne,' Beth announced proudly to Adrian and Paula as we entered the living room. 'She's Daddy's partner and is going to be my new mummy.'

I could see Marianne was as surprised as I was by Beth's comment. For Beth to have accepted this so early was far more than we could have hoped for. Marianne was flustered and didn't know what to say for a moment, and then she recovered and said hello to Adrian and Paula.

'Do you remember me?' she asked Paula.

'You're the lady who brought Beth's swimming costume,' Paula said a little shyly. So she did remember.

'That's right,' Marianne said. 'It seems a long time ago now.'

While I made a cup of tea, Marianne and Derek talked to all three children, asking them about school and what they liked to do in their spare time. When I returned with the tray of tea and biscuits, Adrian asked if he could go and play, which he could – he didn't have to stay with us. Paula wanted to stay.

As we drank our tea we made light conversation, as Jessie had suggested. Beth was sitting on the sofa between her father and Marianne. I'd never seen the three of them together before and not only was it touching, it also seemed very right. There was a strong familial resemblance between Derek and Beth, but Marianne didn't look so different to Beth in colouring and features – she could have been her natural mother. I also noted that the Beth I now saw sitting beside her father was very different to the images in the photographs upstairs, where she was wearing make-up, skimpy clothes and posing suggestively. Now she was just a little girl, dressed appropriately and sitting beside her father who clearly loved her.

Presently, Marianne took a packet of photographs from her handbag. At the planning meeting Jessie had suggested that they bring some recent photographs of themselves and the flat to show Beth. Marianne began going through them and Beth held up each one for Paula and me to see. The first was of Derek and Marianne sitting on a bench in a park and enjoying the sun. The others were of their flat, which they'd thoroughly redecorated since Beth had been living there. Marianne said a bit about each photograph, and when they came to the last one – of Beth's bedroom – Beth's eyes rounded and her mouth fell open in astonishment.

'Wow!' she said.

'I know that's your favourite colour,' Marianne said a little shyly. 'I chose the wallpaper, curtains and duvet to match. I hope you like it.'

'Wow!' Beth said again, for once rendered speechless.

Paula and I didn't wait for Beth to hold up the photograph but went over for a closer look.

'You've got a lovely bedroom,' Paula said.

'You're a very lucky girl,' I said.

Marianne smiled. She'd obviously put a lot of work into decorating and refurbishing Beth's room. From the photographs, I could see that it was a lovely young-girl's room painted in pale lilac, with soft furnishings to match. There was a large lilac-tinted toy box in one corner overflowing with Beth's toys. Neatly arranged on the shelves were Beth's books, cuddlies and other knick-knacks that litter girls' bedrooms.

'It wasn't as nice as that before,' Beth said, clearly impressed and pleased. I thought that, given there'd been issues with Beth not wanting to sleep in her own bed, it was a very good step to refurbish the room. 'When did you do it?' she asked her father.

'When we knew for definite you would be coming home,' he said. 'Marianne chose the colour scheme and bought the duvet and curtains, and I did the painting.'

'It really is lovely,' I said.

'When can I see my new room?' Beth asked excitedly.

'When you come for your visit on Saturday,' Marianne said.

'Can I keep the photograph?' Beth asked.

'Yes, they're all yours. I think they're better than the ones you have with you here in your room,' Marianne said, meeting my gaze. I nodded.

'Would you like to see my bedroom here?' Beth now asked Marianne, as I thought she might.

'Yes, please,' Marianne said.

Beth took Marianne's hand and led her out of the living room and upstairs while Derek stayed with Paula and me.

'You're welcome to go up too,' I said. 'Although there's not an awful lot to see.'

Derek shook his head. 'No. It's better if Marianne does the mummy things. I'm taking a bit of a back seat in all of this. I got it badly wrong before, and I'm not going to risk it again. I hope to return to work before too long. And Cathy, can I just take this opportunity to thank you for all you've done for Beth. Marianne and I very much appreciate it.'

'I'm pleased it all worked out,' I said.

'So am I. I'm so grateful to be given this second opportunity. I know how lucky I am and how close I came to losing Beth. I won't mess up this time.'

When Marianne and Beth returned downstairs and into the living room, Beth was carrying a carrier bag. 'I'm getting rid of my make-up and some of my dressing-up clothes,' Beth declared.

'If that's all right with you?' Marianne said to Derek and me. 'Beth, show Cathy and your father what is in the bag.'

Paula and I peered into the bag Beth held open in front of me. I saw the make-up, bottles of different-coloured nail varnish, black fishnet tights and some see-through tops.

'I'm more than happy for those to go,' I said.

Beth carried the bag to her father and he looked in. He frowned in anguish at the stark reminder of what had been. 'Yes, throw them all out,' he said. 'I can't believe I ever thought you looked nice in those things.'

'Marianne's going to take me shopping and buy me lots of new clothes,' Beth said to me.

'That'll be nice,' I said, although I hoped Marianne wouldn't make the mistake of spoiling Beth too much.

'We'll need to replace the clothes we're getting rid of,' Marianne explained, and I nodded.

As the hour allowed for the visit drew to a close and it was time for her father and Marianne to leave, Beth begged them to stay longer. Aware of Jessie's words on the importance of keeping to the timetable, Marianne and I explained to Beth we had to keep to the timetable, and eventually she said goodbye without a fuss. It was important Beth saw us all working together, and we were.

That night, when it was time for bed, Beth ceremoniously ticked off today's date on her timetable, and then quietly counted the days to the picture of the house when she would be moving home. She didn't comment, but before she climbed into bed she slid out the photograph of her and her father from under her pillow and placed it face down in a drawer.

'Marianne and Daddy don't like these photographs,' she said. 'And I don't now.'

I waited as Beth took one of the new photographs – of Marianne and her father in the park – and, kissing it goodnight, slipped it under her pillow.

'Night, love,' I said, tucking her in.

'Night, Cathy.' She was tired and happy and fell asleep easily.

The following morning, as soon as I woke Beth she leaped out of bed and checked her timetable. 'Yes! Daddy and

Marianne are phoning me tonight,' she said. 'I'll tell Miss Willow.'

Jessie telephoned later that morning to see how the visit had gone, and I was pleased to be able to tell her that it had gone incredibly well. Jessie had already spoken to Derek and had got his and Marianne's feedback, so she knew that Beth had introduced Marianne as her mummy. Marianne was at work, but she'd asked Derek to make sure Jessie knew that they'd be getting rid of the photographs Beth had with her in her room and would be framing new ones for the walls of their flat. Jessie told me she'd advised Derek not to get rid of all the photographs, as they formed part of Beth's history – good and bad.

'So you've got the first joint phone contact tonight,' Jessie finished by saying. 'For Marianne and Derek.'

'Yes. Should I still monitor the call on speakerphone?' I thought to ask.

'No,' Jessie said. 'Stay in the background in case Beth wants you, but there's no need to monitor the call. I'm trusting Marianne and Derek with their child, so I'm sure I can trust them to make an appropriate phone call. You haven't got any worries, have you?'

'No.'

Chapter Twenty-Seven
The Postcard

Beth's rehabilitation home continued to go well and as planned. Indeed, the speed with which she bonded with Marianne, and re-bonded with her father in an appropriate father–daughter relationship, outstripped all the adults' expectations. Jessie told me that the therapy had played a part in this, but so too had the time Beth had spent with my family, as it had shown her what having a mother could mean, and the joys of being part of a two-parent family and having a family life. Beth was now allowing Marianne and her father to make this happen for her in a way she hadn't before. And, of course, Derek and Marianne also now had confidence in their ability to parent Beth.

By the middle of June we were over halfway through the timetable of Beth's rehabilitation home. The previous weekend she'd spent Saturday and Sunday at home, but had returned to us to sleep. The next weekend Beth would be staying overnight for the first time. Jessie had suggested I leave Adrian and Paula at home with their father while I took and collected Beth, so that I could give her my undivided attention. Adrian and Paula would have an opportunity to see Beth's home once she had moved in.

Marianne, Derek and I had been working closely together, and they knew they could ask me if they had any questions. I'd already given them a written outline of Beth's routine, which they were going to follow – at least to begin with – so that Beth didn't have too many changes all at once. Beth had told them which foods she liked and didn't like, although in truth she was a good eater and, apart from Brussels sprouts and cabbage, happily ate most foods. Marianne telephoned me late on Wednesday evening worried that Beth might not want to sleep in her own bed. Beth had seen her newly furbished bedroom when she'd visited the previous weekend and had absolutely loved it, and had spent time playing in it. But Marianne was now concerned that when it came to actually sleeping in her bed, she might refuse and insist on sleeping with her father, as she had done when she'd lived there before. We all knew this couldn't be allowed to happen.

'Start as you mean to go on,' I said to Marianne. 'Once you've established a bedtime routine, it will be much easier. You've already decided that Derek will be reading Beth her bedtime story in your living room, and then you're taking Beth for her bath and to bed, so keep to that. Check whether she wants her curtains fully drawn and her bedroom door closed or open. These little details can be important in helping a child to settle at night. I usually leave a night-light on the landing, as many children don't like the dark. Once Beth's in bed and you've said goodnight, come out. You may have to go in and resettle her, or take her back to bed if she gets out, but don't be tempted to let her go into your bed, or into the living room to watch more television. If you do it once, she'll expect it in the future. Keep to your routine, kindly but firmly, and I'm sure she'll soon settle.'

'Thank you,' Marianne said. 'I'm just a bit nervous.'

'Of course you are. It's to be expected. You may also think about giving Beth a cuddly toy to take to bed, like the Mr Sleep Bear I showed you. I'm afraid I can't let Beth take him, as he was a present to Adrian, but one of Beth's favourite soft toys will do just as well. Use the same toy every night and she'll soon associate it with sleep.'

Marianne gave a small laugh. 'Beth didn't own many cuddly toys, so I've bought her one that looks a little bit like Mr Sleep Bear. I might tell her it's his brother.'

I laughed too. 'Nice one,' I said. 'You'll be fine.'

So everything was going very well, not only with Beth, but also with my life in general. I often thought how lucky I was. I had two happy, healthy children, a loving husband, wonderful parents and enough money that we didn't have to worry constantly about paying the next bill. I appreciated how lucky I was and I assumed my life would continue in the same way. Why shouldn't it? There was no reason for it not to, or so I thought. Perhaps there's a barometer of happiness that registers when you've been happy for too long and brings you back in line. I suppose those who have a religion say they are being tested at difficult times. But whatever the reason, when events took the turn they did, I didn't understand any of it. Nor did I know how I would cope.

It was Thursday lunchtime, the day after Marianne had called, when the telephone rang. As I picked up the handset I thought it might be Marianne again, or Jessie asking for an update – she often telephoned about midday.

'Hello,' I said brightly.

I was surprised to hear John's voice. 'Hello, Cathy,' he said, his tone a little flat. 'I won't be coming home this weekend.'

'Oh dear. Not at all?'

'No. We both need time to think.'

I hesitated, thinking I'd misheard. 'Sorry?' I said.

'We both need time to think about the future,' he repeated in the same flat voice.

'Do we?' I asked, puzzled.

'Yes. We need to think what is best for us in the long term.' I felt the slightest twinge of unease, but I knew this would pass once I understood what John meant.

'Surely we can think about the future when you are home?' I said. 'It would be better to plan any changes together, wouldn't it?'

There was a pause before he said: 'Let's not play games, Cathy. We both know what I mean. We haven't been getting on for some time now. We've drifted apart, and it's obviously time to call it quits. I hope we can be adult about this.'

The unease I'd felt exploded into fear, yet I was hearing the words without fully understanding their meaning. 'I don't know what you mean,' I said, my voice distant and unreal.

'Oh come on, Cathy,' John said. 'I can't put it any simpler. We need to start divorce proceedings as soon as possible. We'll both be happier once everything is sorted out.'

The walls tilted and a loud buzzing noise filled my ears as the floor began to rise up and engulf me. I thought I was going to faint, and Paula was in the house. I mustn't faint. I'd taken the call in the hall, and I sat heavily in the chair by the telephone table and tried to catch my breath.

'So I think it's best if we have a few weekends apart,' John was saying on the other end of the phone. 'It's only natural for us to feel hurt that it didn't work out, but we don't want to say things we may later regret. You may want to talk to your parents. That's OK, but don't let them persuade you into doing something that isn't helpful. We'll sell the house and both find new places. Paula starts nursery in September, so you'll be able to go back to work then.'

I fought for some words; they weren't easy to find. 'When did you decide all this?' I asked, my voice shaking.

'One of us has to plan ahead,' he said. 'I'm going to take two weeks' holiday and I suggest you do the same.'

'I thought we were going on holiday together,' I said stupidly. I wasn't thinking straight and 'holiday' was one of the few words I understood.

'We need time apart,' he said. 'I've booked to go away. I suggest you take the children and stay with your parents for a few days.'

'They've got school, and please don't keep telling me what I should do,' I said, fear morphing into anger. '*We* have children. They're *our* responsibility. You can't just go away for two weeks. What about Adrian and Paula? You should come home so we can talk about what's wrong and sort it out. I'm sure it can be put right.' I was desperate.

'There's nothing to sort out,' John said. 'And it won't help if we argue. I'll say goodbye now and give you time to calm down. I'll phone when I return from holiday. Give my love to the children, and please don't try to turn them against me. It's a joint decision to separate. I'll still see the children regularly. Goodbye.'

He hung up. I went into the kitchen and was violently sick in the sink.

Presently Paula came to find me. 'What's the matter, Mummy?' she said worried.

'It's nothing for you to worry about, love. I'm not feeling so good.'

I wiped my mouth, had a drink of cold water and then took Paula into the living room, where I switched on children's daytime television. I left it on for the rest of the afternoon.

I'm not someone who usually goes into denial; I usually confront any problems I may have, but not then. This was far too big to face. I didn't cry, and I didn't tell anyone – not even my parents or my good friend Kay. I was in shock, numb, and part of me didn't accept what John had said. Perhaps after his holiday he'd come home refreshed and apologize, and we'd carry on as normal. He'd been working too hard, a two-week holiday was what he needed to set him right again. Also, I had the children to look after, and it wasn't long before I had to collect Adrian and Beth from school, then the evening meal to make, homework to help with and the bath and bedtime routine. I didn't have time to think. I had the children to see to.

The following day I steeled myself to tell Adrian and Paula that their daddy wouldn't be coming home at the weekend. They assumed he was working, and I didn't tell them any different. I telephoned Jessie and left a message on her answerphone to say that Adrian and Paula would be coming with me when I took Beth home for her weekend stay, as John was working away. I didn't feel I could ask a friend to look after my children at the weekend, and also I felt I needed to keep them close to me, to make sure they were safe. My world had crumbled with John's words and I felt threatened. I wanted my children close.

I telephoned Marianne and told her I'd be bringing Adrian and Paula with me. 'That's fine,' she said. 'We'll look forward to seeing you all on Saturday, at about ten o'clock.'

'Yes, see you then,' I said.

Outwardly, therefore, I continued as normal. I talked, I ate (though not a lot), I took the children to school, collected them, helped them with their homework, did the housework, and then on Friday I packed Beth's overnight bag ready for Saturday, all the time ignoring the huge dark cloud that hung over me, ready to descend and engulf me at any moment.

On Saturday morning, as arranged, I took Beth home for the weekend. Adrian, Paula and I stayed for about fifteen minutes and admired Beth's new bedroom and the newly framed photographs in the living room – lovely photographs, of Beth playing and with her father and Marianne. I drove us home, then after lunch I took Adrian and Paula to the park, where I pushed Paula on the swings and then the roundabout, while Adrian worked the seesaw and followed the mini assault course. That evening I cooked dinner and then telephoned my parents as I usually did at the weekend. I told Mum that John was working over the weekend and she suggested we went there for Sunday lunch, but we couldn't, as I had to collect Beth at four o'clock.

'We'll come over as soon as Beth has returned home,' I said. By which time I hoped John would have returned home too.

On the Sunday morning I took Adrian and Paula swimming at the leisure centre, as John and I did sometimes at weekends. I swam and pretended I was enjoying myself. Then at four o'clock we collected Beth. She'd had a great weekend and didn't want to leave, but Marianne and Derek explained we all had to follow Jessie's timetable, and that it was only one more weekend before she could move home for good.

'Yippee,' she said.

In quieter moments when I was alone, especially at night, I went over John's words in my head, time and time again, checking to see if I had heard them correctly, and then searching for a clue as to why. Could I – should I – have seen it coming? Had there been indicators that had suggested we weren't happy? Not that

I'd seen. Which made me think I must have been incredibly insensitive not to notice John's unhappiness. How cold I must have appeared to him, not to have seen his suffering. How could I have let it get to this point?

I telephoned John's work number with the intention of acknowledging my failings, apologizing and begging – if necessary – for John to come home so we could talk about what had gone wrong, when I would promise to change in whatever way he wanted. But of course John wasn't there, he was on holiday, and a recorded message said he was on annual leave and then gave the telephone number of a colleague who could be contacted if it was urgent. I desperately needed to speak to John, and I willed the days to go quickly so that when he returned I could apologize and hopefully make everything all right.

Jessie telephoned for feedback after Beth's first weekend stay, and I told her that it had gone very well. She said she was pleased with the way Derek and Marianne were relating to Beth and managing her behaviour. She also confirmed that, if it continued to go well, Beth would return home for good as planned the weekend after next.

On the Wednesday of that week, ten days after John's telephone call, a postcard arrived. I heard the letterbox go, and then found the card lying face down on the mat in the hall with the other mail. I recognized John's handwriting and my heart set up a queer little rhythm – of hope – until I began to read.

Hi kids,
I expect Mummy has told you that Daddy is having a well-deserved rest. I'm staying in a hotel on a beautiful island in the Indian Ocean. You can see from the picture on the front that it has palm trees, blue sea and sky, and miles of white sand. And

tortoises! How about that! I bet you wish you were here. See you soon. I miss you both.
Love Daddy.

It was addressed to Adrian and Paula only.

I turned over the postcard to look at the picture. Clear blue sea and skies, miles of white sand and a giant tortoise, just as John said, and beneath the picture were printed the words: *The Seychelles.*

My hurt and anger rose, not so much for me, but for Adrian and Paula. How insensitive of him. How selfish and thoughtless to send them a card. They were missing their father dreadfully, and they'd never been abroad. Of course they'd wish they were with him, especially on a luxurious holiday. And why hadn't John addressed the card to me as well? Was it because he'd already written me out of his life? It appeared so. I reread the card and then hid it away in a drawer. I wouldn't show the children. It would be too hurtful and would raise more questions than I could answer at present. My eyes filled as I pictured their little faces if I showed them the card – impressed by where their daddy was, but unable to understand why he'd gone on holiday without them.

That evening, when all three children were in bed and asleep, I took the postcard from the drawer and read it again. John's behaviour was so out of character – first the phone call and then the card – that I struggled to believe he was the same person I'd married and lived with all these years. John had never been on holiday by himself before in his life, and he'd said that those who did seemed 'a bit sad'. A 'Billy-no-mates', he'd called them once. While, I supposed, there was a first time for everything, something didn't gel. I returned the postcard to the bottom of the drawer and then went upstairs and into my bedroom, with the intention of searching John's personal belongings.

Like most couples, John and I respected each other's privacy, so I would never normally have gone into his wardrobe or drawers, unless I was putting away his clean clothes. Now, however, everything was different, and although I felt guilty and degraded right from the start, I needed answers – however hurtful they may be – and possibly I'd find them here. I began by going through his wardrobe where he kept his suits, jackets and trousers, dipping my hand into the pockets and taking out and examining what I found. I didn't know what I was looking for and part of me hoped I wouldn't find it – whatever it was. There were receipts from hastily grabbed coffees, chewing-gum wrappers, tissues, Biros and a couple of elastic bands, all of which I returned to the pockets exactly as I found them, loathing myself for being so underhand and sly. Then, about halfway through the rail of hangers, I dipped my hand into the pocket of his leather jacket. It had been my Christmas present to him last year. I drew out a folded receipt and opened it. It was from a jeweller a long way from where we lived and was for a silver bracelet, cost £79. It wasn't my birthday or Christmas, and I hadn't received a bracelet from John, although the receipt was dated two months previously.

I refolded the receipt, returned it to his jacket pocket and continued to the next garment: a pair of corduroy trousers. Both pockets were empty. But in the next pair of trousers I found another jeweller's receipt, this time for a diamond drop necklace, which had cost him £350. It was a different jeweller, but in the same part of the country as the first. In the other pocket of these trousers I found two torn-off cinema tickets – not to any film I'd seen. Then, in a suit pocket, I found a receipt for a restaurant where the bill had come to £107 and had included a bottle of champagne, together with a hotel receipt for £245, for one night. John stayed in hotels while working away, but not five-star hotels on the coast, as this one was. His company put him and his colleagues in budget motels close to their place of work. It was dated the last weekend John hadn't come home, when I distinctly remembered him saying he'd been working in Rugby. This hotel was over a hundred miles from Rugby.

I should have stopped searching then. I'd already found more than enough. We hadn't drifted apart as John had claimed. The reason he wanted a divorce was because he'd been seeing someone else. I now doubted he was on holiday alone. I don't know why I didn't stop searching. It would have been less painful. Curiosity, perhaps – to see what else he'd been up to, and what other gifts he'd bought for her. Or possibly I still didn't believe that John was capable of this, and I'd discover something to show that I was wrong. I delved into the pocket of the next pair of trousers and drew out a neat little gift card with an embossed picture of a red heart on the front. Perhaps it was for me? I opened it. In a delicate script – not John's handwriting – were the words: *To my dearest John. On our first anniversary, a small token of my undying love. Love you forever. Zara x.*

Chapter Twenty-Eight
Couple in the Playground

No words can describe the desperate sadness, the fear of my now unknown future and the sense of abandonment I felt that night as I was forced to accept John had left me for another woman. I knew who Zara was. John had introduced me to her at his firm's Christmas party. She was a colleague, the only female in an otherwise all-male team, and ten years younger than John. I'd always assumed I'd be married for life, and that John and I would grow old together, loving and caring for each other into our twilight years, just as my parents did. All that had now gone. I thought of Dr Jones's praise for my two-parent family and how much Beth had benefited from being part of it. I also thought of all the times I'd defended John to the children when he'd worked away. 'It's because Daddy loves us and wants to give us a better future,' I'd said. How bitterly ironic those words seemed now. Yet while I felt sorry for myself, I felt even more sorry for Adrian and Paula, who would now grow up without their father's presence.

Beth had one more week with us before she moved, and I didn't want to ruin her last days with upset and tears, so I didn't tell anyone that John had left us and continued as best I could. I saved my tears for when I sat alone in the living room at night or lay unsleeping in my bed. Sometimes, during the day, my tears would suddenly well up uncontrollably and I'd rush from the room and upstairs and shut myself in the bathroom until I'd composed myself, rather than break down in front of the children. But as far as Beth was concerned, she'd leave us as she'd found us. And at that time Adrian and Paula were also blissfully unaware that anything had changed.

When John telephoned after his return from holiday it was Friday – the day before Beth was due to leave us. He sounded relaxed and not at all embarrassed. 'Hello, I'm back from holiday,' he said, and then asked if the children had missed him.

'They've missed you,' I confirmed.

'I'll come to see them next weekend,' he said, 'when I've had a chance to sort myself out after the holiday.'

'OK,' I said coolly.

'I'll get there first thing on the Saturday morning and I'll take them out for the day, but I won't stay overnight. Now we've decided to separate, it's not appropriate for me to sleep there any more.' Which felt like a big slap in the face.

'*We* haven't decided to separate,' I said, no longer able to contain my feelings. 'You made that decision. And, John, it didn't have anything to do with us "drifting apart" or "not getting along". It was your choice to end our marriage because you're having an affair with Zara.'

'Who told you that?' he demanded angrily.

'No one told me. I found out. Please give me some credit and stop lying. You've lied enough already.'

It went very quiet on the other end of the phone and, just for a moment, I thought he might admit his affair, apologize, say he'd made the biggest mistake of his life and ask to come back, then I would have forgiven him and put the past behind us. But he didn't.

Clearing his throat, he said stiffly, 'I've made an appointment to see a solicitor next week. I suggest you do the same.' Another big slap in the face.

'If that's what you want,' I said.

'It's for the best. And it won't do the children any good if you blame me. I'm their father and they still love me.'

'I know they do,' I said.

I finished the last of Beth's packing that afternoon. Then Friday evening I made Beth a special tea with jelly and ice cream and cupcakes – a little leaving tea – and then organized some games, with just the four of us. When she went to bed she was excited, but also a little sad and she wanted lots of cuddles, and reassurance that she would still see us, which was only natural. The following morning there was little time for brooding; once we were all up, washed and dressed and had had breakfast, Marianne and Derek arrived – as arranged – at 10.30 a.m.

It was a beautiful summer's day, already warm, and with temperatures predicted to soar. Jessie had told us to keep our goodbyes short so that Beth wouldn't become upset. Marianne and Derek knew I wouldn't be offering them coffee, and I had all Beth's cases ready in the hall. We all helped load their car with a bittersweet excitement, for although Beth was starting her new life, she was leaving ours. Once all her cases, bags and boxes of toys were in the car, I gave her a leaving present, which she said she'd open on the way home.

'Thank you very much,' she said sweetly. 'I will still see you at school, won't I?'

'You certainly will,' I said.

Adrian and Paula hugged Beth first and then it was my turn. I swallowed hard as I felt her little arms around me for the last time. After a while I gently eased her away. 'Bye, love. You're a good girl.'

We stood on the pavement as Derek, Marianne and Beth climbed into their car and fastened their seatbelts. Then they wound down their windows so they could wave. We all waved vigorously until they were out of sight and then Adrian, Paula and I slowly filed back indoors. My heart was heavy, not only from Beth leaving, but now I had to tell my children about their father. I couldn't put it off any longer.

'Can we fill the paddling pool?' Adrian asked, as I closed the front door. He was referring to the children's inflatable pool that we filled with water in the garden when the weather was fine.

'Yes, in a while,' I said. 'First, I need to talk to you both.'

'What's the matter, Mum?' Adrian asked, seeing my expression grow serious.

'Come and sit down, please.' I led the way into the living room, my eyes already filling. I knew I had to stay calm and in control for the sake of the children. I sat on the sofa with Adrian on one side and Paula on the other. Toscha was asleep in the sun falling through the patio window. Stretching out, she lazily turned over without waking.

'Is it about Dad?' Adrian asked, looking at me anxiously.

'Yes, it is,' I said.

The colour drained from his face.

'Daddy is safe and well,' I quickly reassured him. 'He'll be seeing you as planned next weekend. But there are going to be a few changes, and one of them is that he won't be staying the night any longer.'

'Why not?' Paula asked.

'Sshh. Listen,' Adrian said.

I took a breath. 'Sadly, like the daddies of some of the children at your school and playgroup, your daddy is now living in another house, and not with us any more. He will still see you both regularly. He'll come here and will take you out for the day.' Adrian and Paula were so young that I thought it was best to concentrate on the practicalities. 'Daddy loves you loads and that will never change,' I said.

There was a moment's silence before Adrian asked, 'Are you getting divorced?'

'Yes,' I said quietly.

'Why?' Paula asked.

'Because it's what Daddy wants,' I said. I wouldn't criticize John to the children, but I certainly wouldn't lie for him. I was relieved Paula didn't ask why he wanted a divorce, for I wouldn't have known what to say.

'Is that why Dad hasn't been coming home much?' Adrian now asked, his little face sadder than it should ever have been. 'Because he wants a divorce?'

'Yes, and work,' I said. 'He has been working away a lot.' Although in truth I no longer knew how much of his absence was due to work and how much was due to Zara.

I slipped my arms around their shoulders and drew them close. 'If there was anything I could do to change this, then I would,' I said. 'But I'm afraid there isn't. We'll still be a family, just a different one. Please try not to worry. I'll look after you. You two are my world and I'll never leave you, ever.'

'Have you told Nana and Grandpa?' Adrian now asked.

'Not yet. I'll phone them this evening. I thought you two should know first.'

Adrian nodded solemnly and his brow furrowed. I hated John for what he was doing to the children.

'Can we go to Nana and Grandpa's tomorrow?' Paula asked, not fully appreciating the enormity of what I was saying but feeling this might help.

'Yes, if you'd like to,' I said.

'I'd like to,' Adrian said.

I looked at him, suddenly old beyond his years. 'What are you thinking, love?' I asked.

'Nothing much.' He shrugged. 'I suppose if Dad has made up his mind there's nothing we can do. And we'll always have you, Mum, won't we?'

'You will.'

He wrapped his arms around me and held me tight. So too did Paula. We sat on the sofa for some moments, hugging and in silence. Sometimes a hug can say a thousand words. Then I said gently, 'Do either of you have any questions?'

Adrian shook his head, and Paula copied him.

'If you do think of anything, promise me you'll tell me. I'm here for you and I always will be.'

'I'll always be here for you too, Mum,' Adrian said, and the tears in my eyes fell.

I knew the telephone call to my parents that evening would be difficult, although as it turned out they weren't as shocked as I'd expected them to be.

'Your father and I thought John was working away too much,' Mum said. 'You couldn't see it, but we've had our doubts for a while. I'm sorry this has happened to you, of all people. You really didn't deserve it. You gave that man everything he needed.'

'Clearly not,' I said cynically.

'How will you and the children manage?' Mum asked.

'I'm not sure,' I said. 'But we will.' In truth, I didn't know how we were going to manage – financially, emotionally or on any level. There seemed so much to think about.

'You won't have to move house, will you?' Mum asked.

'I hope not,' I said.

Dad, who'd been listening in the background, now asked to speak to me. He said how sorry he was and then – ever practical – offered me a loan. 'You only have to ask,' he said, 'and we'll have the money ready. I don't want you and the children wanting for anything.' Which made me cry again.

I was on the telephone to my parents for over an hour. They were both so kind and supportive that I kept welling up and had to wipe my eyes. Their kindness – such a contrast to John's hurtfulness – was almost more than I could bear. As we wound up, I said we'd like to visit them the following day if they were free.

'Of course,' Mum said. 'We'd love to see you and the children any time. But we don't ever want to see John again. Not after what he's done to you and the children.'

Fiercely loyal and protective as she was, I could understand her view, but it was important she didn't say anything similar in front of Adrian and Paula. 'You won't have to see John again,' I said, 'but the children will be seeing him, and they should have a positive image of their father.'

'I'll hold my tongue when they're around,' Mum said. 'But he's still a bastard.' It was the only time I'd ever heard my mother swear.

With Beth gone and happily settled at home, I was now free to worry about my situation, which I did for the whole of that Saturday night. I didn't go to bed until 2 a.m., and then I tossed and turned until dawn. I knew I had to see a solicitor and I was dreading it. I didn't know what to expect. Divorce was uncharted territory for me; no one in my family had been divorced and I only had one close friend who had been, and she'd had to sell her house and move away. The only firm of solicitors I knew was the one we'd employed for the conveyancing, when John and I had bought our house. At some point I'd have to telephone the firm and make an appointment to see a divorce solicitor, and I tormented myself further with the questions I might be asked.

Despite worrying and having a sleepless night, we had a pleasant day on Sunday, although Mum and Dad went out of their way to avoid mentioning John. He and his crime sat like 'an elephant in the room' – massive and unacknowledged, and when Paula innocently said, 'I'm seeing Daddy next Saturday,' Mum changed the subject and Dad went very quiet. Understandably, it would take them time to adjust, as it would us. They were of a generation who didn't divorce but stayed together through 'better or worse', although I couldn't remember John and I having bad times, which was why this had all come as such a shock.

On the drive home I explained to Adrian and Paula that Nana and Grandpa were upset about Daddy not living with us any more, which was why they couldn't talk about him.

'I know how they feel,' Adrian said quietly, and my heart ached for him.

On Monday morning it was strange not having Beth a part of our weekday routine. Sometimes you don't realize how much a foster child has become part of your life until they are not with you any more. Beth had fully integrated into our family and there was now a big gap. I found myself standing outside her bedroom door, about to go in and wake her and tell her to get ready for school, before I remembered. Then, downstairs, as I prepared breakfast, I automatically reached for the packet of her favourite cereal before I realized. As we ate breakfast, Paula said the table was 'too big' without Beth. And later Adrian caught himself waiting for his turn in the bathroom, as he'd done when Beth had been with us, before remembering he didn't have to wait any more. But as we left for school we were all excited to be seeing Beth soon. The weather was good, so we walked and arrived in the playground before her. Adrian, as usual, ran off to play with his friends – he could see Beth at break and lunchtime.

As I waited with Paula in the playground, I noticed Jenni's mother standing with another mother a little way off, both looking at me as they talked. I had the feeling they were talking about me, possibly discussing Beth's return home, for Beth had told all her friends and her teachers she was going home. The playground continued to fill and I concentrated on the school gates. A few minutes before the klaxon was due to sound I saw Beth come in, smart in her school uniform, walking proudly between her parents and holding their hands. She was smiling broadly, although Derek and Marianne looked serious – hardly surprising given the playground gossip. Jenni's mother and her friend weren't the only ones looking. Possibly it was my imagination, but it seemed the noise level in the playground dropped slightly as others turned to look too.

'Beth's here,' I said to Paula, whose view was blocked by parents.

I took her hand and we walked over to where Beth stood with her parents.

'Cathy, lovely to see you!' Marianne exclaimed as we approached.

'And you,' I said, hugging her. I then hugged Beth and Derek. 'Have you had a nice weekend?'

'Wonderful!' Marianne enthused. Beth was already talking to Paula. 'I should really be at work,' Marianne added. 'But Derek felt a bit uneasy coming in by himself on the first day.'

'I can wait with you for moral support?' I suggested to Derek. 'Then Marianne can get off to work.'

'I'd appreciate that,' Derek said, finally smiling.

'Thanks, Cathy,' Marianne said. 'I've arranged to leave work early this afternoon so I can be here, and I'll be cutting my hours anyway when Derek goes back to work.'

Marianne kissed Derek goodbye on the cheek and then hugged and kissed Beth. Other parents in the playground were still watching and Derek saw them too. 'Bye, love. Have a good day,' Marianne said as she walked away.

'Bye, Mum!' Beth called. 'See you later.'

Interest in Derek and Beth gradually evaporated and the prying stares disappeared as conversations resumed. I waited with Derek, talking about the weekend, until the klaxon sounded, when Beth kissed her father goodbye and ran over to line up with her class. When the teachers came out to lead their classes into school, Miss Willow made a point of looking over and giving Derek a little wave and a smile, which was thoughtful. She was possibly aware that Derek would be feeling uncomfortable on his first day back, and I could see he appreciated her kindness. He returned her wave and smile.

I walked with Derek out of the playground and then we said goodbye and went our separate ways home. That afternoon, when I returned to school to collect Adrian, I kept a lookout for Marianne and Derek with the intention of once again standing with them. The playground can be a lonely place for parents, just as it can be for children, if everyone but you appears to be chatting happily with friends. I saw Derek and Marianne come through the school gates; she had her arm loosely linked through his. I was about to go over when Frances, April's mother, went up to them. Offering her hand for shaking and with a big smile, she introduced herself and then they began talking. I remained where I was. I didn't want to intrude, and it would be good for

Beth if Marianne and Derek got to know her friends' parents. It was thoughtful of Frances to approach them, for she was quite a shy person herself, but having appreciated Beth offering friendship to April, she was now doing the same to Marianne and Derek. I was very touched.

But there was another reason why I was so moved and was having to blink back my tears. For as I looked at Derek and Marianne – now truly a couple – I was reminded of the days when John had come with me to meet Adrian from school. We had stood side by side, together, in the playground – a couple – just as Marianne and Derek were doing now. But as they were at the start of their life together, my life with John had ended. We would never be a couple again, and I was very sad.

Epilogue

A week later school broke up for the long summer holiday, and by the time school returned in September the playground gossips had lost interest in Derek and Marianne. They were just another couple waiting for their child. Derek, now in good health, returned to work at the end of September and Marianne shortened her hours, so they could both share childcare and the school runs. Sometimes Derek was in the playground and sometimes Marianne was, and occasionally they were together. We always chatted if there was an opportunity, and also if we saw each other by chance in the high street or one of the local parks.

Beth's birthday was in October and she wanted a party at home. Marianne had never organized a children's birthday party before and asked me for some advice on games and party food. Beth invited eight friends from her class, including Jenni, who surprisingly was allowed to go. I was pleased Jenni's mother had managed to put her own prejudices aside for the sake of her daughter. I think Derek was pleased too, although he didn't say much.

At the beginning of November, Adrian, Paula and I visited Beth at home. Marianne and Derek made us feel very welcome and it was clear Beth was happy and settled. Beth showed us some photographs of her party, and also of her natural mother, which her father had found and given to her. Marianne told me that she and Derek had spoken to Beth about her mother and had reassured her that if she ever wanted to contact her, they would try and trace her, but Beth didn't want to at present. She told Marianne she was her mummy now.

Marianne and Derek were married at the end of November in a small ceremony at the local register office. Beth was the bridesmaid, and two friends from Marianne's work were the witnesses. After the service the five of them went out for dinner at a nice country restaurant.

Jessie continued to monitor the family for the first year and then, satisfied there were no concerns, the social services' involvement ended.

And what of John and my family? I took some time off from fostering after Beth left so I could concentrate on Adrian and Paula and also get my own head sorted out. But you can't stay upset and angry forever. At some point, you have to put the past behind you, let go and move on. John saw Adrian and Paula regularly and I had to accept that Sunday outings with their father were part of my new life. I kept myself busy on those days, and when I returned to fostering I used the time to give the child I was looking after one-to-one attention, which they appreciated. My parents didn't see John again, and while I never completely forgave him I was always polite when he telephoned to arrange contact or speak to the children, or when he came to the door to collect them on a Sunday. I've never remarried, although I have dated. Like many parents who are deserted by their partners, I think I probably overcompensated for the absent parent and invested all I had in my children. But then I know I must have done something right when I look at the wonderful people they've become.

Emotional incest is rarely spoken of and often missed or undiagnosed, but it is a form of abuse that can, and does, wreck lives. Derek, Marianne and Beth were lucky to receive the help they needed; many others do not. The parent–child relationship is very special and quite distinct from the relationship an adult has with another adult – on all levels. A child can never be used as a substitute or surrogate partner, regardless of how abandoned or lonely the adult may feel. Children need their childhood so that they can flourish and grow into healthy and emotionally mature adults. Well done Marianne, Derek and Beth. You are truly a lovely family.

SUGGESTED TOPICS FOR
READING-GROUP DISCUSSION

Jenni's mother typifies how some people view mental illness. Why do you think she and others feel this way? What could be done to change such attitudes?

The child is always the victim in an abusive relationship. Discuss in respect of what Marianne tells Cathy about the way Beth and Derek excluded her.

Marianne is very unsure of her role as stepmother. Why? What could she have done differently at the start? What could Derek have done to help her parent Beth?

Emotional incest is difficult to identify and is often missed. Why do you think this is?

The parent-child relationship is very different from that between parents. Why is it so important for the whole family to maintain these distinctions and boundaries?

What were the possible reasons for Derek getting it so badly wrong?

The family were given the therapy they needed. What could have been the outcome(s) for each of them if they had not received this help?

It's sadly ironic that while Beth's family was being reunited, Cathy's family was falling apart. Were there any indications in the book that John was about to leave her? If so, why did Cathy miss them?

What did you think of the book's resolution? How did you feel seeing Beth reunited with her father?

Cathy Glass

———

One remarkable woman, more
than **150** foster children cared for.

Cathy Glass has been a foster carer for
twenty-five years, during which time she has
looked after more than 150 children, as well
as raising three children of her own. She was
awarded a degree in education and psychology
as a mature student, and writes under a
pseudonym. To find out more about Cathy
and her story visit **www.cathyglass.co.uk**.

A Long Way from Home

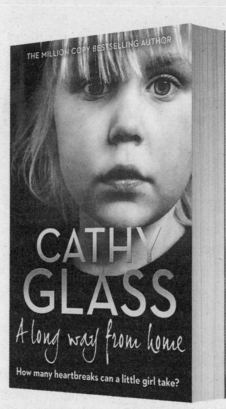

Abandoned in a run-down orphanage, little Anna's future looks bleak – until Elaine and Ian adopt her

Anna's new parents love and cherish her, so why does she end up in foster care?

Cruel to be Kind

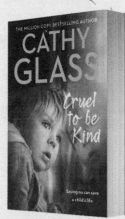

Max is shockingly overweight. Not only is his health suffering, but he struggles to make friends ...

With Max's mother and social worker opposing her at every turn, Cathy faces a challenge to help this unhappy boy.

Nobody's Son

Born in prison and brought up in care, Alex has only ever known rejection

He is longing for a family of his own, but again the system fails him.

Can I Let You Go?

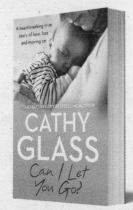

Faye is 24, pregnant and has learning difficulties as a result of her mother's alcoholism

Can Cathy help Faye learn enough to parent her child?

The Silent Cry

A mother battling
depression. A family
in denial

Cathy is desperate to help
before something terrible
happens.

Girl Alone

An angry, traumatized
young girl on a path to
self-destruction

Can Cathy discover
the truth behind Joss's
dangerous behaviour
before it's too late?

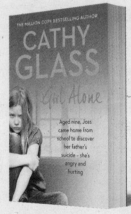

Saving Danny

Danny's parents can
no longer cope with his
challenging behaviour

Calling on all her expertise,
Cathy discovers a frightened
little boy who just wants
to be loved.

The Child Bride

A girl blamed and abused for dishonouring her community

Cathy discovers the devastating truth.

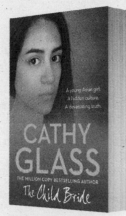

Daddy's Little Princess

A sweet-natured girl with a complicated past

Cathy picks up the pieces after events take a dramatic turn.

Will You Love Me?

A broken child desperate for a loving home

The true story of Cathy's adopted daughter Lucy.

Please Don't Take My Baby

Seventeen-year-old Jade is pregnant, homeless and alone

Cathy has room in her heart for two.

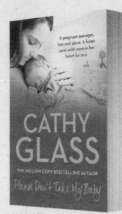

Another Forgotten Child

Eight-year-old Aimee was on the child-protection register at birth

Cathy is determined to give her the happy home she deserves.

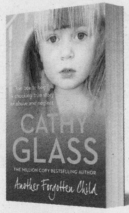

A Baby's Cry

A newborn, only hours old, taken into care

Cathy protects tiny Harrison from the potentially fatal secrets that surround his existence.

The Night the Angels Came

A little boy on the brink of bereavement

Cathy and her family make sure Michael is never alone.

Mummy Told Me Not to Tell

A troubled boy sworn to secrecy

After his dark past has been revealed, Cathy helps Reece to rebuild his life.

I Miss Mummy

Four-year-old Alice doesn't understand why she's in care

Cathy fights for her to have the happy home she deserves.

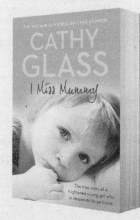

The Saddest Girl in the World

A haunted child who refuses to speak

Do Donna's scars run too deep for Cathy to help?

Cut

Dawn is desperate to be loved

Abused and abandoned, this vulnerable child pushes Cathy and her family to their limits.

Hidden

The boy with no past

Can Cathy help Tayo to feel like he belongs again?

Damaged

A forgotten child

Cathy is Jodie's last hope.
For the first time, this
abused young girl has
found someone
she can trust.

Inspired by Cathy's own experiences...

Run, Mummy, Run

The gripping story of a
woman caught in a horrific
cycle of abuse, and the
desperate measures she
must take to escape.

My Dad's a Policeman

The dramatic short story
about a young boy's
desperate bid to keep his
family together.

The Girl in the Mirror

Trying to piece together her past, Mandy uncovers a dreadful family secret that has been blanked from her memory for years.

Sharing her expertise...

About Writing and How to Publish

A clear and concise, practical guide on writing and the best ways to get published.

Happy Mealtimes for Kids

A guide to healthy eating with simple recipes that children love.

Happy Adults

A practical guide to
achieving lasting happiness,
contentment and success.
The essential manual for
getting the best out of life.

Happy Kids

A clear and concise
guide to raising
confident, well-behaved
and happy children.

Be amazed
Be moved
Be inspired

———